VISTA BOOKS
Elephant In The Room

David Challice

David Challice was born in Brighton in 1960 and has had a varied career, including freelance journalism, working in a quarry, and running his own furniture restoration business, Strip & Wax (which might have been fun but not as much as it sounds).

David has run the Head Office of the UK Independence Party since 2006 and learn't three things along the way.
1... Never send your food back to the kitchen.
2... Don't Google yourself.
3...Things in the media are usually 40% true, 40% tenuous spin, and 20% complete lies.

Elephant in the Room is a sequel to the successful "The View From Here", also published by VISTA.

David lives in a cottage on the edge of Dartmoor with his partner Hilary and their two cats, all of whom appear within these pages.

ELEPHANT IN THE ROOM

David Challice
2016

SBN 978-0-9558091-1-8
vista books
ELEPHANT IN THE ROOM

VISTA BOOKS

Published by VISTA BOOKS

Astarte House

1 Vale Drive

Midanbury

Southampton

SO18 4SW

vistapublishing@btinternet.com

FIRST EDITION JANUARY 2016

The moral right of the author has been asserted

Typesetting and Cover Design by ASTARTE DIGITAL www.astartedigital.com

Set in Bookman Old Style.

Print Management provided by Print by Design Ltd, Bodmin, Cornwall. www.printbydesign.co.uk

INTRODUCTION

I should briefly explain that this book is a collection of pieces from the Trago Column (aka Speaker's Corner) from January 2008 through to December 2016. It is the sequel to The View From Here, covering 2001 to 2007.

The weekly Trago Column appears in thirty or so newspapers throughout South West England, within the larger full-page advert for Trago Mills Shopping Centres, and has a wide readership. Sometimes that readership doesn't always agree (the further Left the reader, the more the disagreement, but I also get criticised by Nazis for being "too soft" so I'm probably hitting the notes right).

I must express my huge gratitude to Bruce Robertson and his staff, among them Henrietta and Rosanne, for all their help, kindness and generosity throughout the years.

Mike Robertson, who founded Trago and originally wrote the Column, stood down as Chairman and was succeeded by his son Bruce. It was in 2001, when Mike finally laid aside his old typewriter, that I stepped in and wrote my first Trago piece. I never thought I'd still be here fifteen years later, but there it is.

The European Union has provided much of the material for this book (It does that just by existing) but it's not all about the EU as you'll see. Most of the pieces are original but a few have been culled from well-known items sloshing around on the internet, and are commonly recognised as that. I make no claims of authorship on those.

Like its predecessor "The View From Here", this is a retrospective so I have not amended anyone's titles or offices. Gordon Brown is referred to as "Prime Minister" rather than "former Prime Minister". What you are reading is the piece as originally written, with all its faults.

My aim has always been to entertain readers, whilst imparting sometimes complicated or tedious stuff, without scaring the horses, and without making their eyes glaze over (the reader, that is... not the horses). I hope I've succeeded and that you will enjoy it.

David Challice
Dartmoor
January 2016

Dedicated to Mother, without whom I would not have been possible

CONTENTS

2008

2009

2010

2011

2012

2013

2014

2015

2003

ELEPHANT IN THE ROOM

David Challice

2008

UP THE POLE

Next time you're wondering what happened to all those taxes you paid, please bear this in mind. Economic migrants to Britain claim £1.4 million a month in child benefit for their children living abroad, and it's rising fast. As reported by the Sun (November 2007) 18,000 workers from new EU countries sent the cash back home to their families in Poland, Bulgaria etc.

In September 2007 there were 6,286 Polish immigrants claiming the benefit, 4,000 more than in July. If each claimed for just one child the cost would be £17 million, but many claim for two or three children. When Gordon Brown declared a war on "child poverty" (whatever that is) few realised that the children he meant were living in Warsaw.

A spokesman for HM Revenue and Customs said: "Under EU rules, an EU national working and paying compulsory contributions in one EU country can claim child benefits for their family resident in another."

So there you go.

January 2008

THROUGH THE KEYHOLE

Here's an email that came into UKIP Head Office the other day. I thought you might be interested...

"Dear Fellow Fruitcakes,

I recently had a letter from the Office of National Statistics regarding the English House Condition Survey, informing me that an interviewer will call uninvited at my home to make unspecified enquiries. The website, www.communities.gov.uk/ehcs reveals this includes questions about my income.

The letter says: "Everything will be treated with confidence". I find that just as reassuring as any other government promise. I am regularly lied to by the State, whose real intention is to take as much taxpayer's money as possible for its cronies. I am therefore not prepared to give private information which could be used against me or others, and I have informed them that I am not prepared to participate in their survey. If this is ignored and the interviewer calls at my home, they will be told politely but firmly to leave. I suggest that other UKIP members do likewise."

I can't speak for you, but that sounds a pretty wise course of action.

January 2008

BOG OFF

Politics can be rough. In Parliament it is said that you face your opponents, but your real enemies are sitting behind you. Winning a seat is difficult. Keeping it is harder. Eric Lubbock (now Lord

Avebury) remarked wryly: "In 1962 the wise, far-seeing people of Orpington elected me as their member. In 1970 the fools threw me out."

Even if you gain power you are constantly at the mercy of "events". Opposition is a luxury where you can promise the earth, safe in the knowledge that you'll never have to deliver; but it comes as a bit of a shock if you win unexpectedly. This happened last year in Israel when the Palestinians turned away from Fatah and voted for Hamas. There was panic in the Hamas camp when they suddenly realised that they now had to start running the place, not just indulge themselves by shouting in the streets, spraying bullets into the air with an AK47 (I've often wondered where all those bullets actually land, but that's for another time).

It's not quite the Gaza strip, but Gordon Brown is about to learn how tough politics can get. He is trying to stuff the renamed EU Constitution through Parliament without asking the people in a referendum (breaking a solemn promise that helped get him elected). This is bad enough, but his hated Treaty will mean that Britain gets the Euro Currency.

Before the inevitable cries of "Codswallop" may I quote from Article 3: "The Union shall establish an economic and monetary union whose currency is the euro." It then expresses the desire of: "ever closer co-ordination of economic policies... pending the euro becoming the currency of all Member States of the Union"...

No wriggle room for Gordon Brown there. Vote for the Treaty and get the Euro as an extra. In other words Buy One Get One Free.

January 2008

THE ORACLE SPEAKS

The Delphi Technique is a sneaky way of pushing through controversial issues. You will find it at public enquiries, school meetings, local government consultation exercises etc; and this guide should help you spot it.

Their aim is to get you, the audience, to vote for a preset decision (hospital closure, new airport, gypsy site, etc). If people believe an idea is their own, they'll support it. If they feel it's being forced on them, they'll resist.

This so-called participation is an illusion and it works like this. They hire a "facilitator". Supposedly neutral and non-judgemental, but in fact he's on 'their' side. He then works the crowd, seeking out those who disagree, making them look foolish, inept or aggressive, sending a clear message to the rest of the audience that they'd better behave unless they want the same treatment. This is 'group dynamics'.

Once the opposition has been identified and alienated, the facilitator becomes the good guy and the direction of the meeting is established without the audience ever realising what is happening. The crowd is then broken up into smaller groups (divide and rule) and encouraged to put down on paper their ideas and concerns, not sharing them openly. That way nobody knows what anyone else has written, and the final compilation of results can be left to those running the meeting. And even if one table disagrees, they are still in a minority.

Lynn Stuter is an education researcher in Washington State, and she lists the way to counter the Delphi Technique. Always be charming, courteous and pleasant. Don't be aggressive or you will lose the audience. Don't respond angrily when the facilitator tries to ridicule you. Be persistent. If the facilitator launches into a long monologue, this is done deliberately. Wait till he finishes, then say: "You haven't answered my question. What I asked was…" Sometimes it helps to have friends in the crowd: "You haven't answered that ladies question." But ignore each other at tea break or they'll soon realise that you're in cahoots.

As Mrs Stuter says: "Citizens believe they are contributing to the result, but in reality the outcome has already been decided beforehand. The goal of facilitators is to make the majority of the group members like them, and to alienate anyone who might pose a threat to the realisation of their agenda."

It is oddly reminiscent of the approach by Europhiles to anyone who dares to disagree with them. Refutation by denigration, Delphi style.

February 2008

DOING A CORBYN IN BRUSSELS

Just before Christmas 2007 a group of 80 Eurosceptic MEPs protested loudly in the European Parliament at the signing of the Charter of Fundamental Rights, which surrenders a huge section of UK sovereignty. Hans Gert Pottering – President of the Parliament - asked them to leave. When they refused, pandemonium broke out. The EU's own TV cameras swung away from the demonstration and killed the sound.

Herr Pottering shouted that the protesters were "anti democratic, because they will not let our guests speak," to which the demonstrators replied: "Let the people speak." Opposing MEPs from the European Peoples Party then pitched in, furious at the protests. One of them dragged an observer from the Independence and Democracy Group out of the chamber, demanding her camera containing footage of the protest.

Nigel Farage, leader of the UK Independence Party, said afterwards: "This is the new EU in action, showing the world a united face as they steamroll towards their own superstate while totally refusing to allow anyone to see a different point of view."

He continued: "The high point of this hypocrisy surely came at the end, when MEPs were invited to stand for the European anthem – the one that's supposed to have disappeared. To their everlasting shame, British MEPs from the Labour, Conservative and Liberal Democrat parties stood ram-rod straight to grant this piece of music 'national anthem' status."

The good news is that TV cameras from BBC and ITV were filming events in the chamber. The bad news is that neither have ever shown it to their viewers. How very odd that a punch up in the EU Parliament is not considered newsworthy.

February 2008

TOOLED UP IN LINCOLN

In Autumn 2007 Bill Newton-Dunn (Lib Dem MEP) asked Brussels for 250,000 euros (£173,000) to promote an EU wide police force.

At the Lisbon Summit in October 2007 the EU

signed a Treaty establishing the Eurogendfor (EU Gendarmerie) and Mr Newton-Nunn clearly wanted a slice of the action.... This is predictable for a Lib Dem, but his UKIP opponent in the East Midlands, Derek Clark MEP, issued an immediate press release: "I do not wish to see Euro-cops, armed with a handgun and legal immunity swaggering around the East Midlands with a European Arrest Warrant from a European prosecutor ready to drag one of my constituents back to a country for a crime that may not even exist in the UK. I will be voting against Newton-Dunn's scheme".

Shortly afterwards Bob Spink (Tory MP) stood up in Westminster and asked the Foreign Secretary: "Will you give an assurance that this paramilitary force will not be allowed to operate on British soil?"

Setting aside his milkshake, wiping his mouth, and standing up, David Miliband replied that he could give no such assurance. Eurogendfor had to be invited into any country by its government.

As Bob Spink said: "This gives no confidence at all to the British people, since we know from experience that we cannot trust this government. I note that they haven't ruled out giving permission for Eurogendfor to enter Britain, for instance during the 2012 Olympic Games."

Still going to vote for one of these Brussels-friendly parties?

March 2008

T'WAS EVER THUS AT THE BBC

It's no secret that the BBC has become dominated by progressive lefties (which explains why much of its output is now unwatchable) but here's an interesting tale...

One of UKIP's supporters is the ex-deputy editor of Radio 4's Today programme. He has spent 29 years in the BBC and was editor of Newsbeat, World Tonight, 6pm News and Today in Parliament. This man knows his onions. He recently attended Today's 50th birthday party in the O2 Centre next to the London Eye.

Then he wrote to us about it: "The event was filled with the 'great and the good', Ken Livingstone, most of the Lib Dem MPs, David Trimble, Lord and Lady Howe etc. Among the many journalists but few Today workers, was a well-known presenter from Radio 5 Live (not sure why he was there, but still).

'When "Europe" cropped up he had the audacity to suggest we could do nothing about it and like a woman being raped, should lie back and "enjoy" it. I was so taken aback, I didn't know what to say – without being extremely rude that is. Regrettably that seems to be the attitude of most people in the UK. Will they ever wake up?"

March 2008

CLIPPINGS FOR THE BONFIRE

In my box of clippings I often have odds and ends that never quite fit in anywhere. Please forgive me if I use up some of them now.

A cross section of the population of the UK,

including Albanians, Turks, Liverpuddlians, Iraqis, etc, were asked if they thought that Britain should change its currency to the euro. The result was enough to gladden the most eurosceptic heart: a vote of 99% said no. They were very happy with the giro, though this was before the Northern Rock fiasco. (Had the bank been called Southern Rock, and its members Tories from the shires, things might have been very different).

The credit crunch has reverberated around the world, with Japan the latest casualty. The Origami Bank has folded; Bonsai Bank has cut many of its branches; and shares in Kamikaze Aeronautics have nose-dived - all this following the recent news that 3,200 employees at the Karate Bank have been given the chop.

Ahem. And now for something completely different. Mark Leonard - foreign policy director of the 'Centre For European Reform' (and a huge fan of Brussels) – said this: "The British House of Commons, law courts and civil servants have become agents of the European Union, implementing European law. By creating common standards that are implemented through national institutions, Europe can take over countries without necessarily becoming a target for hostility".

This all goes to show that you mustn't believe everything you read. (The Origami Bank, for example, does not exist. Sorry about that). But the Mark Leonard quote is the exception that proves the rule. It's totally accurate (source: Christopher Booker, Sunday Times, Feb 2005). And quite frankly if his words don't worry you, then I'm not sure what will. Please try to wake up. The coffee's on, bacon's frying. Over to you.

March 2008

A QUICK FLASH OF TUNGSTEN

They call them 'light-bulb moments'... (St Paul had one on the road to Damascus), the moment when realisation hits and the scales suddenly fall from your eyes. For Roger Knapman MEP (former leader of UKIP) it happened in 1985, shortly before he was elected as a Conservative MP. He was in Germany at the time, as guest of the Konrad Adeneur Stiftung (Foundation).

Along with other British visitors, Roger was observing 6,000 NATO forces on military manoeuvres on the bleak North German Plain. It was a cold day, with a damp mist rolling in across the battlefield, obscuring the action. As time wore on the observers gradually lost the feeling in their toes, so the Bundswehr Colonel invited them into the nearby officer's mess for 'a little something'.

Over a glass of colourless liquid the visitors gradually thawed out. As the others talked with the officers, Roger looked around the mess. He noticed a big coloured map fixed to the wall: "EUROPE OF THE REGIONS", with 116 'regions' listed, stretching right across Europe, from Portugal to Poland, from Finland to the toe of Italy. Yet barely anyone in Britain at the time had ever heard of 'regions'. This was an eye-opener...

We all have our light-bulb moments. For Roger Knapman it came in 1985. I wonder when you'll have yours (if you haven't already).

March 2008

FOUND IN POSSESSION OF EGG AND SPOON

Devon Columnist Toby Landers visited a 'non-competitive school sports day' in Derby last year.... I'll quote him: 'I heard a teacher telling a 9 year old girl: "We don't do that here!" She had been running across the playing field with a 'racing attitude'. It was very obvious this girl had a natural talent and I am sure everybody could see that. Was she encouraged? Not a chance. I felt she was being patronised and put down by her school. She was told to resume passing beanbags around and pouring water into empty buckets. What a waste of time.'

Sometimes it's difficult to feel sympathy for these teachers. When corporal punishment was banned and children suddenly knew their 'human rights', the resultant chaos in the classroom was inevitable. And with a generation of Wayne and Waynetta parents, themselves reared on turkey twizzlers, hopped to the eyeballs with E110, pinning the headteacher against the bike-shed wall, the only solution is to fight like a cat in a sack to get your child into one of the half-decent schools we have left.

Tony Blair didn't hesitate to pull strings for his own offspring. No bog-standard comprehensive for his offspring, and when the prime minister sets the example, who can be blamed for following?

April 2008

CLEAR THE ROOM PLEASE

Thanks to New Labour (and the EU) and its hysteria over man-made climate change, we will soon be losing our traditional tungsten lightbulbs for 'green' bulbs, containing mercury, an extremely poisonous substance...

If you break a mercury bulb you must leave a window open and evacuate the room for at least 15 minutes to let the fumes clear. Here are the official instructions issued to MPs/Lords in Westminster: Don't hoover up the glass. Put on protective gloves and mask, and place the large fragments inside a sturdy box. Then sweep up the splinters using stiff card. Clean the area with a damp cloth, place the cloth in a box, and seal the box with parcel tape. Then – you haven't finished yet – then, label the contents of the box using pen or paper, and then take the sealed box to a waste removal area where it must pass to a licensed waste disposal operator.

There are many problems with these new bulbs. They are hideously ugly, dangerous and poisonous, and won't fit old (antique) light fittings, and are useless on a staircase where you only briefly need illumination. No wonder they save electricity. You'd be better off with a pocket torch...

Ironmonger Barry Forkin added his tuppence: "You'll need to lay in a big stock of 40-watts," he told one of his customers. "British manufacturers won't be able to make them. But in Europe they're not withdrawing them by 2010, so they're making all these low-energy bulbs to sell in Britain. Funny that."

Even funnier, if mercury is suddenly so safe and cosy, why did Brussels recently ban the manufacture of traditional mercury barometers, wrecking a number of British family-run businesses that had been trading for generations?

If you're interested Trago Mills is running a sale of incandescent 100, 60, and 40-watt light-bulbs, for HOW MUCH? A pack of 10 for £1.69.   Now that's what I call a bargain. The only problem is that I intend to zip over to Newton Abbot tomorrow and grab the lot. Sorry about that. Blame the green zealots of New Labour and Brussels.

April 2008

SHIVER ME TIMBERS

It's a real barrel of laughs out there at the minute. France has now banned British border guards in Calais from using an X-ray scanner when checking vehicles for stowaways. Apparently the scanners breach European safety laws, and without written permission from the illegals their use is now outlawed.

Or try this one: in 2010 the British 'kitemark' safety standard will be torn up and replaced by a European 'C.E' mark. As a result, firework displays are now under threat, because the manufacturers must pay to have all their products retested. As Tom Smith of the CBI explained: "Not a single person in Britain will be made safer... but everyone will be affected by it becoming much more expensive and bureaucratic to import fireworks."

Or try this one, from the Guardian, Jan 18th. In the little village of Carnon Downs, near Truro, the local drama group produced a homemade pantomime - a mixture of Captain Hook, Robinson Crusoe and Long

John Silver. But there was a problem. The panto's finale ended with a sword fight across the stage. Under Health and Safety rules, they had to register the weapons with the police: two plastic cutlasses, six wooden swords and a toy pistol that flicks out a flag saying 'Bang!'... Oh, and they also needed to employ a fight coordinator from Liverpool to supervise the fight scenes on Hook's galleon. Now tell me that this country hasn't lost the plot.

May 2008

A LITTLE SLOW BETWEEN THE EARS

The bad weather was closing in from Princetown when the Revenue & Customs official parked his car in the farmyard. He was on a mission, investigating a complaint about a farm labourer being paid less than the minimum wage. He brandished his notebook even as he declined tea in the kitchen. "I'll need a list of everyone who works here."

The farmer thought for a moment, added sugar to his coffee, stirred it, watched the froth as it circulated slowly: "Well," he began, "there's my farm hand. He's paid £200 a week, plus free board and lodging. And the cook, of course. She been here twenty year and gets free board; clothing allowance; cash when needed."

The official looked at him: "I know there is someone else".

"You're thinking of the half-wit. He puts in 18 hours a day, does most of the work around here, makes about £10 a week, and pays for his own accommodation. I buy him a bottle of whisky on Saturday night. Sometimes he sleeps with my wife"...

The official smiled dangerously: "That's the man I want to talk to. The half-wit".

"That'll be me then," said the farmer, raising his coffee cup.

May 2008

SEARCHING FOR AN ALIBI

Roughly 20,000 years ago you could walk from Norfolk to Denmark. People and animals roamed freely in the swampy woodlands. Archaeologists know this because fishing boats often dredge up tree trunks, bones, and man-made flint arrowheads. And then – with global warming - the sea levels rose, the North Sea flooded in, and the locals were forced to higher ground. And then Britain became an island. In the 1600s Samuel Pepys wrote this in his diary: "21st January 1661: It is strange what weather we have had all winter; not so cold at all: but the ways are dusty, and the flies fly up and down, and the rose bushes are full of leaves. Such a time of year as was never known in this world before."

Or on 15th May 1663: "Strange were the effects of the late thunder and lightning, coming with great rain, which caused extraordinary floods in a few hours, bearing away bridges, drowning horses, men and cattle.".

In response to Al Gore's film An Inconvenient Truth, 31,000 scientists republished an earlier petition on climate change: "There is no convincing scientific evidence that human release of greenhouse gases is causing or will, in the foreseeable future, cause catastrophic heating of the Earth's atmosphere and disruption of the earth's climate. Moreover, there is substantial scientific evidence that increases in carbon dioxide produce many beneficial effects upon the natural plant and animal environments." (Daily Telegraph 31/05/08).

I freely admit that I'm no scientist, but if 31,000 scientists (9,000 of them with PhDs) are prepared to endorse this paper, then we really cannot claim that there is still "consensus on this subject."

How about this for an explanation, voiced by an Australian professor recently? Asked why environmentalists kept thinking up new threats to the Earth, he replied: "Well, God died, then Marx, so now they're worshipping the planet".

June 2008

POLES NEED PLODS

The British Police are facing a problem. A few years ago they "fast-tracked" bright young graduates into senior positions, leap-frogging the experienced cops. The senior officers now running the police are committed to political correctness, multi-culturalism and diversity awareness training. Forget catching thieves, most of them couldn't catch a cold.

As a result, crime is rising, morale among "other ranks" has collapsed, and the public have virtually given up. Even worse, many senior officers remain in a state of denial, obsessed with reaching targets imposed on them by the progressive-left.

Ironically, many Poles who emigrated to the UK are complaining of a 'poor or apathetic response' from our boys in blue and are now hiring private detectives from Poland to come here and investigate

the crimes that our lot woefully failed to solve.
To quote the Daily Mail (26/02/08): "Polish private eyes claim that the British police are helpless in the face of Polish organised crime now taking root in Britain. They say that the Poles have received zero support when they become victims of burglars, muggers and other criminals."

My only response to that is: What's new? We could have told them that, years ago. Ask Stephen Earp, of Horsebridge on Dartmoor. Thieves recently broke into his property, stealing various items. He reported the crime, but nobody came. Days later he had a letter from Tavistock police: 'From the information currently available to us there is unfortunately no other active line of enquiry." But if Plod hadn't even stirred from the local cop-shop then how could they possibly know?

As Mr Earp said: "They have done nothing to get evidence. I'd rather they were honest and said they did nothing about it... but they cannot be bothered to send a chap out for half an hour. I am incensed. One assumes the police are getting into the world of standard letters, and are more interested in sending out letters to make someone feel better than trying to stop these people."

I, personally, am so appalled that I have just completed a Victim of Crime report and will be sending it to the Chief Constable. The only problem is that I've mislaid my book of stamps. I put it down just over there, with my wallet, but they both seem to have disappeared. Perhaps I should call directory enquiries and ask for the Warsaw CID?

July 2008

CHOPPING OFF THE OPPOSITION

The Roman poet Lucretius once wrote: "It is pleasant, when the seas are high and the wind is dashing the boats about, to watch from the shore the struggles of another." I see what he meant now. The New Labour Project is collapsing in front of us, and it's rather enjoyable to behold.

The biggest problem with the cultural Marxists running New Labour is that if you oppose them, they call you evil. Disagree with their disastrous immigration policy and you're the BNP. Disagree with surrendering sovereignty to Brussels and you're anti-European or a little Englander.

Reject the lunacy of multiculturalism and you're a racist. Disagree with the Archbishop of Canterbury about Britain adopting Sharia law and you're a religious bigot. Though try opening an off-licence in Mecca and the Religious Police will shut you down and break your legs, even before you can cry: "But I'm a Leftie!"

As someone once said: "Labour has always played the man, not the ball." So I shed no tears if they are heading for political obscurity. The only problem is that it risks letting in the Lib Dems, who are even worse.

Bring back Old Labour? No thanks. For my money UKIP looks the best long-term bet. And that's not so absurd as it may sound. Much depends on next year's European Elections in 2009. If you want to keep alive the voice of political sanity, better vote UKIP. Because if we ever disappear in a puff of smoke, even old Lucretius won't stick around to watch from the shore.

August 2008

But in 2015 Labour members voted 60% for Uber-Left Jeremy Corbyn. The merry-go-round spins and spins.

NEWS FROM THE FRONT

Here are two letters recently received at UKIP Head Office:

"Dear Sir, I'm resigning from UKIP as I'm moving to Northern France. Sorry but I've had a bellyful of New Labour. I'm one of the 700 who are leaving the UK every day. Where I'm going is like this country was in the 1950s. Empty roads, clean streets, no yobs, no litter; friendly polite people and a cheaper cost of living. Even though born and bred an Englishman, I'm being driven out by political correctness, multiculturalism, and untrammelled immigration...

So I'll be thinking of you guys under two more years of Labour. God knows what's going to happen to this country, I despair of it. Nobody seems to stand up for the decent majority, including Cameron."

The other (an email) was shorter: "Hello there. I would love to assist in knocking on doors and meeting the public to add my support on the EU referendum etc.... I do hope that all your efforts bring an end to this madness...If I'm still in this country by the time of the general election, or I have not been murdered by a teenage thug or illegal immigrant, you will be getting my vote."

August 2008

GONE GORDON

The Scandinavians have a saying: "Guests are like fish. After three days they start to smell."... Everything has a shelf life, and Gordon Brown is now looking green about the gills, being avoided by many of his colleagues.

The credit crunch is not his fault, but he blew all our money on a client state of public servants when he should have been squirreling it away for the bad times. Even worse, he moved into 10 Downing Street, saying that politicians must reconnect with voters, then broke an election promise and signed the Lisbon Treaty, surrendering our sovereignty to Brussels... He even lacked the guts to line up with the other EU leaders for the official photograph, deliberately turning up late when everyone had gone home, stepping between the cleaners as they hoovered the carpet around him.

Frank Field and Kate Hoey, both former Labour ministers, were threatened with expulsion from the Party for publicly criticising his decision not to hold a referendum, and both were ordered to attend a "meeting without coffee" to get a carpeting. But then along came the Irish NO vote. Spanner in the works time.

Former German Foreign Minister, Joschka Fischer, then condemned the Irish for voting NO. "A strong European foreign policy, badly needed given the current state of the world, was buried on June 12, for the time being. The nation states will have control over foreign policy once again."

Herr Fischer's words (in an editorial in Dagens Nyheter, June 2008) prove that adopting the Lisbon Treaty means surrendering control of our foreign policy. No wonder David Miliband is scouting around for another job.

August 2008

UNCLE LUDWIG AT NO 10

I read this recently in Christopher Short's superb book The Black Room. The scene is an aristocratic Grand Ball in 19th century Germany.

'Uncle Ludwig came out with Princess Flagstein, looking as dashing and gallant as a man can while dancing with a bear... [Ludwig] created a certain amount of confusion because although he thinks he is a very good dancer, he has no sense of rhythm and as a result turns every dance into a polka, except the polka which he turns into a cavalry charge. No one could have been more gallant in colliding with other dancers, no one more dashing in covering the floor in leaps and bounds, and no one more brave than to attempt what he was doing with the Princess Flagstein.'

Perhaps I've been overdoing it recently, but I now have this image of Gordon Brown as Uncle Ludwig, complete with ceremonial sabre, coal-scuttle helmet, and fixed, rictus-like smile as he cavorts across the floor, oblivious to the disbelieving gaze of everyone else in the room.

September 2008

A SLOW EXPOSURE

Here is a test I was emailed recently. You must give an honest but spontaneous answer to a completely fictional question. This will show where you stand morally:

You are a photo-journalist working for a national newspaper and are caught in the middle of a huge flood caused by a hurricane in a city in the north of England. All around you houses, bridges, cars, people are being swept away. A terrifying situation, but you have your camera and know these pictures will sell across the world...

THE TEST:
Suddenly you see a man in the water, struggling to stay afloat. You move closer. It is Gordon Brown, Prime Minister. The raging waters are about to take him under. You have two options. You can risk your own life to possibly save his. Or you can shoot a series of dramatic shots of the demise of one of the country's most powerful men, and probably win the Pulitzer Prize...

THE QUESTION... and please give an honest answer... Would you select high contrast colour film or go for the classic simplicity of black and white? It's a difficult one, I know.

September 2008

DOWN UNDER WITH SKIPPY'S MATE.

When Captain Cook arrived in Australia he asked the aborigines: "What is that animal called?".

They looked around: "Which animal? Be more specific."

He pointed. "That one over there."

"Kangaroo" said the Aborigines.

The problem is that the aboriginal word 'kangaroo' means: "I don't know." They were telling Cook that they didn't know what it was called (never having been introduced to it, I suppose).

I feel exactly the same way when reading that British Airways have now taken beef off the menu to avoid offending Hindus, and that an Afghan who hijacked a plane to Stanstead airport in February 2000, armed with grenades and a gun, is now working as a cleaner at Heathrow. The only response I have left is: "Kangaroo."

September 2008

LIGHTING A FUSE

You need to be careful in life. Don't look for a gas leak with a match, and remember that your grandmother's 'lucky rabbit's foot' wasn't so lucky for the rabbit. But sometimes it's even more tricky...

Sarah Desrosier, 32, runs Wedge, a hair salon in London's King's Cross. In May 2007 she advertised for a junior assistant. Bushra Noah, a Muslim who wears a headscarf for religious reasons, came along for an interview. Sarah asked if Bushra would remove the headscarf at work. The answer was "No" so she didn't get the job.

Sarah explained: "I needed stylists to reflect the funky urban image of the salon and showcase alternative hairstyles. I'd have done the same if someone refused to remove a baseball cap."

Bushra Noah then took Sarah to an employment tribunal, claiming £34,000 in damages. Sarah, who has spent her savings on this legal battle, was outraged: "I am a small business and the bottom line is that this is not a woman who worked for me."

The tribunal rejected Noah's claim for £34,000, but did grant her £4,000 because of hurt feelings. Sarah was furious: "She is simply someone I met for a job interview, who, for a host of reasons was not right for the job. I never in a million years dreamt that somebody would be completely against the display of hair and be in this industry."

Sarah should have realised that in this insane asylum of political correctness and multiculturalism, to catch a moth you need only to light a candle.

October 2008

"AND WHEN DO WE WANT IT?"

You know something's wrong when female Muslims start claiming equal rights to join al Qaeda as suicide bombers. (This came just after bin Laden's deputy had announced that women should stay at home, do the ironing and finish cooking dinner)...

His comments went down badly. On an extremist Islamic website one woman complained: "When Sheikh Ayman al-Zawahri said there were no women in al Qaeda, he saddened and hurt me. I felt that my heart was about to explode in my chest. I am powerless."

Well, I suppose she should know about chests exploding, but we'll move swiftly on. There is one Muslim male who won't be marching off to war. Abu Qatada, so-called "European Ambassador" for bin Laden, should have been deported to Jordan to face terrorism charges.

But then the Human Rights Act intervened, so now he lives in an £800,000 home in West London, claiming £8,000 incapacity benefit for a bad back. His wife has been claiming £45,000 a year in child benefit, income support, housing benefit, and council tax credit (Daily Mail 23/06/08)...

We taxpayers are also paying £500,000 a year to

provide 24-hr surveillance on him, a man who arrived here 14 years ago on a forged passport. Steve Pound, Labour MP (Ealing) said: "This is adding insult to injury. He abuses us and bleeds us dry at the same time. The sooner he gets back to Jordan the better. I would put him in the boot of my car and drive him there myself."

Steve, I'll gladly share the driving, but let's just strap him to the roof.

October 2008

Qatada was finally deported in 2014 after a face-saving deal, whereby Jordan would put him through a show-trial and then acquit him. And that is exactly what happened, letting everyone off the hook, including Qatada.

SPILL M'GUINESS

You might be interested in a few extracts from the Irish Daily Mail, 14th April 2008. This was before Irish voters later said "NO" to the Lisbon Treaty. A leaked email showed that ministers were planning a deliberate campaign of misinformation...

As the Mail reveals 'Foreign Affairs Minister Dermot Ahern has been personally assured that the European Commission will "tone down" any announcements from Brussels "that might be unhelpful", and ruled out an October referendum because they feared "unhelpful developments during the French presidency.".

The newspaper went on: 'The most controversial aspect is that it will be used to advance the concept of a European army, violating the principle of neutrality that has long been a foundation stone of the State... The leaked email admits that this is one of the issues that needs to be kept from voters.'.

And the editorial comment in the same issue goes even further: 'Whether the Lisbon Treaty is accepted by the Irish public or not, one thing is clear – the Government campaign in its favour is already one of the most deeply dishonest in Irish history. The revelation that the Government has conspired with foreign politicians to deceive its own electorate speaks of profound betrayal. That the Irish people should be the victims of a dishonest alliance between their own government and outside powers is something many will find very hard to forgive quickly.'

November 2008

FIND A BIN TO PUT IT IN

You know it's a good day when you wake up and can still see the bedroom ceiling. But for some people things can suddenly go downhill. Take Keith Hirst, 54, with a heart condition, who recently spent 18 hours in a police cell because he dropped an apple core, was confronted by an apparently "baying" police community support officer and refused to give his name. He was then banged up overnight, with his disabled wife worrying at home where he'd gone.

Meanwhile in Hull, Sarah Davies, 20, was fined £75 after her four-year-old daughter dropped a piece of sausage roll.

Or take canoeist Nigel Conway who paddled along a river in North Wales and refused to pay £3 to a rafting company that leased the banks of the river. He was arrested, questioned for two hours, photographed, fingerprinted, and had his DNA taken. "I refused to pay to paddle the river – it is a matter of principle – everyone should have the right to access water free of charge."

Or how about Victor Abrahams who received a £100 fixed penalty ticket from Barnet Council in London because he had a sign in the window of his Ford Escort: "FOR SALE Escort Ghia Automatic. Very Low Mileage". No price was mentioned in the ad, but he was still accused of "Offering goods for sale in a public place."

The point I'm making here is that because of the Human Rights Act, real criminals are treated with comparative leniency, and ordinary folk like the above are being treated with contempt. This is surely not right.

November 2008

ONLY TOO LIKELY

You'll like this. I only wish I'd come up with it myself.

SCENARIO ONE: Bill and Ted have a fist fight after school...

1978: Crowd gathers. Bill wins. They shake hands and go home.

2008: Armed Response Unit arrives. Mobiles with fight video are confiscated as evidence. ASBOs given to both, even though Ted started it. Videos go onto U-Tube.

SCENARIO TWO: Bill is disruptive in class...

1978: Bill sent to headmaster's office. Given six of the best. Doesn't disrupt the class again.

2008: Bill is prescribed Ritalin and his own personal counsellor. Becomes a zombie in class. Drops out of school. Never gets a job.

SCENARIO THREE: Ted blows up an Airfix kit on an anthill, using an old firecracker.

1978: A few ants die.

2008: MI5 called in. Ted charged with act of terrorism. Parents are investigated and siblings taken into care. Computers are confiscated. Ted's dad goes onto terror list and is banned from any form of air travel.

November 2008

NEWS FROM ENGLANDLAND

"Welcome back to NBC News, America's premier news corporation, and now we're going over to Jeb McGruber our special correspondent in London, Englandland. Jeb, we're hearing that President Norman Brown is in trouble over there."…

"Hi Chad. Good morning America. Yes, President Brown has only been in the job for 12 months. Before that he was Chancellor."

"Like he's German?"

"No, that's what they call their Treasury Secretary over here."

"He's a Conservative like President Tony Blair?"

"No, both are Labour. Blair only pretended to be a Conservative."

"So how did Brown get the job?"

"He just shouted until Blair stepped down. He didn't stand for election because he thought he might lose, but he was elected to the House of Lords by his constituents in Scotlandland."

"So Norman Brown is President of Scotlandland, too?"

"No. That's a guy called Alan Salmon."

"But Brown is Scoddish, right?"

"Affirmative. In this crazy country Brown can make laws for Englandland, but not for his own people in Scotlandland. Not that it matters because he's signed away most of Englandland's lawmaking powers to unelected European bureaucrats in Belgiumland. And the Supreme Court couldn't stop him because it's now in Strasbourg."

"What in the name of Ulysses S. Grant is going on over there, Jeb? Isn't there any opposition?"

"Only a guy called Boris. But he's on holiday in Moscow at the moment."

"Sounds like a Commie takeover. How in the hell did the people of Englandland vote for that? This is the country that gave us the Magna Charta and fought off Hitler."

"There is a guy called Balls who might replace Brown"

"Sounds par for the course, Jeb. And now over to the weather."

November 2008

DO YOU LIKE MY PROFILE?

If you accuse the BBC of bias towards the progressive left, they'll deny it. But they have now confirmed it quite by accident...

Last year 10,580 BBC employees signed up to Facebook, the networking website, where members describe themselves, including their political views if they wish. Not everyone revealed their politics, but of those who did 1,340 described themselves as "liberal" or "very liberal". Only 120 were "conservative" or "very conservative". As for voting intentions it seems that 49% would vote Lib Dem, 38% Labour, and a paltry 3.9% Tory.

I've already said that I like the idea of the BBC and don't mind paying a licence fee, but this inherent bias is a huge problem at the heart of the Corporation. Subjects like euro-scepticism, immigration, even doubts about man-made global warming, are considered off-limits in their liberal-minded comfort zone; and this is unhealthy.

To quote journalist Tim Montgomerie in The Business: "Andrew Marr admitted that the BBC is not impartial or neutral. The BBC's Washington correspondent, Justin Webb, noted that it treated America with scorn, giving it no moral weight. [And] other BBC executives said that the Corporation is dominated by people from ethnic minorities, was anti-countryside, and more sensitive to the feelings of Muslims rather than Christians."

Mr Montgomerie concluded: "Names like the BBC and The Times could stand out in this age of many media voices. But if they want to continue attracting audiences and prevent ever-larger numbers of people from migrating to the new generation of specialist media, they would be very unwise to continue to dumb down."

I couldn't put it better myself, but would just add that if the BBC expects the rest of us to pick up the tab, it's about time they stopped advertising their vacancies in left-wing newspapers like the Guardian.

November 2008

NELLIE THE ELEPHANT IN THE ROOM

On Tuesday 15th July 2008, in Geneva, Britain voted in favour of allowing China and Zimbabwe (among others) to trade in ivory. The British wanted to treat Robert Mugabe as a pariah and were worried that cash would flood into his coffers, propping up his regime. Conservationists had also warned that this legal trade would fuel the illegal trade and "trigger a new poaching bloodbath".

Despite this the British went ahead and voted for the ivory trade. "Why?" I hear you ask. Answer's simple: they were representing the EU, and Brussels had already decided to vote in favour.

As correspondent John Ingham said: "I don't give a damn what the burghers of Luxembourg or Latvia think about elephants. The only view I care about is Britain's because it's the only country where I have any democratic influence. I expect the British government to act according to British interests – and not to vote for a very bad deal simply because it is deemed a good one by a majority of foreign countries. We should either renegotiate our position in the EU or just run up the white flag, tell Brussels to get on with it, and axe our own politicians... If our own government allows itself to be dictated to by the

EU there is no point having it. We should save the money, abandon democracy altogether and become proper Europeans."

And so say all of us.

December 2008

MORE CLIPPINGS FOR THE BONFIRE

Here's another raid on my clippings box; those snippets that I hope you'll enjoy but can't fit in anywhere. Here's one from The Independent: "In Zimbabwe the price of one brick today would have been enough to buy a three-bedroom house with a swimming pool in 1990". The only problem is that it's dated March 2007. These days it would probably buy you one of Robert Mugabe's mansions.

Or try this one, from the Mail on Sunday's 'Quotes from 1982': "The EEC takes away Britain's freedom to follow the sort of economic policies we need. That is just one of the reasons for pulling out." (Tony Blair, before he became prime minister).

Or writer Ayan Rand, quoted recently in the Telegraph: "The difference between a welfare state and a totalitarian state is just a matter of time."
Or finally this one from The Observer 14/9/08: "Thousands of expats aged over 60 will claim more than £10-million in winter fuel payments, even though they live in countries that remain warm throughout the winter... European rules mean that benefits acquired in one member state must be given to those who move elsewhere within the EU."

So if you move to the Algarve you'll still get your coal allowance.

December 2008

LEADER OF THE PACK

One size does not fit all. But in the EU that rule is turned upside down. If you want to take your motorbike test in Britain you must now do it at an off-road centre, not on the public highway. This is because our dozy officials in Brussels failed to notice that the new EU-wide test is taken at 50kph (1.7mph above the 30mph limit). As a result, any hopeful biker cannot be tested on the road because they would be speeding.

It is costing this country £71million to build sixty-six new testing centres, complete with mock-ups of suburban streets. The Driving Standards Agency admitted: "The standard requirements for the new motorcycle test are imposed by EU law", and Matthew Sinclair of the Taxpayers Alliance added: "It's absolutely outrageous that the Government have wasted tens of millions of pounds of taxpayers' money on testing centres for the sake of less than 2mph just because they didn't properly understand the impact of EU regulations."

A delegation from the Motorcycle Industry Association met with Jim Fitzpatrick (Transport Minister) in September, requesting a six-month delay. To quote Motor Cycle News: "but they left with no firm commitment."

You can bet your saddlebags on that. Like the fiasco over Union Jacks on number plates, Mr Fitzpatrick is powerless to act, totally under orders from Brussels. Even if he wanted to, his hands are tied. It makes you wonder why anyone would even want to be an MP, when Westminster has given away most of its powers?

December 2008

A CALM APPROACH TO IMMIGRATION

Phil Woolas, the new Immigration Minister, told The Times newspaper (18/10/08) that he wanted to see a dramatic reduction in the number of migrants coming to Britain. And then the progressive-left squashed him. He was pulled from BBC1's Newsnight and the usual suspects trotted out the predictable stuff that such comments were "potentially racist". Since then (at the time of writing) Mr Woolas has kept his head down, thus proving that the light at the end of the tunnel has just been switched off.

But it's all hot air. Stricter immigration controls won't apply to EU citizens, so the back door is wide open. And as revealed by the Daily Express, Africa News, and Reuters (11/10/08) there is now a secret EU plan to invite 50 million African workers into the EU.

As the Express reported, that same week a tax-payer funded 'job centre' costing 10-million euros opened in Mali as a first step to "promoting free movement of people in Africa and the EU". The Brussels-based agency Eurostat claimed that Britain and other EU-states would need 56-million immigrant workers by 2050, making up for demographic decline due to falling birth rates. Stand by for the rush, ladies and gentlemen, but don't expect Mr Woolas to help. Right now he's probably incarcerated in a political re-education centre somewhere in the Cairngorms.

French MEP Francoise Castex (author of Eurostat's report) said: "It is urgent that member states have a calm approach to immigration." But the fact is that even if we want to panic, it won't do us an ounce of good. Brussels has already decided, and there's nothing we can do about it. This is called Loss of Sovereignty. I just thought you should know.

January 2009

UNIMPRESSED OF BODMIN

Here's an apparently genuine complaint to Devon & Cornwall Police that someone sent me recently. (I needed to cut it down a bit!)...

"Sir, Having spent the past 20 minutes waiting for someone at Bodmin police station to pick up the 'phone, I'm resorting to email. There are three youths in St Mary's Crescent, kicking a football against an iron gate with an earth-shattering CLANG which resounds throughout the whole building. I am unsure of the rules and scoring, because the game is now in its third week.

There are five other mutants spreading bags of rubbish around the wheelie bins, and it's only a matter of time before they turn their limited attention to the bottles of calor gas that someone has kindly dumped there. If they could be relied on to only blow themselves up I would happily leave them to it (indeed I would supply the matches) but they are more likely to blow up the street, and I've just redecorated the kitchen.

What I suggest is that, after replying to this email with worthless assurances that this complaint is being investigated, why not leave it until one night of the year (probably bath night) when there are no mutants around and then drive up the street in a panda car, before doing a three-point-turn and disappearing again.

Whilst I realise there may be far more serious crimes taking place in Bodmin - such as smoking in a public place – is it too much to ask for a policeman to explain to these morons that they might want to play their strange game elsewhere, like the pitch on Fairpark Road, or even at the bottom of Par Dock...

If you want me, I'll be in the Cat & Fiddle."

January 2009

RUNNING OUT OF SOMEONE ELSE'S MONEY

In April 2008 Gordon Brown made an official trip to the USA, but his visit was pretty much overshadowed by the arrival of Pope Benedict XVI. Given the speech that Brown later made within the cloistered walls of Harvard's Kennedy Centre, that was probably a good thing...

Phyllis Schlafly, president of the Eagle Forum, sat in the audience. "Brown's speech impudently demanded that we issue a declaration of interdependence in order to submit to global governance. That's another way of calling on us to repeal our Declaration of Independence"...

Brown's speech used the word 'global' 69 times, 'globalisation' 7 times, and 'interdependence' 13 times. According to Mrs Schlafly: "Brown rejected the concept of national sovereignty, which means an independent nation not subservient to outside control, telling us to replace it with 'responsible sovereignty' which he defined as accepting what he calls our global 'obligations'. Hold on to your pocketbook."

You can understand why the audience felt so

uncomfortable. In 1776 Americans rose up against the British Crown, throwing off foreign rule. Mrs Schlafly again: "Brown wants to increase the power of the United Nations to become 'an international stand-by of trained civilian experts ready to go anywhere, anytime, even to exercise military force'. Americans do not intend to cede such authority to the corrupt UN".

As she pointed out: "The silliest part of his speech was that global society was 'advancing democracy widely across the world'. He doesn't even practise democracy in his own country. Brown refused to let the British people vote on whether they want to accept the European Constitution. Instead of a self-governing nation whose democratic system was developed across the centuries, England is now ruled by what Margaret Thatcher called: 'the paper pushers in Brussels.".

We could do with Phyllis Schlafly around here at the moment. At any rate, it would be an improvement on David Cameron.

February 2009

GOODBYE GRAHAM

MEP Graham Booth recently stood down from UKIP for personal family reasons, to be replaced by Trevor Colman MEP, lead candidate for the 2009 euro elections. In a moving speech Trevor paid tribute to Graham for all his efforts...

"I'd like to wish Graham and Pam a long and very happy retirement. You may not be aware but Graham here is mentioned in most golfing manuals as the inventor of a particular golf-swing, the 'Booth

Scat'. This manoeuvre is totally unique because there is no back-swing. It does not exist...Graham stands over the ball, glowering at it, remaining perfectly still. Then he pushes his arms forward, and by accident the club hits the ball which rolls a few yards...

The 'Booth Scat' is repeated every few steps as he advances down the fairway, muttering, 'I'm giving up this bleep bleep game.' Graham recently played at Churston, his home club in Torbay, where the par is 70. Graham shot a creditable 73, before moving on to the second hole"...

The reason that I am mentioning Trevor's tribute to Graham is to thank Graham Booth for his huge efforts for the last six years, not as a golfer but as a south-west MEP. He has been a great driver (no pun intended) of UKIP over the years and we all wish him a long and happy retirement.

February 2009

THE PEOPLE WHO COUNT

Margaret Thatcher once said: 'The problem with Socialism is that you eventually run out of other people's money', which is very true. But, after the credit-crash when the banks went bananas and blew all our money, unbridled capitalism now stands alongside in the dock. It's not easy finding the right balance, but you can avoid the biggest heffalump traps...

Peter Mandelson (sorry, Lord Mandelson) is still determined to get us into the euro currency. The secret talks were revealed by Jose Barroso, president of the European Commission, who recently said that Britain was 'closer than ever before' to signing up to the single currency. Mr Barroso added that he had had conversations with 'the people who count in Britain' and knew that they were ready to move into the eurozone.

Let's be clear. If we were in the euro the Bank of England could not have cut interest rates to ease the recession. Interest rates for the euro are set in a big bank in Frankfurt, and apply throughout the eurozone. This is why Spain, Italy and Greece are in economic freefall. They need to cut interest rates but can't.

To quote Nigel Farage, leader of the UK Independence Party: 'If Barroso would like to consult the "people who count in Britain" then he can call for a referendum on the euro so the people of Britain can tell him where to go.'

March 2009

SHUT THAT DOOR

Unless you're a hard-line racist, the immigration debate is about two things. Numbers, and multiculturalism, both of which feed extremists. I'm with Sir Gulam Noon (the so-called Curry King) who recently told journalist Andrew Marr: "We should wait for five or 10 years, until all the newcomers have been properly integrated and assimilated into the country. Until then we should just shut the door. We can only accommodate so many."

The big problem is that being in the EU we have lost control of immigration and our borders. Virtually any EU citizen is allowed in, and an immigrant can pitch up in, say, Rumania, be given a passport and a taxi-ride to the border, and that's it. Britain here we come. In short, we've left the back door wide open.

As for multiculturalism, it's a busted flush. When we have a cricket team called the Middlesex Crusaders (so-named for 10 years) being told to change their name after angry complaints from Muslims and Jews, (and then a Muslim suing Tesco's because they made him carry alcohol) this country has gone bananas.

English is now a minority language in 1,300 schools, and in one district of London nine out of ten schools have an intake where the mother tongue is not English for a majority of pupils. It gets worse: one in seven pupils doesn't have English as their first language, and that figure has doubled in a decade. As the Daily Mail reported 29/04/08: "The statistics, compiled by the Dept for Children, Schools and Families show the proportion of pupils whose first language is not English has risen to an all-time high."

Surely it's blindingly obvious that all children in British schools should be taught English and no other language (apart from the ones on the curriculum)? The rest should be taught at home at the parent's expense. Otherwise we are fracturing our education system and sacrificing these poor children on the altar of political correctness.

March 2009

FAREWELL WEASEL, FAREWELL WREN

A primery scool in Glostershire has recently axed spelling tests for its pupils because getting the words rong can leave them feeling like failures. Children at Whitmister Church of England Primary will no longer have to lern lists of words such as Stopping, Between, Planned, Involved, or Smoothly...

The headmistress, Debbie Marklove, explained things in a letter to the parents: "We have taken the decision to stop spelling as homework as it is felt that although children may learn them perfectly at home, they are often unable to use them in their written work. Also many children find this activity unnecessarily distressing."

As one correspondent from New Zealand observed: "If you have any more Nu-Labour governments like the present one, you are going to need all the cannon fodder you can get. Make sure your children get an education so they can apply for a passport and escape."

Adding fuel to the fire is the Oxford University Press which has just culled hundreds of words from its Junior Dictionary, replacing them with entries better reflecting Britain as modern, multicultural and multi-faith. Tradition, religion and the countryside are the worst casualties. Gone are words like Bishop, Chapel, Carol, Devil, Duchess, Emperor, Kingfisher, Lark, Poodle, Raven, Stork, Weasel, and Wren.

Incoming words are: MP3 player, Bullet-point, EU, Bungee jumping, Allergic, Emotion, Dyslexic, Euro, and Food Chain. All I can say is that we will roo the day we surrended our education system to these politically correct spin-meisters.

March 2009

Following the above piece, a couple of Labour luvvies wrote to the newspapers, saying: "How can Mr Challice complain about words when he himself cannot spell?" which reinforces my view of Labour Luvvies. Little sense of humour and even less imagination.

WRIGGLING ON THE HOOK

Brussels has now turned its sights onto sea anglers, wanting them to be part of the disastrous Common Fisheries Policy which has virtually destroyed our entire fishing industry. This will mean that skippers of recreational fishing boats will have quotas imposed on them. Once they reach their quota, no more fishing.

Some 1.4 million Britons go sea angling every year, and the sport sustains a £1-billion industry covering equipment, servicing, accommodation and boat hire. Ports such as Weymouth, Littlehampton, and Arbroath earn millions of pounds a year from recreational anglers. But that doesn't deter the EU.

The man in charge of British fishing is Joe Borg, European Commissioner for maritime affairs and fisheries. From his office in Brussels he says: "Control and enforcement of catch limits should be the cornerstone of the CFP. The future of sustainable fisheries requires us to replace a system which is inefficient with one which really produces results."

Well, this will really produce results, but maybe not the sort that Mr Borg is thinking of....
Fishing was once our greatest self-sustaining natural resource but since we joined the EU our seas have been raped by the Continental armada. As with so much else, we have simply lost control. The idea that sea anglers are threatening stocks is laughable. UKIP will be lobbying MEPs ahead of the debate in April and the party urges you to write to your own MEP warning that if they don't support a CFP exemption for sea anglers they won't get your vote in the Euro elections on 4th June.

April 2009

ROUGH AS A BADGER'S BACKSIDE

There's an old Navajo proverb: "You can't wake a person who is pretending to be asleep", and there are still a few Britons who cannot or will not see the danger posed by our membership of the EU.

Let's look at the legal system. More than 80% of our laws are now made in Brussels, where the votes are taken at such speed that few MEPs know what they are voting on and why they're doing it in the first place.

The former Master of the Rolls, Lord Denning stated: "No longer is European law an incoming tide flowing up the estuaries of England. It is now like a tidal wave bringing down our sea walls and flowing inland over our fields and houses, to the dismay of us all."

If you raise this issue you will get three responses, in order. First, "Don't be so daft. You're spreading alarmist loony nonsense."… Next, a year or so later: "It's just a proposal. It'll never happen."… And finally: "Sorry but it's European law. Nothing we can do about it now."

If the EU was a woman you'd say she was rough as a bag of bolts with a face like a plasterer's radio. It's that bad, believe me. The list of failures is depressingly long: post office closures, landfill tax, Human Rights Act, open-door immigration policy etc...But the people who really make the laws are the European Commission, not the MEPs. And the crucial fact is that when you become an EU Commissioner you are there to serve Brussels, not your own country. It's in the job description.

As the MEP Bill Newton Dunn (Lib Dem) said in 1990: "There is no plot by the European Parliament to usurp powers from the House of Commons. The Commons never had power over European laws. When ministers go to Brussels, they leave their democratic shackles behind them."

That really does spell it out. "leave their democratic shackles behind".

April 2009

THE ROAD TO SEGREGATION

Ask the American Indians what happens when you don't control immigration. The Labour Government has lost control over this vital issue. One small example is that we have an estimated 180,000 illegal immigrants now being granted amnesty, solely because the asylum system went into meltdown and the backlog of cases has grown so huge. To quote the Daily Mail (10/12/08) "The approval rate is 40% and rising, with all those who are successful gaining access to housing and other benefits. Local councils will be expected to find homes for many of them."

One of the problems is the Human Rights Act passed by Labour ten years ago. Many of these people can claim that because of the delay in dealing with their cases Britain is now their home and they no longer have links to their country of origin.

It strikes me that this Government is encouraging our pensioners to move abroad, as few of them vote Labour, and replacing them with illegals who are more likely to preserve it in power, thus ensuring the continued destruction of the British economy.

There is another cost to this, the very structure of British society. In 2004 when the EU enlarged to take in Poland etc the Government estimated that 13,000 would come here for work. Ten times that number came in one year. As Sir Andrew Green, Chairman of Migrationwatch, explained: "This mass immigration is dividing England into two zones. In the countryside, life continues much as usual. In the cities, multi-culturalism is taking over."...

Even Trevor Phillips has suggested that we are "sleepwalking towards segregation." And when we have illegal immigrants vanishing after being given rail tickets and told to "make their way" to a detention centre, this is further proof of meltdown.

April 2009

WRONG WATERING HOLE

G K Chesterton once went to meet someone at an inn called the Dull Man at Greenwich, but he was wasting his time because he should have gone to the Green Man at Dulwich... I know how he feels. After reading a few newspaper reports on benefit scams and pensions, I'm now wondering why I bothered.

The suspected al Qaeda terrorist Hany Youssef has been given leave to stay in Britain (claiming thousands of pounds of benefits) despite the fact that he is on a UN list of people 'belonging to or linked' to al Qaeda. He first came here in 1994, applying for asylum. In 1999 he was held under anti-terror laws. Tony Blair said it was "crazy" he could not be deported. But in 2004 Youssef even received damages after the High Court ruled in his favour because the Human Rights Act - signed by Blair - prevents us kicking him out.

Another report reveals that jobless East Europeans

returning home from Britain are claiming £60 a week dole money from us. That's because we're in the EU and the rules are clear. If you're laid off in one country you can still claim benefits from that country even if you have headed home to look for work.

In Poland they now have workshops on how to claim British Jobseeker's Allowance. Renata Cygan, of the Jobcentre in Opole, Poland, explained: "We work on the assumption that if someone worked abroad they should claim benefits there. Why should we pay? That's why we're organising meetings about how to seek benefits abroad."

For me, the final icing on the cake was that Britain is now scrapping rules allowing wealthy non-EU foreigners from retiring in Britain. So if you're American, or Canadian, or Australian or Indian, or from Hong Kong - anywhere but the EU of course - you won't be allowed in. In retaliation those same locations will probably ban British retirees from going there. So even if you have the money to escape from Nu-Labour land, you might be stuck here with the rest of us. Sorry about that.... Are you coming to the Green Man at Dulwich? I'll buy you a pint. You look like you need it.

April 2009

ANOTHER LIGHTBULB MOMENT

Thanks to the European Union our traditional tungsten light-bulbs will soon be banned, replaced by so-called "green" light-bulbs. But don't be fooled, because these new light-bulbs are highly dangerous. In a world full of health-and-safety laws it is unbelievable that these low-energy bulbs are being shoved down our throats, in spite of the health risks. They are filled with poisonous mercury, which worsens skin disorders, and can trigger migraines and epilepsy.

If you break a bulb you must open the window and vacate the room for 20 minutes. Then you must sweep up the fragments with stiff card and place them into a box labelled "Hazardous Waste" before passing it to a licensed waste operator. Please do not vacuum up the fragments or you will contaminate your hoover bag. Also, it is illegal to throw the waste into your dustbin, because mercury must not go to landfill. It depends who you ask, but some councils insist that you call in the Environmental Health Department before taking any action.

I have yet to see any low-energy bulb that lists the health risks on the packaging, but because it is part of the "green agenda" it is verboten to raise the issue.

This farce has been brought to you by the EU, along with much else UKIP will scrap this crazy law because mercury light-bulbs are highly dangerous. If you've had enough of being treated like a child by these unelected and unaccountable rulers in Brussels then please get out there on June 4th and vote U K Independence Party in the European Elections.

May 2009

THE LIGHTBULB DIMS

Last week I explained how the EU is forcing us to scrap traditional tungsten light-bulbs in favour of low-energy bulbs filled with poisonous mercury. If you break a mercury bulb you must ventilate the room for 20 minutes, then seal the fragments into a box, then send it to a hazardous waste operator. You cannot vacuum up the mess because you'll contaminate your hoover, and you cannot throw it into the dustbin because that's illegal.

Mercury bulbs have caused burning on the skin of those suffering eczema and psoriasis, and are potentially lethal for the partially-sighted (and the rest of us) because they give out a dim, pathetic glow. Take your life in your hands on every staircase. On the subject of dim and pathetic, the British Government rolled over and agreed to this, just to please our masters in Brussels.

It gets better: the EU has listed mercury as a hazardous substance and is currently destroying British firms such as Russell Scientific Instruments because they make mercury barometers. Edward Allen, director of the firm, appealed for help: "Who will be left with expertise to handle and repair instruments if we are stopped? The government must listen to us and fight our case against the bureaucrats of Brussels. Surely the government is fighting to save jobs and not increasing the unemployment figures!"

Unfortunately it doesn't work like that any longer. It's not the Government making the rules.

May 2009

LERN THE BLUDDY LANGUAGE

Sometimes you might feel that Britain's gone so bonkers that it's time to get the local trick-cyclist to book you into the jim-jam clinic for a few weeks till you feel better. But then it gets better, which is nice. Deva Kumarasiri came to Britain from Sri Lanka 18 years ago, becoming a post-master in Nottingham. A union jack flutters from the back of his Landrover. He is encouraging his two daughters to join the RAF and is proud to be British.

A few weeks ago Deva hit the headlines when he refused to serve customers in his shop who couldn't speak or read English, and were making no attempt to try: "All I'm doing is telling people that if they want to live in Britain, be British. Don't boo the soldiers when they come home from Iraq. Don't live your life without embracing our culture. And if you don't want to be British, go home."

He went on: "I decided to make this stand because I think too many British people are afraid to talk out [and] are afraid of being branded a racist."

Making his stand cost him dearly. Deva lost his job as a postmaster, and despite being an elected Lib Dem Councillor the local Liberal Democrats kicked him out of the Party. Nice to see that free speech is still alive and kicking in the East Midlands.

May 2009

GET INTO THE EURO... FAST!

Graham Watson is the South West's only Lib Dem MEP (but I understand that he's so desperate to be next EU President that he recently wrote to UKIP MEPs asking for support. They told him: "We'll get your coat."). In 2006 Mr Watson wrote a different letter, this time to the newspapers: "The best way to protect British jobs is to get Britain into the euro - fast!" This classic is now framed on my office wall. Mr Watson is totally wrong on this. And I'll explain why. Gordon Brown was probably the worst

Chancellor we've had for a century, crippling our pensions industry, shovelling cash into the public services like it was going out of fashion, and abolishing the Bank of England's role of 'banking cop', giving it to the toothless Financial Services Authority.

But at least he got one thing right. He refused to join the euro, and for that we must be grateful. "Getting Britain into the euro – fast!" would mean that the British Government could not cut interest rates. A big bank in Frankfurt would be making that decision for us.

In Marbella, Spain, the waiters and café owners ask: "What has happened to los Ingeles?" Their cafes are empty, with staff laid off. The answer is that 'los Ingeles' wisely kept out of the euro and were therefore free to devalue their currency when it suited. Foreign holidays became more expensive, along with many exports, but it was a price worth paying.

Other EU countries aren't so lucky, but the PIGS are the worst. Portugal, Italy, Greece, and Spain. When one of them crashes out of the eurozone, others will tumble like dominos.

May 2009

ONE-LINERS

The comedian Peter Kay has a number of great one-liners: "When I was a kid I used to pray every night for a new bike, then I realised that the Lord doesn't work that way, so I stole one and asked Him to forgive me." Or: "Right now I'm having amnesia and déjà vu at the same time. I think I've forgotten this before." Or: "At the end of a party there's always a girl crying."

But he doesn't have the monopoly. Lib Dem MEP Graham Watson once wrote to the newspapers: "The best way to protect British jobs is to get Britain into the euro – fast!" Graham, you slay me.
The Buddhists have a great one: "Believe in permanence at your peril."

Or this from Dr Adrian Rogers (not a one-liner): "The government cannot give to anybody anything that the government does not take first from somebody else. When half the people get the idea that they do not have to work because the other half is going to take care of them, and the other half gets the idea that it's no good going to work because somebody else is going to get what they work for, that my dear friend, is about the end of any nation."

Let's return to Peter Kay: "Why is it called Alcoholics Anonymous when the first thing you do is stand up and say: 'My name is Peter and I'm an alcoholic.'"? Or this one: "Old ladies can eat more than you think." Or my favourite: "You've turned into your dad the day you put aside a thin piece of wood specifically to stir paint with."

June 2009

PRE-ELECTION PURPLE

I'm writing this two weeks before the June 4th European Elections, and by the time you read it things might have changed. At the moment UKIP is level in the opinion polls with the Labour government; and we're going up while they're going down. To quote a BBC journalist yesterday: "The UKIP bandwagon is now rolling."

I risk getting omelette on my face when this appears in print, but as more stories emerge of MPs charging us for non-existent mortgages, 88p bathplugs, and porno movies, it seems likely that UKIP will do extremely well. So on behalf of UKIP and all the candidates you voted for on June 4th , may I say a big Thank You to everyone. We couldn't have done it without you, and I promise that UKIP will continue exposing the EU's pernicious influence over this country.

A joke is now running through the EU corridors in Brussels, referring to MPs claims for cash: "What is another name for British MPs?..... Lightweights!"... This is because the MEPs in Brussels know that the system of EU allowances (and the fraud involved) makes Plug-Gate (if I can invent that term) look like somebody fiddling the tea money.

Former accountant Marta Andreasen (hopefully now a UKIP MEP but we'll have to see) was hired to look at the EU accounts. But then she reported back that the system was in chaos, with massive fraud, a vast black hole of money that had simply disappeared, and not even double-entry book-keeping to back it up,. She was then gagged and sacked. For Marta, simply walking back into that EU Council Chamber as an MEP, will be hugely satisfying.

I must take this opportunity to thank Malcolm Wood, SW Regional Organiser for UKIP, who is retiring in June. He's been a superb and tireless worker, a huge asset to UKIP over the years, and he and his wife Jenny will be sorely missed. Enjoy that bottle of Burgundy, Malcolm.

June 2009

POST OFFICE QUESTION TIME

Back in March 2009, in the House of Commons, Tory MP Ann Winterton stood up at Prime Minister's Questions and asked for confirmation that: "…the real reason for part-privatising Royal Mail stems directly from European Union postal legislation, which forced Royal Mail to divest itself of its most profitable business, thereby handing it over lock, stock and barrel to European competitors."
There was hush in the House. An embarrassed silence. Somebody had just back-fired in Church.

The Prime Minister was absent, with Harriet Harperson in his place. She rose, and replied smoothly: "The real reason was the analysis in the Hooper Report, which we commissioned as long ago as December 2007." Then she sat down.

One problem. The Hooper Report makes it clear that EU rules are responsible: "Transformation [of Royal Mail] would have to be carried out under European rules on restructuring aid", which would, "impose considerable restraints". Unless Royal Mail could modernise faster: "a forced restructuring under European rules is highly likely."

The reason for the embarrassed hush in the Commons is that the Tories are voting with the Government, against Labour back-benchers, in favour of privatising the scrag-end of the Post Office. With European Elections looming, the Conservatives were terrified the truth would get out: that the privatisation is driven entirely by EU rules. How would that look to eurosceptic voters?

June 2009

NORTH AND SOUTH DAKOTA

I am very interested in history. My great, great, great grandfather was killed at the Battle of the Little Big Horn. (He wasn't with Custer or Sitting Bull. He was camping in the next valley and went over to complain about the noise).

One of the greatest ever historical machines (along with the Spitfire and the Willys Jeep) is the Douglas Dakota DC3, workhorse of the American Air Force. Twin-engined, designed to fly on only one engine if the other packed up, they served throughout the world and in many wars. In desert, in jungle, across the sea. In 1945 a Dakota broke the world record for flying with one engine out of action (from Pearl Harbour to San Diego, 1,100 miles).

With its on-board loos, and galley to serve hot food, and nose-up beak when on the ground, square windows, and sleek metal fuselage, Daks astonished the world when they first appeared in 1935 – in sharp contrast to the bone-shakers of the day, where passengers huddled under blankets to keep warm.

Veteran pilot Captain Len Morgan says: "The Dakota could lift virtually any load strapped to its back and carry it anywhere and in any weather safely. It is the very human scale of the plane that has endeared it to successive generations. It flies low and slow, and can be landed on a postage stamp."

But in Britain, at least, it is now all over. Finished, thanks to EU rules. The last two Dakotas in service have been banned from flying. Mike Collett, chairman of Coventry based Air Atlantique, has been ordered to ground Romeo Alpha and Papa Alpha because they contravene EU Health and Safety rules. It would be too expensive to fit emergency escape slides and weather-radar systems. Never mind that well-maintained Daks have a great safety record, and when on the ground passengers can step from cabin to runway without effort.

Another casualty of the unelected, faceless bureaucrats in Brussels. They'll poison us with mercury lightbulbs but stick their noses in everywhere else. What a state to be in.

June 2009

GOING TO THE ZOO, ZOO, ZOO

This story is apparently true but it might yet be an urban myth. You must judge... Outside Bristol Zoo there is a car park for 150 cars and 8 coaches. For 25 years there was also a very pleasant parking attendant with a ticket machine, charging cars £1 and coaches £5. Then one day he retired. Bristol Zoo Management phoned up the City Council: "You'll need to send round a new parking attendant."

"No," said the Council. "That car park is your responsibility."...

"No," said the Zoo. "He was employed by you, wasn't he?"

"No," said the Council.

There's now a bloke in Spain, sitting in a villa, who has been taking the parking fees for the last 25 years at an estimated £400 a day. That's what I call private enterprise.

July 2009

TAKING IT FURTHER

In the middle of the European elections in June 2009 a volunteer at UKIP Head Office (near Newton Abbot) took a telephone call: "Good afternoon. UK Independence Party. How can I help?" ...

The lady caller said pompously: "I am not giving my name, but as a County Councillor in Devon, I am appalled, absolutely appalled, that Sir Winston Churchill is on the cover of your election leaflet. I shall be taking this further!"

UKIP's official response is: "Fine. Go ahead."
In September 1945, in Zurich, Winston Churchill made a speech: 'The first step in the recreation of the European family must be a partnership between France and Germany. In this way only can France recover the moral leadership of Europe.' But he continued: 'Great Britain, the British Commonwealth, mighty America, and I trust Soviet Russia, must be the friends and sponsors of the new Europe and must champion its right to shine.'

Churchill saw France and Germany leading the new Europe, but crucially with Britain (and the Commonwealth) as friend and sponsor, not as a member. When we were conned into joining the EU (under the guise of a 'Common Market') Edward Heath and his Conservative Party promptly turned their backs on the Commonwealth. That would have appalled Churchill.

Since the 1970s the three big political parties have colluded in handing our sovereignty to unelected officials in Brussels. But it was never theirs to give away. Sovereignty lies with the people - Churchill knew that better than anyone – and at the June 4th

European elections we saw that many British people agreed with him, and voted UKIP.

After the recent revelations of Plug-Gate (non-existent mortgages, 88p bathplugs, and porn movies being charged to the taxpayer) I should also explain to that anonymous Devon County Councillor that this Party will take no lessons in probity from her lot.

July 2009

ON THE BOX

These contestants' answers from TV and radio quizzes confirm that our education system has much work ahead of it....

Presenter: "Where do you think Cambridge University is?"
Contestant: "Geography's not my strong point."
Presenter: "There's a clue in the title."
Contestant: "Er... Leicester?"

Or try this one. Presenter: "What happened in Dallas on November 22nd, 1963?"
Contestant: "I don't know. I wasn't watching it then."

Or this from University Challenge: Jeremy Paxman: "What was Ghandi's first name?"
Contestant: "Goosey?"

Or this one: Presenter: "Name a film starring Bob Hoskins that's also the name of a famous painting by Leonardo Da Vinci."
Contestant: "Er... Who framed Roger Rabbit?"

And lastly my favourite, from Denham's Drivetime

(Virgin Radio):
Denham: "In which country would you spend shekels?"
Contestant: "Holland?"
Denham: "Try the next letter of the alphabet."
Contestant: "Iceland? Ireland?"
Denham (helpfully): "Did you say Israel?"
Contestant: "No."

July 2009

PLODS ON TOP

Being a frontline cop can be a dirty business. Would you like to be out there on a Saturday night, shovelling drunks into the back of a Transit van, or dealing with snotty little thugs who "know their rights"? Nope, thought not.

So I'm not criticising the troops out there on the ground. My complaint against the Police is how they've been turned into target-driven, politically correct enforcers of discredited Labour policies.

When they're not pulling over motorists who display a Union Jack on their numberplate, or sending out standard letters of response, or criticising the victim: "Well, if you must leave your car radio installed when you pop into Sainsbury's, what do you expect?" they get up to other things...

The splendidly named Ministry of Justice recently confirmed that almost 1,000 prisoners are now on the run, but (to quote the Norwich Daily News 8/7/09) "Many forces have refused to release details of the wanted men's identities or offences, saying it could be considered a breach of privacy." Ah, diddums. Poor dears.

Another story in the same newspaper also caught my eye. In the little village of Brancaster, Norfolk, they were holding a scarecrow festival. One of the organisers built a 7ft scarecrow, dressed in a dayglow yellow jacket, wearing a peaked cap, and armed with a plastic pop bottle painted to look like a speed camera.

Norfolk police didn't get the joke. They took PC Gummidge into custody, explaining: "The owner of the scarecrow used a plastic bottle to symbolise a speed radar gun. As a result an officer removed the scarecrow as it portrayed an incorrect and inappropriate message. Speed radars are used to prevent casualties on our roads and to address the irresponsible actions of motorists – they should not be re-created by the roadside in jest."

And they say the Germans have no sense of humour.

July 2009

HALFWAY HOUSE?

The Lib Dems are seen by many voters as a 'safe alternative' to Tory or Labour. But I wonder why?

The Lib Dems support the EU Arrest Warrant, which allows you (or me) to be taken to face trial in another EU country without any evidence of a crime needing to be shown to a British court, even for a crime that's not an offence in this country.

The Lib Dems are in favour of the Lisbon Treaty, which gives more powers to Europol (the EU police force) whose officers are immune from prosecution when engaged on official police business.

The Lib Dems support EU Communications Data Directive (2006/24/EC) which gives state agencies the right to monitor who you've been emailing and what you've been accessing on the internet.

And the Lib Dems, of course, are pledged to help fund the second Irish referendum on the Lisbon Treaty (the one where the Irish already said "No" so the Lib Dems will be asking them again, until the Irish get it right).

So, if the Lib Dems aren't liberal and aren't democratic, what are they actually for?

July 2009

THE BATTLE OF WODGET HILL

The Stone Age didn't end just because we ran out of stones. It is hard-wired into us to adapt, change, and survive (though the cavemen took a few thousand years to get going). If I invent a widget, you'll invent a wodget, so I must invent a widget that also wodges...

The driving force behind this is private enterprise and the market-place, not governments using our money to fund research. Governments don't know how to innovate and should keep their nose out. The Concorde aircraft might have been a technological triumph, but it never made a profit and the taxpayer picked up the bill.

Constant change is the only permanence. Back in 1939 the Spitfire (and, yes, the Hurricane) blasted the Luftwaffe out of the Battle of Britain. But one year later the Germans introduced the Focke-Wulf 190, a far better plane which blew our guys out of the sky. Churchill saw the threat and cancelled all fighter operations over Northern Europe.

Had the Nazis been using Focke-Wulfs in 1939 we'd have lost. But then in 1941 the new, improved Spitfire Mark 1X entered service, and it was our turn to kick butt again... as you can possibly guess, otherwise I'd be writing this in German, nicht wahr?

So I'm not averse to change, and do accept that mobile 'phones have pretty much killed off the old red telephone kiosks. It's a shame, but things move on. But one thing that does rile me is when UKIP is accused of wanting to return to the past and of being 'phobic' about being sucked into a "modern, dynamic European superstate". Rather than misplaced nostalgia, UKIP is showing plain common sense. Much of what is wrong with 'modern' Britain can be laid at the EU's door, and to quote President Obama: "It's time for a change".

August 2009

THE FREEDOM TO STARVE

Back in the 1960s and 70s (and little has changed since) Africa was wracked by disease, illiteracy, poverty, lawlessness, and endemic corruption. But Rhodesia was different. There were productive farms, schools, hospitals, an honest police-force, and a booming business life, partly due to the Indian and Pakistani community that formed an integral part of Rhodesia's success, not just rich whites as some might imagine. And most black Africans enjoyed a far higher standard of living than millions in neighbouring countries.

But then along came Robert Mugabe, and all the bleeding heart liberals were satisfied. Guardian readers could buy Zimbabwean apples again. There was only one problem. He totally messed it up. Socialists always do. Labour did it to Britain in the 1970s and have done so again.

As for Mugabe, he transformed Rhodesia from "bread basket of Africa" to basket case of that poor benighted continent. I'm willing to bet that most Zimbabweans today would prefer Smith's Electoral College system, with healthcare, decent schools, etc, to the brutal, murderous and repressive regime they are currently saddled with.

When he was Prime Minister, Ian Smith used to walk to work in the morning, carrying his briefcase, saying hello to those he met en-route. Robert Mugabe needs motorcycle outriders and an armoured Mercedes.

Smith pointed this out to President Mugabe years later. President Mugabe smiled.

August 2009

PORKY PIG IS UNWELL

I'm no scientist but I'm getting a nasty feeling about swine flu. On July 12th 2009 the Sunday Times ran the headline: "Swine flu vaccine to be cleared after five-day trial".

Given that most medicines take years to get from laboratory to GP's surgery, this seems a tad rushed. But regulators at the European Medicines Agency are apparently unworried: explaining that this "fast-track approval" follows clinical trials of a similar 'mock-up' vaccine.

Now call me Mr Picky but that's not good enough.

What does "similar mock-up vaccine" mean exactly? The last mass vaccination against swine flu was in the USA in the 1970s, when they halted the campaign after some people suffered Guillain-Barres syndrome as a side effect (a disorder of the nervous system).

And very recent research in Britain now estimates that 1-in-20 young children will suffer acute vomiting as a reaction to the vaccine, leading to possible dehydration if symptoms persist. For young children in particular this can be very serious.

Dr Peter Holden, the BMA's specialist on the disease, said that although swine flu was not causing serious illness in patients, health officials are eager to start a mass vaccination campaign. But why?

To quote the Sunday Times: "About 15 people have died of swine flu in Britain, but most of those infected get only mild symptoms. According to the latest figures from the Health Protection Agency, the UK has had 9,718 confirmed cases of the disease." Given the figures, why the rush to mass vaccinate the entire population?

August 2009

IN THE CITY

Following the credit crunch the EU has now decided to muscle in on Europe's finance, insurance, and banking sectors. Its plan is to impose EU rules directly over this area of business, which is like giving the fox the keys to the hen coop, considering that for 14 years running the EU's own auditors have refused to sign off the accounts.

Bill Cash (Tory MP) wrote to The Times on

10/07/09: "The whole framework for financial regulation is being driven by the overarching jurisdiction of the European Union that will hand over the ultimate decisions to majority voting and the lethal use of co-decision."

In other words the City of London will be fatally undermined, the idea being to move business to Paris and Frankfurt etc. But the probable result is that much of the financial sector will flee Europe altogether and go to the emerging nations such as India and China, whose economies are doing very well (much better than ours!).

Bill Cash raised this with the Chancellor, Alistair Darling, and received this reply: "We are governed by European directives, whether we like it or not."

Thank you, Darling.

August 2009

AN ACCURATE CHARACTER ASSESSMENT

The writer, Anita Bruckner, once said that people who live cautiously and conscientiously are punished for their virtue, while the selfish get away with it: "Haven't you noticed that? Think of Tony Blair. Unrealistic. Selfish. Happy as a clam!"

Britain's immigration policy is a great example. Tony Blair threw open the doors and surrendered control, with dire results, but little blame ever stuck to him. In the first ten years of New Labour, 71% of all new jobs went to foreign-born workers. (source OECD). In Australia it was less than 30%, which makes me think that our lot had a couple of kangaroos loose in the top paddock. So much for "British jobs for British workers".

The Home Office already makes payments of up to £4,000 for failed asylum seekers who agree to go home, but we are now paying people to leave before they have even arrived. Together with the French we are funding the Global Calais Project which targets the migrant camps near Calais. It's very simple. If someone enters Britain illegally they should be returned to the last country they passed through. In this case, France.

To all Guardianista readers who disagree with this policy, why don't YOU go and stand at the dockside in Calais and open your own chequebook? The rest of us have better things to spend our money on, like doctors, nurses, teachers, and body armour for our troops.

September 2009

COUGH UP, MOTHER

A UKIP member recently sent Head Office an email...

"Dear Nigel Farage, You will undoubtedly have heard of the 'Digital Britain' policy of the present government. Having conversations with colleagues in the communications industry, this seems a disaster waiting to occur.

When Mr Brown says everyone should have access to high-speed services, all that will happen is that the present service will get clogged up with people playing games and watching porn etc, with serious users needing a second level (at great cost) to escape the 'noise' of Mr Brown's voters.

The proposed surcharge of £6.00 (plus VAT?) is outrageous. Why should my 87-year old mother help finance everyone else when she has no intention of using the internet?

Why must we lose AM and FM analogue services, with an estimated 70 million radios that will become obsolete? There will be a lot of recycling to do.

The argument of more radio and TV stations is a non-starter. When we had just four or five channels of TV there was always a programme of a standard to shine throughout the world. Now we have literally dozens of channels of drivel.

I also feel that the drive towards digital access from home may be for more sinister reasons. Internet service providers can watch your every move: read your emails, see what you're watching, general surveillance.

This year I joined a political party for the first time in my life. That party was yours, and I trust you will be committed to sorting this mess out as a priority. Wishing you all the best, a UKIP member".

I can't speak on UKIP policy, but the digital switchover (and 'Digital Britain') comes from the EU, in a direct attempt to establish a common digital broadcasting system. It doesn't matter whether it's a good idea or not. In a collective, everyone must be the same. And that's why UKIP is driving to get us out, before the roof crashes in.

September 2009

NEEDLE STUCK IN GROOVE

What is Britain's most exclusive club? The "mile-high"? Or perhaps White's in St James? Nope. It's the Cabinet of the Labour Party...

They prattle on about social mobility and equality; but it's like the mafia giving morality lessons. These guys keep it in the family. As journalist Jeff Randall recently explained: "the Labour Cabinet includes the Miliband brothers, Edward and David; the husband-and-wife team Ed Balls and Yvette Cooper, daughter of Prospect's former General Secretary; Harriet Harman, niece of Lord Longford (former Labour leader of the House of Lords) and the spouse of the party's treasurer, Jack Dromey; Douglas Alexander, sibling of Wendy, the former leader of Labour in Scotland; Hillary Benn, son of Tony, who served as Harold Wilson's industry secretary, and Peter Mandelson, grandson of Herbert Morrison, Clement Atlee's deputy prime minister."

A recent report by Alan Milburn, former Labour minister, concluded: "Social mobility has slowed down in our country. Birth, not worth, has become more and more a determinant of people's life chances."

So to recap: the Labour Government abolished most grammar schools, dumbed down GCSEs and A-Levels, and re-branded tech colleges and polytechnics as "universities" (which then offered non-degrees such as skateboarding or ice skating).

They also poured vast sums into expanding the public sector, at the expense of the private sector which actually makes the cash in the first place. Despite everything, despite all that money, all those initiatives, all the quangoes, all the fine words, Labour has failed in its own central aim of increasing social mobility. Labour has done it again. Give them the public purse and they will empty it in one generation. For the good of the country, they must never be trusted with power ever again.

September 2009

A WORLD OF ISMS

The world is full of 'isms', or is that just a truism?
Socialism is that you have two cows and give one to
your neighbour. Communism is that the State takes
both cows and gives you some milk. With Nazism,
if you're not a Nazi, the State takes both cows and
shoots you, and Surrealism means you have two
giraffes and the State pays for your harmonica
lessons.

This all seems pretty loony. But remember that we
live in the 21st Century, where – despite the fact
that the planet has been cooling for the last 11 years
– "global warming" is the new religion and scientists
who object (thousands of them) are jostled in the
University canteen, though not all at the same time.
Quite right too. Heretics should be jostled.

The EU was feeling a bit left out in the "knitting
with only one needle" stakes, so they recently
issued a booklet to all MEPs and staff, banning the
use of "Miss" and "Mrs" as sexist. Also outlawed
are "Madame", "Mademoiselle", "Frau", "Fraulein",
"Senora" and "Senorita".

"Sportsmen" and "statesmen" are also outlawed,
along with "man-made", which should be "artificial"
or "synthetic". And please remember that you are
paying for this at the cost of £40-million a day.

Ahem. Back to reality and cows: In a French
Corporation you have two cows but want three, so
you riot and block the roads until the government
agrees. In a British Corporation you have two cows
but both are mad. In an Italian Corporation you
have two cows but don't know where they are, so
you go to lunch. In a Swiss Corporation you have
5,000 cows hidden underground but none of them

belong to you, and in an Iraqi Corporation you have no cows but everyone thinks you're lying so they bomb the bejeebers out of you until they realise their mistake. That's enough cows for now.

September 2009

THAT'S ALL FOLKS

Here's a brief gallop through the latest British loony tunes: Muslim prisoners in Norfolk police cells are being issued with compasses so that they can face Mecca in the east when praying. (They don't trust the existing compass already painted on the ceiling). Along the same lines, many police forces are introducing Braille notices in the cells. I have asked a number of ex-cops in the course of their career how many blind people had they ever banged up in a cell. In every single case the answer was: "None."

A survey of 600 teachers revealed that pupils at one school had to wear goggles before handling Blu Tack. In another, a 5-page guide was issued to teachers before they could issue Pritt Sticks, and empty egg boxes were outlawed due to salmonella risk. Children cannot use shaving foam in some art classes because they might "drown" in it. Many teachers also reported bans on footballs, running in the playground, and snowball fights.

To show how crazy it's become, even half the teachers themselves thought that Health and Safety rules were holding back the children, and Judith Hackett (boss of the Health and Safety Executive) described the examples given as: "Frankly ludicrous".

Another example is Bill Malcolm, an allotment owner in Bromsgrove, who put up a single strand of barbed wire around his cabbages to deter thieves and vandals. The council ordered it taken down because they could get sued if a thief scratched himself. Mr Malcolm said: "I told them to let the thief sue me. At least I'd know who was breaking into my allotment. But everything I said fell on deaf ears."

West Mercia Police added their bit: "We can confirm that five thefts from Round Hill allotments have been reported in the past year. Our advice to allotment holders is to leave nothing of value there."
Thanks, guys, for that Crime Prevention advice. But given that logic perhaps we should all live in a yurt with no possessions, just in case a burglar ever pops in while we're out.

2nd October 2009

EAT THE CHILDREN

Certain fundamental truths cannot be denied. When you drain out the washing-up water there's always something hiding among the suds (usually a tea-spoon). Or for every twenty people who call the Swine Flu Hotline at least one of them will hear nothing but crackling. Or in Afghanistan, destroying the poppies won't help. We need to buy them from the Afghans and turn them into pain-killing drugs, then introduce alternative crops. Not cheap, but cheaper than fighting an interminable war.

Some things seem true, but are hard work. Will Clower, author of "The Fat Fallacy", advises on the wisest way to eat. Buy the best you can afford, preferably organic. But then he spoils it: "If it's not food, don't eat it. Sodas are not a food. It never grew. It has no mommy or daddy." Bang goes my Trago liquorice allsorts then.

The greatest truth of all is that when you give money and power to a collective, disaster is inevitable. And the EU is probably the greatest collective on the planet. Take this letter from Daily Telegraph Motoring recently: "Sir, my Vauxhall Zafira CDTi is a fine car, in all but one detail. To comply with EU emissions, Vauxhall has fitted it with a diesel particulate filter that will clog up unless you regularly take the car for a 20-minute motorway thrash. I have to make unnecessary detours to keep the car going and am burning up 100 miles of fuel in the process. Is this the daftest bit of EU motoring law yet?"

The short answer is "No" but I've run out of space to explain.

October 2009

A SPIFFING IDEA

The Trago Column has banged on about Britain's immigration policy for years now (mainly that it would be a spiffing idea to have one). The usual suspects denounce this as racist. But they can be ignored. As someone once said: "A conservative is just a liberal who got mugged."

There's nothing "racist" about government controlling its borders. One of the core duties of a government is to protect its citizens, but if they don't even know who's in the country they'll fall at the first hurdle...

Judge Ian Trigger recently summed it up in a court case, while jailing drug-dealer Lucien McClearley (an illegal immigrant from Jamaica) for two years: "Your case illustrates all too clearly the completely lax immigration policy that exists in this country. People like you, and there are literally hundreds and hundreds of thousands of people like you, come to these shores from foreign countries to avail themselves of the generous welfare benefits that exist here."

He went on: "In the past 10 years the national debt of this country has risen to extraordinary heights, largely because central government has wasted billions and billions of pounds. Much of that has been wasted on welfare payments."

Thanks to Labour's response to the credit crash, this country is in greater debt than in 1945, just after the war. We simply cannot afford to lose all this money. We must balance the books, and that means making big cuts or we're all in deep trouble.

October 2009

HOW GOLD IS MY VALLEY?

There's gold in them thar hills. Since 1994 Glenys and Neil Kinnock. have made a cool £8m of taxpayer's money in pay and allowances from the EU, as revealed by the Sunday Times last June. Former MEP Glenys Kinnock is currently Europe Minister in the cabinet, but she is also entitled to £67,835 a year from her EU pension (we're paying for that, along with husband Neil's pension of £80,000 a year as a former EU commissioner). If you tried buying that sort of pension you'd need £4.4 million in cash. The campaigning group Open Europe also discovered that while in Brussels the Kinnocks claimed a housing allowance on top of their incomes, yet they both occupied the same home. Funny that.

Tom McPhail, of financial consultants Hargreaves Landsdown, said: "Wow. Not bad for a failed Party leader and his wife. But people will find this scale of indulgence nauseating, especially when British workers are having their pensions cut."

Couldn't put it better myself. More on Neil Kinnock next week.

October 2009

A DEEP AND SEPULCHRAL SILENCE

In 2001 Marta Andreasen was hired by the EU as their Chief Accountant. Her first job was to approve the previous year's accounts. But she couldn't do it. Her predecessor had been shunted off to Siberia or somewhere equally remote, and looking at the figures she realised there was a massive financial black hole. No professional accountant of repute could possibly have signed that document.

This went down badly. Marta suddenly became as unpopular as a ham sandwich at a bar-mitzvah. In fact, the EU made her life a misery, gagged her, then finally kicked her out. To read the full story you'll need to read her book, Brussels Laid Bare (St Edward's Press) but I'll quote a piece near the end, her final hearing in front of the whole College of Commissioners:
"We moved into the rather cramped hearing room, taking our places at one end of a long oblong table, round which sat 21 of the 24 Commissioners. At our end, on our left, was Commission President Romano Prodi. Several places away on our right, sat Kinnock, whose behaviour appeared to have regressed to that of a schoolboy. He made exaggerated and dismissive gestures with his arms, as if to register his disgust

at what I was saying and alert his colleagues that the lady in front of them was completely mad.

"Other Commissioners occupied themselves with reports or paperwork that were clearly nothing to do with the matter in hand. Some, who had not bothered to turn off their mobile phones, would occasionally wander off to have telephone conversations in the corridor outside."…

When the Chairman finally asked if anyone had any questions there was a sepulchral silence. And that rather sums it up.

October 2009

KEEP THEM SMELLING SALTS HANDY

The French riot police have now cleared the 'Jungle' camp near Calais, where a small army of illegal immigrants had gathered, prior to crossing the Channel and claiming asylum.

But if you think that's the end of the matter then I'll get the smelling salts. I'm afraid it's business as usual. Most of the migrants had already dispersed before the TV cameras turned up, and they didn't travel thousands of miles just to sample the undoubted delights of Normandy cuisine. These guys mean business…

As you've probably guessed, the EU is involved. Jacques Barrot, Justice Commissioner, is demanding a change in the law to allow 'Britain-obsessed' asylum seekers into the UK at their earliest convenience (Daily Mail 21/09/09).

Mr Barrot said: "In order for the closure of the jungle to make sense, it is necessary to share the burden between France and Great Britain. There should be solidarity within the EU over asylum. National solutions are not viable."

His comments might be unpalatable but Mr Barrot is dead right. Membership of the EU means exactly what he says. That's why our fishing grounds have been raped by the Spanish armada and the industry virtually destroyed. A political union (which is what we've signed up to) means that national governments must yield to the greater interests of the wider EU.

November 2009

POSITIVE SPIN

Here's another email we had at UKIP Head Office from a member: "Dear Sir, I am a 2008 graduate with a 2:1 in computer games development and have been unable to find work for over a year now. So I decided to check out the Graduate Talent Pool website, which seems a good scheme..."

There was only one vacancy, a graduate intern at Yorkshire ITV, so our hero clicked on the website and found this: "The Foundation Placement Scheme is delivered under Section 37 of the Race Relations Act and is therefore designed specifically for applicants from Black, Asian or Minority Ethnic backgrounds."

As our UKIP correspondent wrote: "Specifically designed for anyone who isn't white? How is that fair? And how can the government or companies expect people to NOT become racist when they see garbage like this. It is blatantly racist. This is pure discrimination and I fear this kind of ignorance will lead to a rise in fascism."

And he's absolutely right. If you look at the scheme it lists who can apply (above 18, from the Yorkshire region, a UK resident, or from a Black, Asian, or Minority Ethnic Background.) but it's quite clear that if any blue-eyed Caucasians are called for interview they'll be wasting their bus fare.

Just for the record: the UK Independence Party is totally opposed to 'positive discrimination', partly because it acts as a recruiting-sergeant for Nick Griffin's lot.

November 2009

IN LIKE FLINT

You'll enjoy this one. Back in March 2009 Caroline Flint was Labour's Europe Minister. She was being quizzed by her Tory shadow, Mark Francois, in a European Committee session, and he was getting cheesed off because she wouldn't answer the questions.

Eventually he asked: "I am a little surprised at the continuing vagueness of the Minister's answer. This is a really simple question: has the Minister read the elements of the Lisbon Treaty that relate to defence?"

Ms Flint shifted in her chair: "I have read some of it but not all of it."
Mr Francois: "What!"
Ms Flint: "I have been briefed on some of it."
Mr Francois: "That is an extraordinary answer. The Minister for Europe has not read all of the Lisbon Treaty. That is an absolutely extraordinary revelation. It's a bit like the Irish Prime Minister saying that he had not read it before the referendum.

That is an incredible answer. If she is Minister for Europe, why has she not read the treaty?"
At which point the Labour chairman tried to save her: "Order. The Lisbon Treaty is not entirely relevant to the documents under debate."

Mr Francois again: "With respect, it is mentioned a number of times in the documents."
And then, incredibly, Ms Flint jumped back in again with both feet: "The Lisbon Treaty's mutual assistance clause, article (1)49, is in accordance with article 51 of the UN charter..."

Mr Francois: "You're supposed to be Minister for Europe: how can you not have read the treaty?"

Chairman: "Order."

Ms Flint is no longer the Minister for Europe.

November 2009

PEDAL TO THE MEDDLE

Redbridge Council (in Essex) is buying a fleet of bicycles so that staff can cycle to work in the mornings... Sorry, let's try that sentence again: COUNCIL TAX-PAYERS in Redbridge, Essex, are buying a fleet of bicycles so that Council staff can cycle to work in the mornings (also paying for helmets and bicycle pumps). This is total madness. Britain is deep in debt and local councils must be making cuts, not squandering cash on absurd schemes like this.

In Doncaster the new mayor is showing the way. Peter Davies was elected to slash council spending, clear the street of yobs, and dump politically-correct schemes.

On his first morning he cut his own salary from £73,000 to £30,000 then closed the council's own newspaper because it was "peddling politics on the rates." He now wants to cut the number of town councillors from 63 to 31, saving a cool £800,000. As he says: "If 100 senators can run the United States of America, I can't see how 63 councillors are needed to run Doncaster".

Mr Davies has saved another £200,000 by withdrawing the city from the Local Government Association and the LG Information Unit: "Just talking-shops," he called them.
He added: "Doncaster is in for some serious un-twinning. We are twinned with probably nine other cities around the world, and they are just for people to fly off and have a binge at the council's expense."

November 2009

BUT I WASN'T LOOKING

In 1840 the journalist Alphonse Karr wrote a satirical piece attacking Hyppolyte Colet, elderly professor in the Paris Conservatoire. The article so enraged the Professor's young wife, Louise, that she marched round to Karr's lodgings and when he opened the door to let her in, stuck a kitchen knife into him.

The journalist disarmed her, then summoned a cab. In his next article, he wrote: "I certainly would have been gravely harmed if my attacker had struck with a direct horizontal blow instead of lifting her arm high over her head in a tragedienne's gesture, surely in anticipation of some forthcoming lithograph of the incident."

After some persuasion Karr agreed not to prosecute. But he kept the knife, displaying it in a glass case, labelled: "Given to me by Mme Colet – in the back."

Alphonse Karr coined the saying: 'Plus ça change, plus c'est la mëme chose.' ('The more things change, the more they stay the same'), and he was right, given all those people lining up behind Gordon Brown, hatchet in one hand, a hatchet labelled: "Given to me by my colleagues – in the back".

December 2009

THE MOUTH OF THE EXE

Terry Griffin is a prolific letter-writer to the newspapers, with an opinion on everything under the sun. In October 2009, in his best Lifemanship 'plonking' voice, he informed West Country readers that Britain should join the euro. Sit down, Terry. I'll get you some tap-water. "Joining the euro" would mean that the British Government could not have cut interest rates during the recent housing collapse. A big bank in Frankfurt would have made that decision for us, and they'd have said, "No".

In Marbella, Spain, the waiters and café owners ask: "What has happened to los Ingeles?" Their cafes are empty, with staff laid off. The answer is that 'los Ingeles' wisely kept out of the euro and were free to devalue their currency when needed. Foreign holidays got more expensive, along with imports, but a price worth paying.

The euro is a one-size-fits-all currency, like assuming that a single pair of trousers fits everyone in the room. And once the exchange rate is fixed, that's it. Regardless of future events, you're well and truly stuck. Germany and France may be doing reasonably well at the moment but others aren't so lucky. Ireland's economy is being crucified because they can't cut interest rates; even worse are the PIGS (Portugal, Italy, Greece, and Spain) whose economies are in freefall.

Every Briton is free to "join the euro" tomorrow. They can get on a ferry, buy a house in France, and leave the rest of us with our own currency. The alternative to joining the euro is very easy. It's called: "Not joining the euro." Simples.

December 2009

2010

I HAVE A LITTLE LIST

Ever been had? Here are some of the things that Gordon Brown signed away in the Lisbon Treaty. In every case, Brussels either now controls it or, at the very least, has a big say in how they should be run – which means that in time they'll control it totally.

Among the things we've deferred (partially or wholly) to Brussels are: Administrative cooperation, Civil protection, Climate change, Energy, Humanitarian aid, Space, Sport, Territorial cohesion, Economic services, Self-employment, Tourism, Security, Right to life, Right to family life, Protection of personal data, Freedom of thought, Freedom of speech, Freedom of assembly, Freedom of movement, Freedom of occupation, Property rights, Asylum, Extradition, Cultural and religious diversity, Children's rights, Rights of the elderly, Disability rights, Workers' rights, Collective bargaining, Unfair dismissal, Healthcare, Public services, Environment, Right to vote, Consumer protection, Presumption of innocence, Diplomatic and consular protection, Fair trial, Criminal offences and penalties...

And David Cameron is no better, promising "no new treaties without a referendum". But what he doesn't say is that Lisbon is a self-amending treaty, which means it can be changed, added to, and amended. Lisbon is the last treaty they'll need, and they don't want one from David Cameron. Like I said, ever been had... or treated like a mushroom?

January 2010

WISE WORDS INDEED

I thought you might be interested in these words by US President Theodore Roosevelt in 1907. They still apply today:

"We should insist that if the immigrant who comes here in good faith becomes an American and assimilates himself to us, he shall be treated on an exact equality with everyone else, for it is an outrage to discriminate against any man because of creed or birthplace or origin.... But this is predicated upon the person's becoming in every facet an American, and nothing but an American.... There can be no divided allegiance here. Any man who says he is an American, but something else also, isn't an American at all. We have room for but one flag, the American flag. We have room for but one language, and that is the English language, and we have room for but one sole loyalty and that is a loyalty to the American people."...

These words of wisdom will probably get right up the nose of many Guardianista readers, and ultra PC Labour politicians, but after what they have done to this country, frankly I couldn't care less. We face a massive job of demolishing the house that Blair built, and if a few leftie quangoes raise objections that's par for the course. Roll on the election.

January 2010

THE DYING OF THE LIGHT

In his book about death ('Nothing to be frightened of') Julian Barnes writes: "We shall probably die in hospital, you and I", a recognition of the huge advance of modern medicine. Me, I'd rather go out guns blazing than finish up in a Home somewhere with a care-assistant wiping Ready Brek from my chin. But I probably won't have much say in the matter.

The diarist, Marie Bashkirtseff, knew when it was time. Watching the candle at her bedside, she predicted: "We shall go out together."

On the subject of last words, US General Sedgewick famously cried: "Nonsense. They couldn't hit a barn door at this dist..." while just before the Battle of the Little Big Horn, General Custer is meant to have exclaimed: "We've caught them napping!" (but treat this with caution; none of Custer's lot survived!).

More modern examples are Oscar Wilde, expiring in a drab Parisian hotel room: "Either that wallpaper goes, or I do.", or Edward Horley who instructed his executors to send half a lemon to the taxman, with the note: "Now squeeze this." Or the anonymous music critic whose final words were: "You're so lucky. You'll find out what happens to Charlotte Church."

Not everyone gets to utter those famous last words. The main architect of the European Union was Jean Monnet, who died in 1979, leaving us no words. So I'll suggest a few on his behalf. How about: "Chaos. Confusion. Disorder. My work here is done."...?

As for the EU itself, well that's more tricky. I could have used Walter de la Mare's: "Too late for fruit; too soon for flowers." but it wouldn't be true. The EU is still very much alive, kicking, and dangerous. Instead let's steal and adapt from T.S. Eliot: "This is the way the EU ends. Not with a bang but a whimper."

January 2010

TRUTH HURTS

A few months ago I reported that our useless Labour government had secretly allowed men with multiple wives to claim State benefits despite the fact that bigamy is illegal in Britain. A few people complained, calling the article 'racist' or 'offensive'. Refutation by denigration is easy but lazy. If you Google "David Challice" it's probably still bubbling away there somewhere... the usual fulminations of the Left. I laugh in their face, call them a silly thing, and their daughters smell of elderberries.

The article was based on reports in the Daily Mail, Sunday Telegraph, and Times newspapers, with no hint of racism. The mention of Islam and Muslims was strictly factual. Or were these complainants disputing that a Muslim can come to this country with a harem of wives, and claim state benefits for each of them? The taxpayer, of course, picks up the tab.

Of the estimated 1.25 million readers of the Column (which has been running for 40 years in thirty-six different newspapers) there has never been a single complaint from any Muslim reader.

Far from criticising Islam, I was castigating the Labour government and the 'useful idiots' of the progressive left who embraced the lunacy of multiculturalism. This is an old tactic. Ignore the genuine complaint. Invent another.

At the moment we still have a comparatively free press. Let us hope that these few individuals never get their hands on it.

February 2010

THIS LITTLE PIGGY WENT TO MARKET

Last year I wrote about swine flu, questioning why our government planned to inoculate, well, virtually everyone really. In 2009 the UK's Chief Medical Officer, Sir Liam Donaldson, warned of 65,000 deaths from swine flu, and suspended normal rules so that anti-flu drugs could be issued without prescription. Health and local authorities were told to prepare for a major pandemic. Morgues were put on high-alert, so was the Army. Concerns about side-effects on young children were quietly dismissed as "exaggerated".

But it's nice to know I wasn't alone.. Dr Wolfgang Wodarg, head of health at the Council of Europe in Strasbourg, has now called for an investigation into this, branding it: "One of the greatest medical scandals of the century. We have had a mild flu – and a false pandemic."

According to the MailOnline (11/01/10) only 251 deaths have been caused by swine flu in the UK. In the report Dr Wodarg accuses the drug firms of unduly influencing the World Health Authority (who announced the pandemic), and also many governments of then panicking: "[the drug firms] have made them squander tight healthcare resources for inefficient vaccine strategies, and needlessly exposed millions of healthy people to the risk of unknown side-effects of insufficiently tested vaccines".

February 2010

A SHORT BREAK AWAY

After 'Prudence' went on gardening leave, and Gordon Brown ran our economy into the ground, you probably feel like going on holiday for a while. But don't. Julian and Samantha Mosedale, with their three sons, left their terraced house in Tottenham, North London, to spend Christmas with friends. Bad move...

When they returned on January 3rd they found the house occupied by a group of Romanian squatters. As Mrs Mosedale said: "We called the police as soon as we found out. An officer suggested I was racist when I asked if they were Romanians, and did they have a legal right to be in this country. We are hard-working citizens yet get treated like criminals when our home is stolen. We feel let down by the law, the government, and by the police. The kids are upset at the idea that other children are playing with their toys in the garden."

The Mosedales went to the County Court and got an eviction order. But as Mr Mosedale explained: "When the papers were served on them they tore them up and threw them back at the guy who'd taken them round."

The squatters were interviewed by a journalist: Speaking broken English, Luminitsa Vaduva said: "I don't understand the problem. We have paid for this home. If they move us out, then my children will not have a home. We are from Romania, we have no money for another home."..

Thanks to our EU membership, any EU citizen has an absolute right to travel within the territory of the EU. Romania is in the EU.

February 2010

CAN I HAVE THE NUMBER FOR PICKFORDS REMOVALS PLEASE?

Last week I did a piece on Julian and Samantha Mosedale, who went away for Christmas. When they came back to their terraced house in Tottenham, they found seven Romanians in residence, refusing to budge. The police accused Mrs Mosedale of being racist when she questioned whether the Romanians should even be in this country (the answer to that is a big fat "Yes" because Romania is in the EU and every EU citizen has an absolute right to travel here).

Mihaela Vaduva explained in her broken English: "We saw a handwritten sign on the gate and then met the landlord in McDonalds. We gave him £2,000 for rent and a deposit". The 'landlord' then deleted his number from their own mobile phones and told them any future business should be conducted in the same McDonalds (Daily Mail 14/01/10). They told journalists that they had no money but had applied "for all the benefits we are entitled to." Phew, that's a relief. I was worried there for a moment.

You'll be pleased to know that the squatters have now been evicted from 76 St Margaret's Road, pictured wheeling a shopping trolley laden with belongings from the Mosedale's home. But they didn't have far to go. Just down the street, in fact. The two husbands disappeared into another house 100 yds away, one with estate agent's boards outside.

Later that day they refused a council offer to 'assess their housing needs'. "We are going to stay with relatives," announced one of the women, Luminita Miclescu, turning to the cameras to make a splendid gesture involving her ring finger, doubtless some traditional Romany valediction. I wonder if those 'relatives' live in Bucharest. What do you reckon?

February 2010

THE PROTOCOLS OF BLAIR

According to Andrew Neather, former advisor to New Labour, Tony Blair and Jack Straw sat down in 2000 and dreamt up a secret plan; secret because if it went public there would be a huge backlash. Our borders were to be thrown open to millions of immigrants, changing the racial and cultural profile of the country, possibly forever. Those who objected (such as Tory leaders William Hague and Michael Howard) would be branded as racists.

This was nothing less than the secret multiculturalism of Britain, and is probably the worst crime committed by New Labour in its entire term of office (and there is stiff competition: Iraq, Devolution, Lisbon Treaty, bloated welfare state, wrecked pensions industry etc).

The immigrants pitched up on our shores, secretly encouraged by the government. UKIP had always opposed this dangerous social experiment, but in 2001 William Hague, Tory leader, said that Mr Blair was turning Britain into a 'foreign land'.

As reported by The Mail on Sunday (25/10/09) the New Labour spin machine went into action, accusing him of 'playing the race card'. His successor, Mr Howard, was called "a racist" when he visited Burnley and denounced Labour's stance on asylum seekers. The very existence of this secret policy was usually denied, or (in some cases) strategically defended by insulting any opponent as a Nazi, leading to the inevitable backlash that we now see. And it was entirely predictable. But the sad fact is that while we stay in the EU, our borders remain a yawning gap.

March 2010

RIDING ON A DONKEY

If you think that some British MPs are masters in spending our taxes on bizarre things (moats, bathplugs, porno movies), think again. The EU knocks 'em into a cocked hat. Last year it awarded a grant of €980,000 to Intertango, a Finnish dance project, to further "the internationalisation of Finnish tango".

There's plenty more: Italian dentist, Giovanni Lupo, invented a solar-panel business and was then given millions of euros by Brussels. There were no solar panels. He blew everything on fifty-five luxury cars including a yellow Ferrari Testarossa. That's it, baby. If you got it, flaunt it.

The EU gave €850,000 to the Swedish town of Orsa for a 'gender equal' wood design centre, which ran out of funds before it was finished. Brussels also awarded €400,000 to "AlterEgo" a project encouraging teenagers to "explore different and varied identities by creating a double portrait – a portrait of themselves and someone from a different cultural background" to raise awareness of "the importance of developing an active European citizenship".

Perhaps the worst of all is Donkeypedia, yet another art education project. Asino, the blogging donkey, travelled through the Netherlands, meeting people en-route, every day making postings on 'his' electronic blog. You might have expected entries such as: "Tuesday, ate some straw. Wednesday, refused to move. Let 'em call me stubborn" Not a bit of it...

Asino's postings were the sort of PC twaddle to delight a Guardianistas' heart. Here's one now: "I was under a chestnut tree sleeping in sand. When I opened my eyes there were animals looking at me. I was embarrassed. Now I understand a little how people from different cultures may feel in the Netherlands".

The campaigning group Open Europe unearthed these gems. As they said: "Too often, EU money is wasted on inefficient projects based on unrealistic expectations or for which there is no real demand [and] the focus of the EU budget is to get the money out the door, not to spend it wisely".

March 2010

THE RUST BELT

It has been said that the 19th Century was Britain's, the 20th was America's, and the 21st will belong to China (along with India and Brazil). That's probably true. China is the world's factory, India has the English language, and Brazil has just discovered vast oil-fields off the Atlantic coast. And all three have a huge labour force willing to work for peanuts.

In the USA the decline is obvious: Dan Kildee, treasurer of Genesee County, recently dreamt up a plan to bulldoze derelict areas of many cities and return them to nature, in an 'adapt or die' strategy. He outlined the scheme to President Barack Obama and has now been approached by the US government. (Daily Telegraph 12/06/09). There are

50 cities on his hit list, many in the 'rust belt' such as Detroit, Pittsburgh, Baltimore and Memphis. Mr Kildee's own city, Flint, was the original home of General Motors. The car giant once employed 79,000 people. Today that's fallen to less than 6,000, with unemployment at 20%, and an exodus of young people causing property prices to collapse. Flint has already demolished 1,100 houses. Kildee estimates another 3,000 must go for the city to avoid bankruptcy.

I'm telling you this because if America is contracting, then the next British Prime Minister should pause a moment. The plan to build thousands of new houses in overcrowded Britain is sheer madness. If you visit many cities in the industrial north, there are still huge areas of wasteland from factories bulldozed when the jobs moved abroad decades ago. Rather than increasing our population from 60 million to 70 million, we should be reducing it (along with the rest of the world). And don't forget: immigrants and asylum seekers get old, too. Will we invite another 5 million to come in and look after them?

March 2010

ON THE BEAT

'Evenin' all,' as Dixon of Dock Green used to say. But these days he'd be up for 'cultural diversity awareness training'. The police have recently issued a handbook for officers, POLICING OUR COMMUNITIES, banning certain words. Officers cannot say 'Evenin' all,' because: "Terms such as 'afternoon' and 'evening' are somewhat subjective in meaning and can vary according to a person's culture or nationality". The words 'child', 'youth', and 'youngster' are also on the blacklist. So is the word 'blacklist', along with 'laymen's terms', 'taxman', and 'housewife'.

It's even worse if you're in the Metropolitan Police: the word 'homosexual' is banned ('gay' should be used) but confusingly 'straights' must be called 'heterosexual'. You work it out.

Here are a few words that Plod hasn't got around to banning yet: 'Intaxication' (euphoria at getting a tax refund, which lasts until you realise that it was your money to start with).

'Reintarnation' (coming back as a hillbilly)

'Sarchasm' (the gulf between those making a cruel joke, and the Victim who doesn't get it)

And my own favourite: 'Bozone' (the substance around stupid people that stops bright ideas from penetrating).

And given POLICING OUR COMMUNITIES, the bozone layer shows little sign of breaking down in the near future.

April 2010

BANNING THE BURKA?

On January 16th The Times ran this headline: "UKIP woos white working class with call for total ban on burkas". The Times went on: "The policy, which a number of European countries are also debating, is an attempt by UKIP to broaden its appeal and address the concerns of disaffected white working-class voters".

Lord Pearson of Rannoch, UKIP Party Leader, explained: "We are not Muslim bashing, but this is incompatible with Britain's values of freedom and democracy," going on to say that the fabric of the country is under threat from Sharia and that forcing women to conceal their identity in public is not consistent with traditional Britishness.

Three days later UKIP Head Office received an email from Shahhed Boksh from the Client Contact Centre at Tower Hamlets Council, London (the address was Shahhed.Boksh@towerhamlets.gov.uk) ...

"Subject: YOU WILL BE BANNED UNDER ISLAMIC RULE. ISLAM IS THE DOMINANT RELIGION IN THE UK AND THE WORLD. MAY ALLAH THROW YOUR MOCKING BACK ON YOUR SOUL".

Beneath it, in small type, was the equally superb: "Working Together for a Better Tower Hamlets"...

When a council employee feels able to send such an official email (thus dragging his employer into national politics) it rather proves that multiculturalism is a busted flush. Ah well, man was born to toil as the sparks fly upward.

April 2010

WASHING UP AT THE TSB

Nigel Farage MEP recently stood up in Brussels and criticised the new EU President, Herman van Rompuy: "I'm sorry, but after that performance you gave earlier. I don't want to be rude, but really you have the charisma of a damp rag, and the appearance of a low-grade bank clerk. I mean: who are you? I'd never heard of you. Nobody in Europe had ever heard of you."

The media loved it. "The rudest man in Europe",

they howled. And when he appeared on BBC1's Question Time the audience was primed and hostile. Even at UKIP Head Office we had many emails from "disgusted" voters, who felt that personal attacks were wrong.

But then things changed, as they often do, with messages of support coming in (particularly after the Question Time ambush) "Well done, Nigel. I've never voted UKIP before, but I will from now on!" Or: "At last. A politician who talks straight. You've got my vote." Or more simply: "Hurrah!"

I do understand that many people deplore rudeness, but I ask you to remember that UKIP has often been insulted (little Englanders; anti-Europeans; BNP in blazers; cranks and gadflies; David Cameron even called us "Loonies and racists mostly", which seems a huge insult to all UKIP voters, some of them Conservatives). It also seems an odd sense of priority to get steamed up about a few colourful words yet blithely ignore the sell-out of the country to a foreign power.

Mr van Rompuy is a president who got the job because Gordon Brown broke an election promise and rammed home the Lisbon Treaty, backed up by David Cameron, who - faster than a scalded cat - then dropped his own "cast iron pledge" on holding a referendum. Quite frankly, sometimes we need more than genteel politeness and sandwiches with the crusts cut off. Sometimes we need to speak bluntly.

A line was drawn beneath the matter a few days later when Mr Farage was summoned to the headmaster's study. Jerzy Buzek (President of the EU Parliament) demanded an apology. Farage declined: "I have been called many things in my time – that's politics." And he was then fined £2,700 in allowances, upon which he immediately apologised... to every bank clerk in Europe.

April 2010

MORE GLOBAL WARMING

If you were among the thousands of Devon motorists stranded in snow drifts on Haldon Hill last January, you'll be forgiven for uttering a hollow laugh the next time some idiot wibbles on about global warming. And how odd that owning a 4x4 has suddenly become socially acceptable. Landrover sales are booming.

The truth is that climates always change. It's what they do. "The worst rain in 40 years" simply means that today's heavy rain has happened before. 40 years ago.... The ancient kingdom of Nubia (now in northern Sudan) was one of the greatest empires of the ancient world, rivalling the Pharaohs. Their symbol was the cow, found carved onto thousands of temples and ruined palaces. But the Nubian Empire collapsed when the desert turned their pastures to sand.

At the recent UN World Climate Conference in Geneva, 1,500 climate scientists gathered for a meeting. Mojib Latif (a top climate modeller) announced that we are about to enter possibly two decades of cooler temperatures: "People will say this is global warming disappearing. I am not one of the sceptics. However, we have to ask the nasty questions ourselves or other people will do it."

Latif predicted: "In the next few years a natural cooling trend will dominate the warming caused by humans." As reported by New Scientist magazine (September 2009): 'The cooling would be down to cyclical changes in the atmosphere and ocean currents in the North Atlantic Oscillation. Breaking with climate-change orthodoxy, Latif said that the NAO was probably responsible for some of the strong warming seen around the globe in the past three decades'

Another conference delegate, Vicky Pope (from the Met Office) warned that dramatic Arctic ice loss in recent summers was partly a product of natural cycles rather than global warming. There was much less melting last year than in 2007 or 2008. Funny that...

It's taking time, but one by one, our scientists are regaining their nerve and creeping out from under the sofa.

March 2010

THE NORWICH CONSPIRACY

On 12th October 2009, Paul Hudson, a regional TV weather forecaster, received an email (in response to his earlier article: "Whatever Happened to Global Warming?", which had argued that for the last 11 years there had been no increase in global temperatures).

Opening the email Mr Hudson was confronted by thousands of leaked documents from the Climate Research Unit at East Anglia University. These seemed to show that scientists had skewed the data on climate change, shutting out those who disagreed. In one email, Phil Jones, director of the East Anglia climate centre, wrote that sceptical research was unwelcome: "We will keep them out somehow – even if we have to re-define what the peer review literature is!".

The scientific method is meant to work like this. I

say: "If you drop a 50-lb rock on your bare foot it will hurt." Others then take a similar rock (preferably the same one) and repeat the experiment, thus proving it. These East Anglian scientists have not done that. Instead they tried to freeze out anyone who disagreed with them.

Lord Monckton was unimpressed with these so-called scientists. "For years they have refused to reveal their data and their computer program listings. Now we know why: the programs and data are a hopeless, tangled mess. In effect, the global temperature trends have simply been made up."... Regardless of the truth about man-made global warming, this is bad science. As UKIP has been warning, it lends weight to the view that 'Climate Change' is just another way of extracting taxes from a terrified public.

Don't take it from me. The Daily Mail's headline (28/01/10) ran: "Climategate scandal scientists broke the law by hiding data from global warming sceptics" following an investigation by the Information Commissioner, which found that the East Anglian scientists had broken the Freedom of Information Act.

So to sum up: the scientists concealed their data, in breach of the scientific method, then conspired to destroy that data when requested to reveal it, in clear breach of the law. Judging by this sorry performance, I wouldn't trust them to produce the chemical formula for Ovaltine, let alone award them taxpayer's money to play at 'climate-change' research.

April 2010

BANGERS AND MASH

In 2009, in the darkest days of the recession, the Labour government introduced the "scrappage scheme" to help the ailing British car industry. If you owned an old banger they'd give you £1,000 towards a spanking new vehicle from the showroom, with the dealer giving a further £1,000.

Because most UK cars are imported, the scheme was a disaster. Economist Karen Ward was interviewed by the Independent newspaper: "Latest data shows that more than a third of the deterioration in the trade in goods in September was owed to a sharp rise in car imports". And HSBC (the UK's largest bank) blamed the scheme for Britain's sluggish recovery.

Another consequence, glossed over by the Green lobby, was that thousands of perfectly good older cars were scrapped, encouraging manufacturers to build even more vehicles. Talk about 'reducing your climate footprint'.

Even worse, hundreds of classic cars have been crushed, when most could have been saved or used as spares. We know that a 36,000-mile Riley Elf recently went to the breakers, along with an original Morris Minor pick-up (rare as hen's teeth) and a mint 12,000-mile Morris Marina (though Top Gear won't mind, as long as a falling piano was involved).

The government minister responsible, Ian Lucas, was unsympathetic: "Owners of older cars should not be blocked from participating in the scheme" he announced, though conceding that once the car had been 'de-polluted' the actual scrappage could then halt.

'De-polluting' means hacking out the catalytic

converter (usually with a disc cutter), draining out all fluids, and removing tyres and battery. And because the vehicle has been scrapped it can never be licensed again for road use anywhere in the world.

Call me old fashioned, but who in their right mind would buy a 'heritage' car without tyres or battery, that's been left standing in the rain in a breaker's yard without oil or water, and cannot be driven on the road without Plod calling round? Top Gear probably.

April 2010

LOSING YOUR MARBLES

Unless you've been living on Mars, you probably know that Greece is bust. They lied about their public finances just to join the Euro Club, and now the bank manager is kicking down their door. Italy, Portugal and Spain could be next.

At least by keeping out of the euro we were free to devalue our currency when needed (the one time 'Prudence' made the right decision), but now a White Knight has come riding to Greece's rescue. Jim Croft, a London city trader, has launched a £100-million charity appeal website to help bail out the country.

"Greece is in deep financial trouble" he explains.

"Donating here will help go a long way to helping those poor people who have lived beyond their means for the last ten years and are now struggling to pay their bills. Please think of them as they avoid their taxes and then blame evil speculators rather than face up to the fact that lying about their national statistics was probably more of a factor."

The Daily Telegraph (10/04/10) revealed that many donors have stepped forward: Mr Anthony Chisnall pledged a tenner, but only if the Greeks stop smashing all that crockery. The British Museum contributed £10 (apparently) but asked: "Have you lost your marbles?" and 'Mr Turkey' volunteered £10 to the fighting fund in return for an island. We'll await developments.

May 2010

EGG ON FACE TIME

I'm writing this three weeks before the general election 2010, and it will come out after the results are announced. Yet again I risk getting egg (though by now it's omelette) all over my face. But what the heck. I've been right in the past. Let's see this time...

Predictions then: there will now be a hung parliament; Nigel Farage UKIP MEP will either win in Buckingham against John Bercow (the Squeaker) or will miss beating him by a gnat's whisker, and all across the country the smaller parties (UKIP, Greens, BNP) will hugely increase their vote.

Because of the First Past the Post voting system it is hugely difficult for newer, smaller parties to muscle aside the Lib/Lab/Consensus but at least they can upset the apple-cart. And with a hung parliament, to quote Sherlock Holmes, "the game's afoot".

Many people wanted shot of Labour but were afraid of letting them back in again, so they voted for the least worst option, the Conservatives. UKIP's response is that it doesn't matter which of them won. Burger King or McDonalds. Coke or Pepsi. Same bloke, different hat. All are committed to the EU. All have renounced being leaders in favour of being managers for a distant boss. And all were wibbling about £3-billion cuts here or there when we owe £176-billion and rising. Ladies and Gentlemen, we're broke. Bust. Wiped out. Totally snozzled. Yet we have 'ring-fenced' Overseas Aid to countries such as India and China, each of whom runs a Space Programme.

Ahem: after all those predictions, I'll be fascinated to see how wrong I got it!

May 2010

WIPING OFF THE EGG

A couple of weeks ago I risked my neck with some predictions about the 2010 general election. You win some. You lose some. Yes, I predicted a hung parliament, but certainly got it wrong with the Buckingham campaign where I felt that Nigel Farage MEP had a real chance of overturning John Bercow's 18,000 majority. In the end Nigel took 17% of the vote but nowhere near enough (though crashing in an aeroplane on polling day morning probably didn't help).

The Lib Dems were the biggest losers, and in a way I sympathise. Despite the huge advantage of Nick Clegg getting equal billing on the three TV debates (unlike UKIP or the Greens), and despite reaching 30% in the polls, they ended up with five fewer seats than they started with.

The Lib Dems took only 57 seats (with 23% of the vote) but how odd that Labour could grab a whopping 258 seats with only 29% of the vote (a paltry 6% more). There must be thousands of angry voters out there. Or take UKIP: with 3.1% of the vote nationally, we didn't take a seat, yet in Scotland the SNP got 6 seats with only 1.7% of the vote. In Wales it was far worse, where Plaid Cymru took 3 seats on only 0.6%. Perhaps we shouldn't be lecturing the Afghans on how to run a democracy.

May 2010

A BLACK AND WHITE MINSTREL

It's a funny old world, and my recent diggings, back-filling as I go, confirm the theory. I've just read a story from 2009 where a musical telling the story of Al Jolson's life (Jolson & Co) fell victim to the PC police.
Al Jolson was white, but blacked up to portray a Negro jazz and blues singer. But because blacking up is now off-limits, actor Allan Stewart was forbidden to apply the boot polish. The irony is that Jolson was a great campaigner for equal rights in America when racism was rife. To quote the Daily Mail (19/02/2009) "When he read in a newspaper that Blake and Noble Sissie were refused service in a Connecticut restaurant, he tracked them down and took them out to dinner, insisting he would punch anyone who tried to kick them out."

Further proof of world-oddness came from an apparently genuine report on tenants complaining to their local Council: "I wish to report that tiles are missing from the outside toilet roof. I think it was bad wind the other night that blew them off."
Or this one: ""I am writing on behalf of my sink, which is coming away from the wall."

Or: "This is to let you know that our lavatory seat is broke and we can't get BBC2".

Or try this one, from a Bootle newspaper:
"Commenting on a complaint from Mr Arthur Purdey about a large gas bill, a spokesman for North West Gas said: "We agree it was rather high for the time

of year. It's possible Mr Purdey has been charged for the gas used up during the explosion that destroyed his house."

Or my own favourite, an announcement made by a driver on the London Tube: "Let the passengers off the train FIRST!" (Pause.) "Oh go on then. Stuff yourselves in like sardines. See if I care – I'm going home.".....

May 2010

BUTTERING YOUR PARSNIPS

In the land of the blind, the one-eyed man is king, and the blindness over global warming is a great example of myopia. In the wake of various scandals (Climate-Gate, glaciers not melting, non-flooding in the Netherlands etc) we now have another turnabout. Backfiring cows are not destroying the planet, the UN has admitted, despite previous claims that meat-eating is warming the planet.

As reported by The First Post (25/03/10) "Vegetarians less smug after scientist points out cow farts are not as destructive as they thought". The UN had originally claimed: "The livestock sector is responsible for 18% of greenhouse gas emissions. This is higher than transport" (measured at 13% by the UN). Air quality scientist Frank Mitloehner shot down the UN with one well-aimed bullet: "While the figure for meat production included emissions from all associated activities, such as growing fodder, methane, and meat processing, the figure for transportation only included emissions from the burning of fuel, ignoring carbon produced by the manufacture of vehicles or building of roads etc".

Mitloehner went on: "Transportation actually contributes 26% of carbon emissions in the US, while raising pork or beef are only responsible for 3%. Producing less meat and milk will only mean more hunger in poor countries."

Pierre Gerber, one of the authors of the UN report, admitted: "He has a point – we factored in everything for meat emissions, and we didn't do the same thing for transport."...

The last word goes to Dr Patrick Moore, founder of Greenpeace, who explained that even though the amount of carbon dioxide in the upper atmosphere is rising, global temperatures have been falling since 1998. Asked if man was definitely causing global warming, he replied: "the answer is a resounding No."

And if that doesn't butter your parsnips then I don't know what will.

June 2010

WRONG ARM OF THE LAW

Michael Mancini was stuck in a queue of traffic with a runny nose. He fastened the handbrake, drew out a hankie, and was then immediately fined £60, for being "not in control of his vehicle". The cop who collared him (PC Gray, Ayrshire police) is renowned for this. A few months earlier he issued a fixed penalty notice for littering, to unemployed Stewart Smith... who had accidentally dropped a £10 note as he left a shop.

If you're eager for more brushes with the law, there are great opportunities out there. Leave more than one pay-and-display ticket on your windscreen, you'll get fined. The City of London Corporation's website says: "It is a requirement that only a single ticket is displayed. If more than one ticket is visible, the civil enforcement officer will issue a penalty charge notice and it is unlikely that we will withdraw it."

Or take grandmother Joan Higgins, 66, pet shop owner, who sold a goldfish to a 14-year old boy and was given a £1,000 fine, placed under curfew, and ordered to wear an electronic tag, in a prosecution estimated to have cost taxpayers £20,000. We are assured that the goldfish was later adopted by an animal welfare officer and is in good health. That's a relief. I was worried it might have been done for aiding and abetting.

But all these people can be thankful they weren't sent to prison, where things are getting rather fraught, if you believe BBC journalist Andrew Gilligan. "Muslim gangs imposing Sharia law in British prisons" ran the Telegraph headline (15/03/10).

At Long Lartin high security jail, non-Muslim prisoners have been forced by Muslim gangs to stop playing Western music and take down pictures of women from their cells. Prisoners are allowed to cook their own meals, but pork is off the menu, as you'd expect.

Chief Prison's Inspector, Anne Owers, reported on the increasing influence of Muslim gangs. One prisoner told her that Long Lartin was "turning into an American-style jail, where if you're not in a gang, you're in trouble. People are converting to Islam for protection."

One Catholic prisoner who refused to convert was seriously assaulted after repeated threats. A prison officer explained: "He said every so often they would come up to his cell and hold the Koran up through the small window in the cell door and start running their fingers along their throats." Multiculturalism, eh. Isn't it great?

SO FAR LEFT HE GOT LEFT BEHIND

You might be interested in this one from The Sunday Times (2008), particularly as the Miliband boys are now contesting the Labour leadership. Under a freedom of information request the newspaper unearthed a few facts about the Miliband dynasty. 'Grand-dad Miliband' Samuel, was (probably) born in Warsaw in 1895. When the Soviets invaded Poland in 1919, he joined the Red Army, fighting alongside the Communists. The years passed and Samuel had a son, Adolphe, raising him in Belgium, until 1940 when the Nazis came marching in, Samuel and Adolphe then fled to England, where son Adolphe (understandably) changed his name... to Ralph.

Still with me? Good. After the war Ralph stayed in England but his father returned to Belgium. But then Samuel realised that the war had destroyed his business, so he tried to get back to England. And then the trouble started. The Home Office refused his application for citizenship. Samuel then claimed that he was suffering anti-Semitism in Belgium, so could he please come in now?

"Nope" said the British. They didn't believe him, despite further letters and pressure from son Ralph (who later became a prominent Marxist academic). Belgium at the time was run by a Socialist government that did not discriminate against Jews. (Europe had had quite enough of that business). One Home Office report from 1948 states: "Miliband and son have so misrepresented the case in the past, I am afraid we can place no reliance on their statements", and when embassy officials interviewed Samuel he admitted his claims of persecution were untrue and he was not being expelled from Belgium. Ernest Bevin, foreign secretary, decided in 1948 that the Miliband's claims were "without foundation". Samuel Miliband tried nine times to get in, and in 1954 eventually succeeded. The old boys of British Socialism had roused themselves, rallied round and pulled strings. So to recap: the next leader of the Labour Party will probably be David Miliband, whose own grandfather made nine false applications to be a British citizen, supported by misleading statements from Ralph (father of Ed and David). I'm beginning to understand why David Miliband might be so keen on increasing immigration to Britain.

June 2010

I was quite wrong of course. David Miliband lost the leadership to his brother Ed, who had Union backing... Ed then went on to a crushing defeat in the 2015 general election, losing Scotland for Labour in the process.

NICE WORK IF YOU CAN GET IT

When the 27 members of the European Commission are sworn in, they take an oath to: "be completely independent in carrying out my responsibilities, in the general interest of the Union."

They also pledge: "neither to seek nor to take instructions from any government or from any other institution". And just for the record, when they step down as commissioners they get a massive lifetime pension, but if they bad-mouth the EU that pension is forfeit, so they are silenced with a velvet gag. Peter Mandelson, for example, pockets an annual pension of £31,000.

For those who still think that the EU is a harmless

club, may I point out that from October 2010 the British Chancellor of the Exchequer will have to show his budget to the EU before he unveils it to the country and parliament.

Under new EU "budgetary surveillance" proposals the budget will have to be "peer reviewed" by other EU finance ministers. David Cameron, admitting this was on the cards, then revealed his cunning 'wheeze'. "We will show it to the Commission at the same time as we show it to Parliament." Brilliant. But there was one problem.

Your EU President, Herman van Rompuy, a man of hidden shallows, he was unhappy. He even pursed his lips. This was unacceptable, informed Mr Cameron. Treasuries would be required to hand over the budgetary information "well in advance" to allow time "to adjust the plans before the final budget is presented".

Let's recap. The British Chancellor of the Exchequer is about to lose the power to set his own budget. Brussels will take a big red marker pen to it, saying: "That bit must go. And that. You can have this part, but not that section at the end."

When UKIP bangs on about loss of sovereignty, this is a classic example of why. You recently voted in the general election, expecting whoever formed a government to make their own economic decisions, without asking a distant boss for permission. Now perhaps you realise why 'Europe' was airbrushed out of that election campaign?

July 2010

MINE'S A DOUBLE

Following the credit crunch and all that talk of hedge funds, leverage, etc, here is your quick guide to how Derivatives work. Bill runs a pub but all his customers are unemployed alcoholics, so he offers them credit. "I'll put it on your tab".

Bill keeps a ledger, a record of all these loans. Word gets out and soon every lush in town is drinking in 'BILL'S BAR', pushing sales volumes through the roof. When Bill puts up the prices the customers don't mind. It's 'drink now, pay later' so they keep on drinking, and gross sales increase massively.

Down at Bill's local bank a whiz kid with gelled hair, pimples and a too-big collar and tie, realises that all these customer debts are a valuable future asset, so he increases Bill's overdraft and alerts his trader friend at Bank HQ, who then bundles up the debts and sells them as ALKIBONDS on the international derivatives market. Investors snap them up, not realising that they are buying the debts of unemployed alcoholics who, even at this very moment, are cheerfully getting plastered with no prospect of ever paying their bar tab.

But then it all goes wrong. A risk manager at the local bank looks carefully at 'BILL'S BAR' and decides to call in the debt. Bill can't get the money from his drunken customers so he goes bankrupt. ALKIBONDS drop by 90% overnight, which means that the banks have no spare cash and cannot offer new loans, thus freezing the entire economic sector.

Bill might be gone, but he owed money to his suppliers (who had also invested their pension funds in ALKIBONDS because they knew it was a good thing). His wine merchant goes bust, and the brewery is forced to close, laying off 150 workers.

Others are luckier. Because they have cronies in government the banks and brokerage houses are bailed out by £-millions in no-strings-attached deals.

This money is created by imposing new taxes on sober, hard working people who have never crossed the threshold of BILL'S BAR in their life.   I hope that makes it very clear.
July 2010

THE GREECEY POLL

Here is a very recent quote from Gunter Verheugen, former vice-president of the EU Commission: "It is hard to convince people in Germany to work until they are 67 to allow people in Greece to retire at 61." And he's right. But it's not only Germans. It's us, too. Luckily we never joined the euro - which helps – but we're still bailing out Greece and the eurozone with £-billions of taxpayers' money, when our new coalition government is scrabbling around trying to make £6-billion in cuts.

The euro is a political currency. If it had been a financial enterprise then the Germans would never have allowed Spain, Greece, Italy or Portugal to join. Berlin would have told them: "Your finances are shot. Go away, clean up your act. Don't come back till you do." But Berlin didn't tell them that, because the EU made the classic Socialist mistake of thinking that money grows on trees, and that nothing should get in the way of the brave new euro-state.

As UKIP's Godfrey Bloom MEP commentated: "Boiling a tin of beans without puncturing the lid will eventually lead to an explosion. No point in watching it bubble away for the first few minutes and persuading yourself all is well."

Whilst I'm quoting other people, let's end with this one from EU President, Herman van Rompuy: "Nobody ever told the proverbial man in the street that sharing a single currency was not just about making people's lives easier when doing business or travelling abroad, but also about being directly affected by economic developments in the neighbouring countries."

UKIP and the Trago Column have been saying this for years, but Lib-Dems and Labourites always dismissed it as nonsense. Now that the President of the EU has confirmed it, perhaps they'll partake of a large slice of humble pie, with extra custard, and then say: "Sorry for getting it sooooo wrong."

July 2010

TIDDLING WITH FAIRIES

If you spend some time looking at newspapers and tiddling away online, you'll find some real gems out there. Here's one now: Carl Truman, 19, of Los Angeles won $74,000 plus medical expenses when a neighbour ran over Truman's hand with a Honda car. The court decided that the driver should have realised Truman was trying to steal the Honda's hubcaps at the time.

Or consider Kathleen Robertson of Austin, Texas, who broke her ankle tripping over a toddler who was running around inside a furniture store. She sued, and won huge damages in court. The store owners were miffed at the verdict because the toddler was her own son. Personal responsibility?

Or perhaps this one, from journalist Claire Ellicott, reporting on traditional fairy tales: one in ten parents think that Snow White and the Seven Dwarfs should be re-titled, because "dwarfs" is un-pc, Rapunzel is 'too dark' and Cinderella is 'outdated because she does all the housework'.

July 2010

COCKING THAT LUGER

There are some great laughs out there, if you can keep your sense of humour. Take this one, from the MailOnline (8/2/10): "Bus delayed after Muslim driver pulls over so he can pray in the aisle". It happened on the number 24 in Gospel Oak, North London, when the driver pulled over, took off his fluorescent jacket, laid it on the floor, removed his shoes, then prayed to Mecca (not the Bingo hall, the other one) for five minutes.

Passenger Gayle Griffiths, 33, stared at him in amazement: "I was gobsmacked and quite bewildered. He hadn't addressed the passengers at all. I didn't say anything and nor did anyone else. It even went through my mind that this might be some sort of terrorist attack with the bus blown up because I had heard suicide bombers prayed before attacks. He was also blocking the exit, so if something had happened we wouldn't have been able to get off. Everyone was looking round in a mix of shock and amazement. It was truly bizarre, ludicrous..."

A spokesman for Transport for London said: "TfL apologises to passengers for any inconvenience. TfL and the individual bus operating companies acknowledge and value the diversity of their staff." What a relief. I was worried there for a moment.

Or try this one from North Humberside, where shopkeeper Graham Taylor was chasing two teenagers who had just stolen spirits from his newsagents. He stopped a police officer in a patrol car and asked for help. But he was told: "You had better call the Police." Having recovered from this strange advice Mr Taylor then, indeed, rang 999, but the officer assigned to deal with the crime missed the radio call because he was "celebrating at a colleague's retirement party."

And if you heard a 'ker-click' just then, it was me, cocking that Luger.

July 2010

SAY CHEESE

Smile. It's not that bad. Ask Irene Graham, of Boscombe, who delighted an audience with her reminiscences of a German POW who was sent each week to do her garden: "He was repatriated at the end of 1945," she recalled. "He'd always seemed such a nice friendly chap, but when the crocuses came up in the middle of our lawn in February 1946, they spelt out 'Heil Hitler'."

Or how about Stuart Isbister, who runs a small gift shop in Nottingham? When the smoking ban was introduced, he refused to display a "No Smoking" sign on his window. "We just don't think it necessary to have a sign. We have a small amount of space and wanted to keep the door area simple and uncluttered. It is completely disproportionate and totally unnecessary. People just don't smoke in shops. We don't have signs on the door saying no thieving and no dropping your trousers, yet both of these are against the law."

As part of its war against smokers the previous Labour government generated a massive bureaucracy and an army of enforcement officers employed by councils (that means YOU in case you hadn't realised) requiring all stores, public buildings, even churches, to display a No Smoking sign. Nottingham Council took Mr Isbister to court, and lost, because they hadn't followed the correct procedure, but it's only a matter of time before smoking is banned totally. Already the EU zealots are getting into the act. As reported by the News of the World last year: "Brussels chiefs want to outlaw beer-garden ciggie areas – and even extend the ban to open air concerts like this weekend's Glastonbury Festival. It says non-smokers in outdoor areas are still in danger from passive smoking."

Sorry if I lose a few of you here, but this is utter madness. I can accept that shops, churches, restaurants etc should be non-smoking, but pub landlords (and private clubs) should be free to allow smoking if they want; and banning smoking in the open air is health fascism gone mad.

Please remember the first person to ban smoking in Europe was Adolf Hitler (though only among women; his generals warned him that if he wanted to lose the war, all he had to do was prevent the troops from lighting up and the Russians would be in Berlin by next Wednesday).

But with the eurozone in meltdown, I suspect this proposal has been temporarily stubbed out, so let's keep smiling and light up another jolly old gasper.

August 2010

WE'RE DOOMED... ALL DOOOMED

Next time they ask for your money to combat 'climate change', please remember a few cataclysmic predictions that have already been made. The ecologist Kenneth Watt announced: "We have about five more years at the outside. By the year 2000 we will be using up crude oil at such a rate that there won't be any more crude oil."

Or try this one, from North Texas State University's, Peter Gunter: "Thirty years from now, the entire world, with the exception of Western Europe, North America and Australia, will be in famine."

Or this one, from Dr S. Ripley, secretary of the Smithsonian Institution: "In twenty-five years between 75% and 80% of all species of living animals will be extinct."

The clincher comes from Kenneth Watt again: "The world has been chilling sharply for about 20 years. If present trends continue the world will be about 4 degrees colder in 1990, but 11 degrees colder in the year 2000. This is about twice what it would take to put us into an ice age."

The common thread running through the above quotes is that they all date from 1970, and reflect fairly common scientific opinion at the time. I'm not criticising scientists but they sometimes they get it wrong. Even worse: when those who disagree are termed 'deniers' or 'heretics', it means that the scientific method has been turned into a religious dogma of unthinking, blind faith, fed by political pressure from those with their own agenda.

September 2010

NEWS AT SIX AND SEVENS

"Good evening. This is David Challice on the newsdesk, and now we'll go across to Germany for the latest developments. Widespread unrest has been reported across the country as German taxpayers begin to understand the possible disaster facing their economy.

'In recent mid-term elections the German Chancellor, Angela Merkel, was punished heavily at the ballot box when voters realised that they were effectively bank-rolling the rest of the eurozone, including the so-called 'Club Med' countries, Greece, Spain, Portugal, Italy, all of them in economic meltdown. Our Germany correspondent, Andrew Gilligan, now reports from Westphalia: Good evening, Andrew".

"Good evening, David. Yes, day after day, week after week, the main German tabloid, Bild Zeitung, has been metaphorically stripping naked the same victim, then pouring cold baked beans over her head. Chancellor Merkel has had probably the worst seven days of her life. The deal she has done was only after repeated prodding by Mrs Merkel's great European rival, French President Nicolas Sarkozy, who reportedly threatened to pull out of the euro.

'We are again the idiots of Europe!' shrieked Bild, which has the power of the Daily Mail, The Sun, and the Mirror added together, and whose official slogan can be broadly translated as: 'We think up your opinions so you don't have to'."

"So what's the mood on the streets, Andrew?"

"Well, one of those I interviewed was Hendrick Bohmig, in the attractive old town square of Bielefeld. He told me: 'Greece is only the first state that is going down, the next one will follow very soon and Germany will end up paying for them all. People don't realise what's coming. When their kindergarten closes to pay for Greece, people will go on the streets'... Mr Bohmig sells BMWs. When the luxury car salesmen start talking about taking to the streets, you know you have a problem."

"Thank you, Andrew. And now, it's across to Sharon for the weather."

August 2010

ONE POSSIBLE SOLUTION

It's very strange. During the mad cow epidemic our government had the technology to trace a cow born three years earlier, tracking its entire history from farmyard to plate. But for years now they have been unable to locate hundreds of thousands of illegal immigrants who pitched up here looking for work or benefits. Rather than granting them amnesties (the Lib Dem solution) why not just give each of 'em a cow?

On a different subject, someone pointed out that as we are determined to give Iraq a new Constitution, why not sell them ours (Magna Charta and the Bill of Rights etc)? We don't need it anymore, because Brown and Cameron have saddled us with the Lisbon Treaty. It's certainly an idea. Recycling?

20th August 2010

A SILLY WEIGHT

Thanks to new rules from Brussels we might soon be prevented from buying "a dozen eggs". Foreign MEPs have just outvoted our own MEPs and imposed regulations on us, forcing retailers to sell eggs, oranges, bread rolls etc by weight, not by the number contained in the packet.

If you think this is crazy, you're right. It will cost producers £-millions and mean that they need to weigh every box or packet before offering it for sale. Instead of a carton of eggs saying "6 Eggs", only the weight may be displayed. Showing the amount (i.e.: "6 Cup Cakes") will be illegal.

The Food Standards Agency said: "It is important that information is provided in a way that is meaningful and beneficial to customers. The issue is still being considered by EU member states and it will be some time before the regulation is finalised."

We must hope that sanity prevails but how interesting that such a proposal should even need to be discussed let alone given any sort of consideration.

August 2010

A WELL-FOUNDED PERSECUTION COMPLEX

"I'm not paranoid, it's just that everyone's out to get me!" The words of Len Deighton's 'Bernie Samson' back in 1985. But these days the paranoia has spread. De Lisle Catholic school in Loughborough recently banned a father from their school sports day because he hadn't undergone a Criminal Records check. We all know that paedophilia is horrible, but when a dad is physically prevented by the head teacher from watching his own son in the sack race, or the egg-and-spoon, then surely it's gone too far.

The dad, a taxi driver, said: "Rather than kick up a fuss and embarrass my son I just turned around and walked away. I was fuming. She made me feel it was wrong to want to watch my son take part in his first sports day."

But even if you are genuinely paranoid, they might still be gunning for you anyway. For example, the NHS in Wales is banning sugar from vending machines because sweetened tea and coffee "offer no nutritional benefit". Water and juice will be offered as an alternative. Since when did tea have to be nutritional? And what about the Burger King franchise in these hospitals? And why won't these health fascists leave us alone?

Further lunacy is that the EU has now banned the insecticide, methyl bromide, vital for the production of traditional willow cricket bats. The firm J S Wright & Sons is the world's oldest and largest supplier of bat willows. The owner, Nick Wright, said: "40 jobs depend on this. I give our industry twelve weeks to survive." Given that the cricket bat industry will now move to India (the only other source for willow, though inferior) Mr Wright could be forgiven his paranoia for thinking that someone in Brussels was out to get him.

September 2010

HANDS AT TEN-TO-TWO

If you've ever seen the light at the end of the tunnel, it was probably Mother.

Years ago she advised me on how to drive in the dark: "Straddle the white line, and don't dip your lights 'til you see the whites of their eyes!" She ran an old Lotus back then (Lots Of Trouble Usually Serious) and the locals soon learnt to identify her at a distance. Today she drives around East Devon in an armoured car, and is only slightly less dangerous.

Unlike my Mother, the European Union is still a

huge and growing threat – folk have just taken longer to recognise it. Evidence of this is that Brussels has insisted on getting a preview of Chancellor George Osborne's future budgets, before they are presented to parliament, which proves they've got us by the short and curlies.

Further 'proof of threat' is that Britain has just been fined £150-million for not flying the hated, blue Ring of Stars flag above a number of 'EU-funded' schemes such as the Eden Project. Two problems: we are net contributors to the EU; and for Britain there's no such thing as 'European Funding'. It doesn't exist. It all comes from UK taxpayers. The fact that we have been fined £150-million for the EU's stupid bureaucratic rules, at a time when UK hospitals and schools are crying out for renovation, is enough to make one see red.

My suspicions are that a UKIP government would refuse to pay, tell them to sue, and then leave the EU. As a final fall-back position – the so-called nuclear option - they might send in my Mother.

September 2010

MAN FOR THE NEW MILLENIUM

In 1982 the rock band RUSH wrote the song New World Man: "He's old enough to know what's right, but young enough not to choose it. He's noble enough to win the world, but weak enough to lose it. He's a New World Man."

You'll find the New World Man everywhere. He thinks Overseas Aid should be ring-fenced, but not that it props up corrupt and violent governments. He opposes war but cannot see that arms make peace. He'll spend 'government money' at the drop of a hat, without realising that business-people were needed to create it. He is passionate about open borders and 'strangers into citizens', but can't see that multiculturalism creates division and anger.

The New World Man knows that the euro makes it convenient to travel across countries, but not that it would bankrupt his own. He signs up to Human Rights, yet is blind to the rights of the victim. He says sorry for slavery - though he is blameless - yet is silent when he should be apologising. The New World Man presses pedal to the metal and concentrates on his vanishing-point, yet ignores his mirrors and the trail of destruction left in his wake. He's "in the 21st Century now", but does not recognise the old mistakes he is about to repeat. He has faith in progress, but doesn't do religion.

As RUSH said: "He's noble enough to know what's right, but weak enough not to choose it. He's wise enough to win the world, but fool enough to lose it."

May the good Lord protect us from New World Men.

October 2010

SMOKING BAN?

Lawyers are smart people but sometimes they meet their match. An American lawyer bought a box of 24 rare and expensive cigars, and then insured them against fire. Then he smoked them all, and filed a claim against his insurance company, stating they had been "lost in a series of small fires."

The case went to court and, incredibly, he won. The judge summed up: "I agree that the claim is 'frivolous', but the company had warranted that the cigars were insurable and also guaranteed that it would insure them against fire, without defining what is considered to be unacceptable fire. The company is therefore obliged to pay the claim." The insurance company paid $15,000 in settlement. But then came the best part. Once the lawyer had cashed the cheque the insurance company had him arrested on 24 counts of arson. With his own testimony on record, he was convicted of intentionally burning his insured property, given two years in jail and walloped with a $24,000 fine ($1,000 per cigar).

But unlike pub-goers in Britain, at least he was permitted to smoke inside the building, though by that time, of course, the very thought might have choked him.

The only enclosed public space in Britain where smokers are free to light up is on Crown Property, eg: within HM Prisons and the Palace of Westminster. In other words, it doesn't apply to the very MPs who introduced the law in the first place.

It seems to me that pub landlords and private clubs should be free to decide for themselves whether to allow smoking. Many pubs would choose to retain their smoking ban, and that is a matter for them. But others would be places where grown adults can choose to go out in the evening and light up a cigarette without the health police feeling their collar.

The Labour Party still doesn't understand, but partly why they lost the election was because they thought they had the right to tell us how to live our lives. They didn't; now they are paying the price, and good riddance to them.

October 2010

DUCK OR GROUSE

It's vital to heed warnings. Red sky at night: Shepherd's delight. Red sky in the morning: Shepherd's house on fire. UKIP constantly warns of the dangers of EU membership, and here's another one.

The British government is signing up to a new deal called the European Investigation Order. This will enable foreign police forces to come here, mount surveillance operations on you, bug your 'phone, monitor your bank account, even participate in your arrest, even if the 'crime' doesn't exist in Britain.

Some will ask, isn't this just a more organised Interpol? But there are huge differences. Anyone refusing to comply with a foreign police force is likely to be arrested by the UK police. And this is all part of Eurojust, a common legal system that will eventually stretch across the entire EU.

UKIP leader, Lord Pearson, blasted this handover of police powers: "It now appears that Continental police forces really do have ways of 'making us talk.' The fact that Theresa May, Home Secretary, is trying to suggest that defending ancient British liberties is being 'soft on crime' is a disgrace."
The campaign group Fair Trials International added: "Under the new rules it would be possible for Spanish police investigating a murder in a nightclub to demand the ID of every British citizen who flew to the country in the month the offence took place.

They could also force the UK to search its DNA database – containing nearly one million innocent people – and send off samples belonging to anybody who was in Spain at the time".

Some of you might still believe that everything in the EU garden is lovely, but for me it's rather like explaining the Christmas agenda to a well-fattened turkey thumbing through a fancy-dress catalogue to decide what costume will look good at the New Year's Party.

October 2010

A GAILY-PAINTED GYPSY CARAVAN

When the EU expanded to take in ten new states, only UKIP objected. The other British Parties all voted YES, which led to a huge influx of eastern Europeans. Take Lavinia Olmazu, 30, a vocal campaigner for Roma rights. She has an MSc in European Social Policy from the London School of Economics, has addressed the UN on Roma issues, and was funded by the Foreign Office to live and work in Britain. Enough to gladden a Guardianista's heart...

On 26th July 2010, at Southwark Crown Court, she was convicted of masterminding a £2.9million scam, enabling gipsy migrants to come here and fraudulently claim benefits. Along with her boyfriend, Alin Enachi, she charged £80 a pop to provide false employment documentation, charging another £70 to attend the Jobcentre interview alongside the client.

One client was Stelian Dumitru, 26, a failed Roma asylum seeker who was earlier deported from Britain but then returned in 2007 when the borders opened up. Along with his girlfriend (a convicted thief and shoplifter) he obtained £27,048 of our money.

In all Lavinia Olimazu had 200 claimants all lined up, ready to go. Luckily her scheme was discovered, but it could have cost UK taxpayers a potential £12million. Olimazu will probably be deported, but under EU law she will soon be free to travel back here again, when she'll probably claim benefits. And thanks to EU law there's not a damn thing we can do about it.

October 2010

FROM BABES AND SUCKLINGS

It could turn teachers to drink. Here are a few recent exam questions, and the answers given by students:

"What type of attractive force or bond holds sodium and chloride ions together in a crystal of sodium chloride?"
Answer: JAMES BOND.

Or: "Briefly explain what hard water is."
Answer: ICE.

Or: "What happens during puberty to a boy?"
Answer: HE SAYS GOODBYE TO HIS CHILDHOOD, ENTERS ADULTERY..

Or: "What is the meaning of varicose?"
Answer: CLOSE BY.
Or: "What is a fibula?"
Answer: A LITTLE LIE.

But it's not only in the exam hall. Take Ken Clarke, Tory Lord Chancellor. He plans to jail fewer criminals because he thinks short sentences don't work, which is enough to drive us all to the bottle, not just teachers. Mr Clarke ignores that before a petty criminal is sent to jail they will have been convicted many times already. Relying on community sentences is the very punishment that has failed earlier.

From personal knowledge, I can assure you that

many offenders passing through the Probation Service already have a file six-inches thick. Under Mr Clarke that file will grow even thicker. A decent government would build more prisons, and then teach the inmates how to read and write - something the schools should have done years ago.

Let's finish with some more exam answers: "Name one of the early Romans' greatest achievements." Answer: LEARNING TO SPEAK LATIN.

And finally: "Where was the American Declaration of Independence signed?"
Answer: "AT THE BOTTOM".

November 2010

SMASHING MORE PLATES

When Greece went bust, after years of living beyond her means, the eurozone (basically Germany) bailed her out, but then also ran out of money. German voters were so furious with Angela Merkel, Head Frau in Berlin, that they deserted her in recent mid-term elections.

Having run out of cash, the eurozone (Germany, remember) then called in the International Monetary Fund. Within days the IMF offered emergency funds. Because we belong to the IMF, this hit UK taxpayer's in the pocket. But then things got even worse...

The Acting Chancellor, Alistair Darling, was summoned to a crisis meeting in Brussels where they ordered him to provide £13-billion to prop up the euro, even though Britain had never joined the Single Currency. Mr Darling was forced to capitulate because a clause in the Lisbon Treaty ("exceptional occurrences") has stripped Britain of its veto, and his former boss, Gordon Brown, had signed up to it.

To quote the Daily Telegraph (10/5/2010) 'Britain escaped being sucked into the wider bailout loans but was forced to underwrite the "stabilisation mechanism" which - added to an existing facility of £43-billion – makes British taxpayers liable for £13-billion of a new £95-billion fund.'

In other words, the EU rammed through its political project, the euro, knowing that it wouldn't work in many countries, and now expects us to pick up the tab. A UKIP government would politely tell Brussels to get lost, place the Lisbon Treaty into the cylindrical waste-disposal facility, and leave the EU. But then you probably guessed that already.

November 2010

STATE OF THE UNION

If you study a political map of Britain, following the 2010 election, you'll notice something odd. Vast areas of England and Wales are now Tory blue or yellow Lib Dem. Apart from a few industrial areas like Manchester, and eastern areas of London with its client-immigrant population, Labour were gravely damaged in England.

Yet in Scotland things were different. North of the border red, red, red was the colour of their carpet, proving that many Scots live - or at least vote - on another planet. You might have expected an SNP victory, for independence from the hated English, but nope, that didn't happen. The Scots weren't daft. They voted Labour, for the English chequebook.

When people such as tennis player Andy Murray announce they support ANY football team against England (and he's not alone; during the World Cup another Scot told the cameras: "I'd rather have my legs sawn off than support England") one can be forgiven for asking if the Union is worth preserving. I suspect the real threat to the Union comes not from Scotland but from south of the border. To quote journalist Bruce Anderson: "If it becomes clear to the English that Scotland is culturally hostile and economically ungrateful, they will cease to see the point of the Union."

He's probably right, but it would be a disaster. Because of our shared history and culture, the Union is vital for England and Scotland. The real key is getting the Scots back onboard, not just as Labour-voting clients but as full partners in the future success of this country. But it won't be easy.

November 2010

But come the 2015 General Election the Scots voted SNP en masse, virtually destroying Labour and the Lib Dems. The Tories clung on to their usual solitary seat in Scotland.

AN EQUITABLE SOLUTION

There's always a way out. For Britain to escape the European Union, all we need is a majority of MPs in Westminster voting to overturn the European Communities Act 1972. And that's it. We're out. But not until enough people vote UKIP instead of for the three bigger parties. Regardless of small differences between them, please remember that the Lib/Lab/Con have all relinquished 'governing' the country. Now they are just managers, taking orders from a distant boss.

A different type of escape route is what's happening in New York. Muslims are trying to build a mosque near 'Ground Zero' (created by the 9/11 attacks). Millions of Americans (some of them Muslim) were appalled. But President Obama approved the proposals, stating that under the law they had every right to build there and that all Americans should honour the principles of religious tolerance.

Let's leave aside how 'tolerant' it is proposing to build a mosque there in the first place. Let's even ignore whether there's an ulterior motive behind it. Let's concentrate on journalist Greg Gutfield, from Fox News, who has the perfect solution: "As an American, I believe they have every right to build the mosque. After all, if they buy the land and they follow the law, who can stop them? Which is why, in the spirit of outreach, I've decided to do the same thing. I'm announcing tonight that I'm planning to build and open the first gay bar that caters not only to the west, but also Islamic gay men. The bar will be situated next to the mosque."

He went on: "As you know, the Muslim faith doesn't look kindly upon homosexuality, which is why I'm building this bar. It is an effort to break down barriers and reduce deadly homophobia in the Islamic world. An entire floor will feature non-alcoholic drinks, since booze is forbidden by the faith. I hope that the mosque owners will be as open to the new bar as I am to the new mosque. My place, however, will have better music."

December 2010

TRAIN-SPOTTER

Here's a quote from film-maker and journalist Luke Johnson (Management Today magazine, Oct 2010): "I have always been an EU and eurosceptic so I am not surprised at events in Greece. It is a beautiful country but the idea that Greece is as creditworthy as Germany was certain to lead to disaster. You only have to look at its national train company for a case-study in how dangerous European monetary union really is.'

He went on: 'Hellenic Railways wins my award for the most preposterous organisation of the year. It loses roughly €1bn annually on revenues of just €200m. That's right – its yearly deficit is five times its turnover. It carries a vast debt-load [equivalent to] 5% of Greece's GDP, because misguided foreign investors believed that the Greek government would never permit it to fail – and the EU would never permit Greece to fail."

Mr Johnson is absolutely right, but the EU has learnt nothing. It now wants to increase its budget by 5.9%, an extra £900million from Britain alone. The money will pay for Baroness Ashton's new EU diplomatic Service, £399million next year (which will see British embassies closing all around the world), a 90% increase in the EU entertainment budget, a new palace for EU President Herman van Rompuy (£280million), and a European Banking Authority (£11million next year alone). These new quangos will join the EU's existing 47 quangos, just as David Cameron promises a 'bonfire of the quangos' here in Britain.

But just remember that whatever the EU spends, it's not their money, so they don't care. And with David Cameron rolling over like a one-trick performing poodle, keep your hand on your wallet, because 'Europe' has its greedy eye on the contents.

December 2010

THERE IS A GREEN HILL FAR AWAY

If you're thinking of staging a nativity play or carol service this Christmas, you'll need to know the latest

Health and Safety requirements (like most things these actually come from the EU, but you'd never know it by reading the document).

Live performances of Jingle Bells may not involve a "one-horse open sleigh" unless a satisfactory risk-assessment has been completed. If on private land, the land-owners' permission must be secured beforehand, with valid insurance policies in place. The sleigh operator must be fully conversant with all relevant animal welfare legislation regarding stabling, fodder, rest periods, standards of bedding, and easy access to veterinary care. (It is advised that a vet be present 24 hours a day but this is not a statutory requirement).

The carol 'While Shepherds Watched their Flocks by Night' is another minefield. The European Shepherd's Union has objected that watching their flocks by night, 'all seated on the ground' may lead to piles or other medical problems, unless appropriate seating arrangements have been made (cushions, padded benches, orthopaedic chairs etc). In bad weather a facility must be in place, allowing them to watch their flocks by CCTV cameras.

You may think the above examples are extreme but it's not all imagination. This country has just announced that convicts in prison will be entitled to vote in future general elections, thanks to the Lisbon Treaty incorporating the European Convention on Human Rights into EU law. Just one disenfranchised prisoner could take our Government to court and we'd be forced to pay 78,000 convicts £750 in compensation.

Enough to make you choke on your turkey. Merry Christmas. See you next year.

December 2010

FRENCH'S MUSTARD ON MY HOT-DOG SAUSAGE

Here's a conundrum: you are driving in a car at a constant speed. The ground to your left falls away 18 inches. To your right there is a fire engine, travelling the same speed. Ahead of you is a galloping horse. You cannot overtake. By turning, and looking behind, you observe a galloping zebra, travelling the same speed as you, the horse, and the fire engine. How do you escape this dangerous situation?

Here is the solution. You are either drunk or stoned. Get off the merry-go-round.

Our membership of the EU is another merry-go-round. They are trying to push through a rise of 5.9% to their budget, when most countries are making cuts. Prime Minister David Cameron called it "completely unacceptable" but then went to Brussels and rolled over, saying that he'd agreed with the French and the Germans to pay only an extra 2.9%.

Mr Cameron can huff and puff until he's blue in the face but we'll be spending more than that before these negotiations are over. But even if he gets his 2.9%, it's still an increase when the EU should be cutting and cutting. Instead we could be facing an extra £900million, on top of our current massive contributions.

UKIP's Nigel Farage asked: " Did anybody who voted for Cameron vote for criminals to get the vote? Did they vote to increase the EU budget? Did they vote to hand over our aircraft carriers to the French? Of course not. Every single Tory must feel betrayed. Mr

Cameron's foreign policy can only be described as 'Surrender, Surrender, Surrender'."

Ladies and gentlemen, if we want to have enough left for a candy-floss, hot-dog, and a last ride on the dodgems, it's time to get off that merry-go-round.

January 2011

SITUATIONS PRETTY VACANT

You can't always believe what you're told: "Bacon and Eggs, best start to day" might be true, but be on your guard if it comes from the Pork and Hen Council.

Market research company OnePoll.com recently compiled a list of job titles. For some employers, window cleaners are now Transparency Enhancement Facilitators (perhaps they should be working at the Houses of Parliament?)

Factory workers are Mass Production Engineers. Housewives are Domestic Technicians. Dinner ladies are Education Centre Nourishment Consultants, and shop workers are Customer Experience Enhancement Operatives.

But it doesn't stop at daft job titles. When Nicole Mamo, boss of her own recruitment agency, drafted an ad for a hospital cleaner, she ran it past the local Jobcentre, just to be sure. They turned it down, because she had included the phrase: "Must be reliable and hard working."

In today's lunatic asylum, the ad discriminates against those who are unreliable and not hard working (Mail Online 27/01/10). Mrs Mamo said: "In my 15 years in recruitment I haven't heard anything so ridiculous. I need people who are hard working and reliable – and I am pleased to discriminate in this way. The reputation of my business is on the line."

How about this ad (suggested by "Rob" from Barcelona): "General layabout required. Duties include filing nails, placing feet on desk, being abusive around the office. Punctuality not essential. Preference given to those of unkempt appearance and work-shy attitude. Applications in whatever language you choose. Interviews held next week, or whatever time suits you best."

January 2011

NO MORE BEEF IN BLUE CHEESE SAUCE

The scene is a boating lake, with two attendants standing beside their hut. The first one raises a megaphone to his lips: "Come in Number 99, your time is up." His colleague looks at him: "We ain't got a Number 99."

The first attendant thinks for a moment, then speaks into the megaphone: "Are you in trouble Number 66?"

Right now we're all aboard Number 66, and in deep trouble. The Food Standards Agency has just released a report saying we should move towards a vegetarian diet and cut out beef and cheese: "The switch is necessary as part of a diet low in greenhouse gases, which are associated with climate change."

The report came from the University of East Anglia, discredited after years of illegally concealing data on climate change and conspiring to skew the peer review process (revealed by leaked emails). In my opinion this seat of learning cannot be trusted to produce the chemical formula for Ovaltine, let alone pontificate on the nation's diet.

As a further example of climate 'spin' in August we had the headline: "Italian Alps melt in Heatwave". After a hot summer the snow had melted on the high passes, revealing a 'long-talked about but never seen before' nest of bunkers and barracks built by Austro Hungarian troops during World War I. The frozen body of an Italian soldier, from the same war, was also found, all paraded as proof of global warming.

Think about this for a minute. Eighty years ago it was sufficiently warm for the Italian Army to need fortifications on a high mountain pass, because they feared Austrian troops crossing through. Not only that, but it was also technically possible to actually build the structure. But then it got cold and the ice grew and covered the fort for years. And now it's just got a little bit warmer - though not as warm as it was 80 years ago - and we're all told to eat baked beans and cabbage to reduce methane gas (Eh?).

And this follows the Icelandic volcano that was estimated to have pumped out more greenhouse gases in the first week of its ash-cloud than had been saved by the 'green' efforts of every human being on the planet for the last five years.

Yes, I know. Let's all have a group hug. And then a T-bone steak. You can even have baked beans with it.

January 2011

SPRAYING IT AROUND LIKE BOLINGER

They say: "Always borrow money from a pessimist. He won't expect it back", so we'll have to be downbeat about ever getting our cash returned by the EU. That's a pity, because there's so much of it. Here are a few examples from the £8billion we gave them last year.

British taxpayers paid £43,000 to a "hip-hop laboratory" in Lyon, France, to ease the "lack of co-operation in European hip-hop". And well done, I say. I've been worried about the situation in Lyon for some time now.

Or how about the £350,000 paid to the Flying Gorillas dance troupe, whose speciality is the Smelly Foot Dance? Or the £14,000 we paid to Austrian farmers in the Tyrol, to "increase their emotional connection with landscapes", or the £352,000 we gave to a Hungarian IT firm "to improve the lifestyle and living standard of dogs."?

But what really takes the cannabis flapjack is the European External Action Service (a sort of EU diplomatic force), led by our very own Baroness Ashton, whose only previous achievement was as former treasurer of CND. The EU Action Service plans to open 200 embassies across the world, with 7,000 employees, at a cost of at least £5.8billion. Baroness Ashton is spending £33million alone, on more than 150 armoured limousines for EU officials across the world.

In London the EU bought the old Tory Party HQ, at 32 Smith Square, for £20million, then spent another £5.6million doing it up, including Herman Miller Mirra office chairs for each member of staff (a very reasonable £800 a throw)... But hey, it's not their money. It's yours. And until you do something about it they'll keep right on doing it. Over to you....

January 2011

ANYONE FOR BULLSHIT?

Nod off during those long, boring meetings and conferences? No problem. BBC Journalist John Humphrys has the answer, a new game, a sort of office Bingo. You must draw up a 5x5 grid of words such as "Best Practise", "Proactive", "Client-Focused", "Mindset", "Win-Win", "Fast-Track", "Value-Added", "Leverage" etc.

During your next meeting or seminar, tick off each word as someone uses it. Once you have completed a full line - vertical, horizontal or diagonal - stand up and shout: "BULLSHIT!"

Here are a few testimonials: "I had only been in the meeting five minutes when I won." (Bob)... Or: "What a gas! Meetings will never be the same after my first win." (Bill)... Or: "The atmosphere was tense in the last process-meeting as 14 of us waited for the fifth word". (Ben)... Or: "The speaker was stunned as eight of us screamed: "BULL****" for the third time in 2 hours." (Kathleen).

I'm very taken with this, and intend to suggest to UKIP MEPs that they adopt it next time they attend the EU Parliament in Brussels. It might make that dreadful experience slightly less awful. You never know, the BBC might even broadcast the highlights

February 2011

I'D LIKE THE ONE WITH THE RED FRONT DOOR AND 16 BEDROOMS

Helena Horvatova, 27, would like a bigger house. She has only three bedrooms for herself, her unemployed husband, and their seven children. Peterborough Council gave them the place a few days after they arrived here from the Czech Republic. She said: "My husband is claiming Job Seeker's Allowance. Back in our country he was a school cleaner but in Peterborough they say there are no vacancies."

But the Horvatora's aren't the only ones jumping the queue. At least 10,000 eastern European immigrants have arrived in Peterborough since the EU expanded its borders seven years ago, with a similar story repeated across much of England. This is a scandal. Even in good times it would be indefensible, but in days of cutbacks and austerity it is complete and utter lunacy.

Equally mad is that by the end of 2009 some 40,000 children living in Poland were receiving British child benefit, with the Government now cutting it for those of you who have at least paid for it in past taxes. Guardianista readers may think this is OK, but if I agreed with you we'd both be wrong.

February 2011

TEA, MR SHIFTER

Britain is making huge cuts in most areas, and jacking up VAT and other taxes. The government tells us it is necessary to balance the books after years of Labour incompetence. But one fact that they still ignore is immigration. Between 2004 and

2031 (by official UK government figures) 86% of population increase will be due to new immigrants, forming 39% of all new households.

This is a shocking statistic, but it might even be an underestimate. As the Daily Mail revealed last summer, England has been named most crowded country in the EU, with net immigration rising by 33,000 in one year, putting huge pressure on hospitals, schools, social welfare, crime etc. This also costs us £billions because of the estimated five million British adults who don't work but are on various benefits.

The real key is that because we belong to the EU we cannot prevent their citizens coming here for jobs. And it might be yours next. Ask the 236 workers at the Twinings tea factory in North Shields. They had a double hit. Not only did Twinings move their production to Poland but they also asked the existing staff to train up their replacements before they left. Talk about 'trouble brewing'...

February 2011

GROOMED FOR OFFICE

I was speaking to a family of Lib Dems the other day, and asked their little girl what she wanted to be when she grew up. "I want to be Prime Minister", she told me. Her parents looked on approvingly.

So I asked: "If you were Prime Minister, what's the first thing you would do?" and she said: "I'd give food and houses to all the homeless people." By now the parents were beaming with pride.

"That's a really worthy goal," I said. "But you don't have to wait until you're Prime Minister. If you come over to my house and mow the lawn, pull up some weeds, dig over my veggie patch, I'll give you £50. Then I'll take you down to the park where that homeless man hangs out, and you can give him the £50 towards food and a new house."

She thought it over then looked me straight in the eye: "Why doesn't the homeless man come up here and cut the grass himself? Then you could just pay him the £50 direct."

I said: "Welcome to No 10, Prime Minister."

Her parents saw me in the street yesterday. They didn't speak.

February 2011

STAY UNDER THAT DUVET

If you think it's OK to come out from under the duvet, better think twice. The European Court has been at work again. Not only have they given votes to prisoners and ruled that women drivers pay the same car insurance as men (despite having fewer accidents), they have now stripped Britain of the right to deport asylum seekers to other EU countries.

The judges ruled that we cannot deport illegals to Greece because Greece treats them to "inhumane or degrading treatment". We're not talking Zimbabwe here. Greece is a member of the EU (for the moment!) and if we cannot deport people to Athens it opens the floodgates for thousands of asylum seekers to either move here from Greece or to simply claim that they've come here from that country.

Sir Andrew Green, of the Migrationwatch think-tank, said: "This opens a gateway into Europe and Britain for asylum seekers. Future asylum seekers will enter the EU through Greece safe in the knowledge that we cannot send them back. Their cases will have to be settled here at the expense of the British taxpayer."

Immigration Minister Damian Green said: "We are disappointed with the judgement.". Then he went and had a cup of tea.

March 2011

SATELLITE UNDER HOUSE ARREST

The EU has a space satellite programme called Galileo (one that the Chinese know all about, and the Americans have threatened to destroy if they ever go to war with China). It was meant to be completed by 2010 but it is running late, way over budget, and beset with technical problems.

Brussels has already admitted that the annual running costs have increased to €800million, but now it needs an extra €1.9billion from taxpayers. Sure. Take it. The money was just sitting around. We weren't doing anything with it. Do you need any more?

Following the Wikileaks affair it emerged that a chap called Berry Smutny, head of OHB Technology (a German satellite firm involved with Galileo) told US officials that the project was "stupid", "doomed to failure", "a waste of EU taxpayers' money" and "driven by French military interests". Mr Smutny is no longer employed at OHB.

The campaigning group Open Europe has calculated that the total cost of Galileo will hit at least €22billion. So far we have paid £2.95billion to the project. The original plan was for private investors to come on board and pay the lion's share. But most of them have run a country mile, "citing a lack of commercial prospects".

It's the same sad tale of everything the EU touches. And when they foul up, the poor beleaguered taxpayer has to pick up the tab.

March 2011

INSERTING THE PARSON'S NOSE

You might be interested in a few Government initiatives apparently in the pipeline. It is rumoured that the Prime Minister intends to make it more difficult to claim benefits. From October the forms will be printed only in English... This seems unlikely, given that the National Census was printed in 57 languages, including Tagalog, Igbo, and Shona.

One view might be that this reflects Britain's rich multicultural diversity. Another might be that if these people travelled thousands of miles to come here, the very least they can do is learn the language, rather than have everything translated for them at a cost of £millions.

There's a big change coming for the NHS where doctors are being expected to act as accountants/project managers rather than simply knowing the business end of a thermometer. They are not happy. The Allergists voted to scratch it. The Dermatologists advised against such rash moves. The Obstetricians said the Government was labouring under a misconception, and the Psychiatrists thought it was madness. You can probably guess the reaction of the Urologists.

If you were wondering why the Government is getting so involved in revamping the NHS, partly it's because it accounts for a massive part of public spending. But the other reason is that as we are now ruled from Brussels it's one of the very few areas where the EU hasn't yet inserted its nose. But give it time..

March 2011

LONG-RANGE VISION

If you want a classic example of idiotic waste, try this one. The Nimrod was a long-range RAF spy-plane. Recently they were publicly scrapped (news footage showed brand-new ones being smashed to bits by heavy demolition equipment).

So what replaces them, you ask? I'll tell you. Three ageing Boeing Stratotankers are to be fitted out as spy-planes and then leased to the RAF. The planes are American and the refitting work will be done in Texas.

The SNP defence spokesman, Angus Robertson, said: "It's nothing short of scandalous that the Ministry of Defence would rather spend money buying second-hand aircraft from America than supporting jobs and bases here. Given the amount of money that has been wasted over cancellation and destruction of Nimrod it is increasingly difficult to believe these decisions can even be justified in terms of cost-cutting."

You can say that again, Angus...

But it's not just the present government. Under Gordon Brown's Labour shower we had such gems as a Walking Co-ordinator (Islington council: £31,935 salary), European Projects and Tourism Officer (Medway council in Kent, £36,313) Climate Change Officer (Braintree council £38,556) and the classic Nuclear Free Local Authorities Secretariat, Policy and Research Officer (Manchester City Council) at a cool £37,543. The job description is: "Identifying nuclear hazards and pressing for existing binding international agreements on nuclear weapons". I wonder if Manchester Council isn't straying a tad beyond its remit of emptying the bins and keeping the library open?

March 2011

LETTING IN SOME LIGHT

The Independent newspaper is sponsoring a philosophy and music festival in Hay-on-Wye, in Wales, this June. Among the speakers is Anjem Choudray, a leading figure in the banned terrorist-supporting al-Muharjiroun. Just for the record (though few of you are likely to attend) they're calling the festival: "How The Light Gets In".

I'm not sure which light they mean, unless it's Mr Choudray's, because he's a leading one in Islam4UK, a group working to scrap Christianity in favour of Islam (You probably guessed that already. There's a clue in the title).

But who else should they invite? Gert Wilders, the anti-Islamic Dutch politician, for a balancing viewpoint? Or Robert Mugabe, for his take on secular, specifically non-Islamic democracy in post-colonial Africa?

That nice Mr Bin Laden would have been a star turn, but is lost to us now, thanks to the Americans. Perhaps the organizers should pencil in Abu Hamza (aka Captain Hook) before the CIA book him first. Get in quick, guys. This is good advice.

I'm sure Mr Choudray will go down like a led zeppelin with the progressive lefties in the audience, though the ultimate irony is that if Islam4UK ever succeeds in taking over the UK it will be the 'useful idiots' in the audience who get put against the wall first. The one group they hate more than Christians are secular atheists.

April 2011

NOT A VERY FUNNY JOKE

Thanks to Gordon Brown signing the Lisbon Treaty, the (non-EU) European Court of Human Rights has now effectively been absorbed by the European Union. Any rulings from the court are now "justiciable", which means they're binding on us and we can't say "No". Thanks Gordon.

Here are two consequences. Firstly, Rebecca Powell lives in a council flat in Hounslow, West London. She's on benefits, yet ran up a bill of £3,500 in rent arrears. The Council tried to evict her but failed, because it was in contravention of her human rights. This means that thousands of council tenants could stop paying rent, then claim "Human Rights" when threatened with eviction. This could potentially cost £millions.

The second example is failed asylum seeker, Aso Mohammed Ibrahim, 33. Despite being banned from driving (and convicted of harassment and possession of drugs) he was at the wheel of his car in 2003 when he smashed into 12-yr-old Amy Houston, leaving her dying under the wheels. Then he did a runner.

The dead girl's father, Paul Houston, battled for seven years to get Ibrahim deported. But the courts have now ruled that this gentleman's human rights would be impinged if he was sent back to Iraq, so now he is allowed to live in the UK permanently.

Mr Houston was unimpressed: "I'm really angry. We should all be angry. This is a perversity of our society. What are the judges saying here? That it doesn't matter what you do when you come here, who you kill, what laws you break? You work hard, pay your taxes, and this is how you get treated. What does that say about politicians, our leaders and the legal system? It's a joke."

But if it is a joke it is not a very funny one.

April 2011

SLIGHTLY LESS UNFUNNY JOKE

In these days of cuts, austerity, blank cheques to the eurozone etc it's important to lighten up a bit. Here's my contribution to the general smilieness of Britain. A friend recently 'phoned Lib Dem HQ, asking for a copy of their manifesto. The lady said: "I'm very sorry but we've sold out." My friend replied: "Yes, I know that. But can I have a copy of your manifesto."

Well if that don't float your boat, how about these simple homespun remedies: Avoid cutting yourself when slicing vegetables by getting someone else to hold them while you chop. Or: a mousetrap placed on top of the alarm clock will prevent you from hitting the snooze button and drifting off to sleep again. Or: if you can't fix it with a hammer you've got an electrical problem.

Or this one: Austrian Helmut Griese, 63, was recently fined £700 for yodelling whilst mowing his lawn. A court in Graz decided that his yodelling activities were insulting his Muslim neighbours. "It was not my intention to imitate or insult them. I simply started to yodel a few tunes because I was in such a good mood," he told his local newspaper.

Even more rib-tickling (if not exactly side-splitting) is that Brussels has allocated £8.3billion for countries such as Serbia and Bosnia that want to join the EU. Turkey has already been granted £3.2billion.

William Dartmouth MEP (UKIP) failed to see the funny side: "British families facing difficult financial times and possible job losses will be dismayed to discover that we are being forced to give money to countries like Albania and Serbia. It must seem like a bad joke, with them as the butt."

April 2011

GAUGING THINGS PROPERLY

I read this recently and thought you might be interested: "The US standard railroad gauge (distance between the rails) is 4 feet, 8.5 inches, a very odd number. Why was that gauge used? Because that's the way they built them in England, and English expatriates designed the US railroads....

Why did the English build them like that? Because the first rail lines were built by the same people who built the pre-railroad tramways, and that's the gauge they used.

Why did 'they' use that gauge then? Because the people who built the tramways used the same jigs and tools that they had used for building horse-wagons, which used that wheel spacing.

So why did the wagons have that particular odd wheel spacing? Well, if they tried to use any other spacing, the wagon wheels would break on some of the old, long distance roads in England, because that's the spacing of the wheel ruts.

So who built those old rutted roads? Imperial Rome built the first long distance roads in Europe (including England) for their legions. Those roads have been used ever since.

And the ruts in the roads? Roman war chariots formed the initial ruts, which everyone else had to match for fear of destroying their wagon wheels.

Since the chariots were made for Imperial Rome, they shared the same wheel-spacing. Therefore the United States standard railroad gauge of 4 feet, 8.5 inches is derived from the original specifications for an Imperial Roman war chariot.

The next time you are handed a specification/procedure/process and wonder 'What ass came up with this?' you're nearer than you'd think. Imperial Roman army chariots were made just wide enough to accommodate the rear ends of two war horses. (Two horses' asses, in fact.)". Bureaucracies live forever.

Ahem… normal service will be resumed next week.

May 2011

LET'S INVADE SOMEBODY

British prime ministers often do this. They win an election and within a year or so take us to war. It could be happening again in Libya where (along with France and the USA) we are interfering in an Arab civil war.

Colonel Gaddafi is a very bad man, but we've known that for years. Britain has had plenty of reasons to attack him (when his gunmen shot dead WPC Yvonne Fletcher in a London Street, or when funding the IRA, or when his agents blew up a Jumbo Jet over Lockerbie) but from where I'm sitting it seems likely we are again being dragged into yet another shooting match, with Libya slated for "regime change".

We tried it in Iraq, with Saddam, plunging that country into chaos. And we're still in Afghanistan when we should have left years ago. And I am deliberately avoiding the price in human blood paid by our own troops. Their job is to fight wars, not "rebuild" entire countries that resent our very presence.

There's another cost. Because Gordon Brown blew all our money (along with the American banks) we're broke. Our Harrier Jump Jets are being scrapped, along with Ark Royal, and the Tornado squadrons will soon follow, with an estimated 42,000 redundancy notices to be issued to the Armed Forces by 2015.

And what does Mr Cameron do? He pledges £650million to Pakistan's education budget, and agrees to pump £billions into the EU to prop up the euro, when we don't even belong to that doomed currency. Madness.

May 2011

UNDER-RATED

Last week my partner said she was leaving me because of my obsession with the 60's pop group The Monkees. I thought she was joking. And then I saw her face.

I was equally amazed when the credit-rating agency Moody's took a closer look at Portugal's economy on 12th July and down-graded Lisbon's government bonds to "junk" status, which means that if you're holding them you've now sorted out the problem of wallpaper for the back bedroom. Think of it as a conversation piece.

Reacting in the only way it knows, the EU lashed out. Jose Barroso, President of the Commission, said: "I deeply regret the decision, both in terms of its timing and its magnitude. With all due respect to that specific rating agency, our institutions know Portugal a little bit better."

German Finance Minister, Wolfgang Schauble, sent his troops in on the left-flank: "The oligopoly of the rating agencies needs to be broken." And then, yet again, he floated the idea of the EU running its own credit-rating agency.

Let's be clear. These agencies are an industry-standard in banking and finance across the world (the big three are Moody's, Standard & Poor's, and Fitch). They don't always get it right. Sometimes they get it very wrong indeed, but they are the best we have. And at least they are in competition with each other, which probably helps.

For the EU to have a hissy-fit over Moody's, and then propose inventing their own agency is like owning a tumbledown cottage, being angry when a structural surveyor condemns it, and then setting up your own surveying business, just so that your own dangerous wreck can get a clean bill of health. Never mind reality. Pieces of paper are all that matter. Lunacy.

June 2011

BIRD CHOPPERS ARE "WHOOFERS NOT TWEETERS"

The answer, I'm afraid, is not "blowing in the wind". Wind farms are a total waste of money. No country that has opted for wind energy has ever managed to shut a single conventional power station as a result, partly because even the best wind turbines operate at only one-third of their stated output, and partly because the wind isn't always blowing when we want to put on the kettle or cook dinner. A conventional power station is always needed to provide back-up.

In the June edition of Business Network magazine, Dr Bernard Juby described a few of the health risks of wind turbines: "The tip of the blade (usually three) the length of a Jumbo's wing, travels at 150 mph. It inevitably makes a substantial sound. Within a few feet it encounters an obstruction in the form of the tower as a blade passes every one or two seconds, giving a pulsating quality to the aerodynamic sound which many people find deeply disturbing."

Dr Juby goes on: "Some developers state that noise isn't a problem, but they rely on ETSU-R-97 which is not a fit instrument to assess it since this screens out lower frequencies. Clusters of windfarms can produce further interaction of sound periodicity as the rotors of different machines go into and out of phase (amplitude modulation) generating the "whoomph, whoomph" at one or two second intervals, an effect which can be likened to the bass "whoofer" speaker in a sound system."

Dr Juby also raises concerns about the "sub whoofer" frequencies which affect all animals (including birds and humans) and the flicker rate of combined multiple spinning blades which have blighted the lives of some people who live near these monstrosities with the risk of epileptic seizures.

To read the full article please visit www. businessnetworkmagazine.com
It's quite an eye-opener.

June 2011

ANDREX FOR THE BABY-SITTER

Here's a comforting tale for two. Abdisamad Sufi was born in 1987 in Somalia. In 2003 he entered Britain on a fake passport and claimed asylum. This was rejected but he appealed. In June 2005 his appeal was dismissed as "not credible" but in October (same year) he admitted two counts of burglary and five of fraud and was sentenced to 18 months in prison.

In February 2006 he was convicted of making threats to kill and sent down for another six months. In October 2007 he was jailed for three months for indecent exposure, and in July 2009 was given a further three years for a string of thefts and burglaries.

And now to Abdiaziz Elmi, 42, another Somali. He claimed asylum in 1989 and was allowed to stay. In 1996 he was sentenced to five years in the slammer for handling stolen goods, fraud, robbery, and carrying a replica gun.

In November 2000 he was sent down for three months for perverting the course of justice, in 2001 put on a curfew for theft, and in 2002 convicted on eight counts of supplying heroin and cocaine, and jailed for three years. In 2004 he was jailed for a year for burglary and theft.

At this point (2006) the authorities woke up and realised that Mr Elmi was not a man you'd want baby-sitting for the children, so they tried to deport him. He appealed to the European Court, which dragged things out. And then in 2008 he was convicted of possessing Class A drugs and jailed for 18 months. In July 2010 he was also charged with possession of Class A drugs with intent to supply.

In case you're wondering, both these men (and 200 other Somalis) have just been given permission by the European Court of Human Rights to stay in Britain because if they are deported to Mogadishu they might find that Somalian loo-paper isn't as soft as the Andrex they've grown used to. And this is why a UKIP government will scrap the Human Rights Act and withdraw from the ECHR.

June 2011

SENSE OF HUMOUR BYPASS

I sometimes worry this country has lost its sense of humour. A few months ago schoolboy Ed Stuckey, 14, was hit in the shoulder by a javelin on the sports field. It was an unfortunate accident and thankfully he wasn't seriously injured. An ITN reporter interviewed the headmistress, Mrs Staab, but neither seemed to notice any irony in any of the surnames. Or perhaps they did, but were afraid to comment. Here might be why....

Financial advisor Filip Slipaczek was recently telephoned at home by a Nat West call centre, offering him new services. But when the girl tried to pronounce his name she laughed and said it sounded like 'Slip a cheque'. Innocent enough, you'd have thought. But Mr Slipaczek clearly disagreed, complaining to Nat West: "This is totally unacceptable behaviour". So the bank had to apologise and pay compensation. Oh well.

Restoring my humour was the fact that Steve Hilton, the Prime Minister's senior policy advisor, has now backed calls for Britain to pull out of the EU. Following the 2010 general election Mr Hilton was "shocked to discover how much sovereignty has switched from Westminster to Brussels." A few examples are votes for prisoners; women paying increased car-insurance premiums despite being safer drivers; and our own Chancellor of the Exchequer having to "clear" his budget with Brussels before announcing it to Parliament.

Just before someone objects that the above relates to the (non EU) European Court of Human Rights, please remember that under the Lisbon Treaty all rulings from the Court are now "Justiciable" throughout all 27 member states. In effect, Brussels wrapped a great big welcoming arm around the Court, said: "Come inside and have a cuppa", then slammed the door shut, locked it, and dropped the key down its cleavage.

June 2011

BEWARE THOSE BEARING GIFTS?

A friend of mine recently admitted to being a brake-fluid addict - but he reckoned he could stop at any time. Unlike the eurozone piling cash into Greece. They can't stop, and for one reason. Greece might be bust, but if she defaults then international banks will take the hit, and they don't want that.

Alex Andreou (who spent years in the USA before coming home) recently wrote an impassioned blog, explaining that the Greek situation is far more complicated than many think. He wrote (and I'm editing it slightly): "What is going on in Athens is resistance against an invasion. The invading army wears suits instead of uniforms, and has lap-tops instead of guns, but make no mistake – the attack on our sovereignty is as violent and thorough. Private wealth interests are dictating policy to a sovereign nation which is directly against its national interest".

He went on: "We did plenty wrong. I returned in 2006 and saw an entirely different country to the one I left behind. [Low credit was everywhere] We took this bait, hook, line, and sinker. We were going to be the most European, the most Capitalist, the most Western. I did not see a pair of sunglasses not emblazoned with Diesel or Prada, a pair of flip-flops not bearing the logo of Versace or D&G. The cars were BMW or Mercedes. If anyone took a holiday anywhere closer than Thailand, they kept it a secret."

He went on: "That irresponsibility was only a small part of the problem. [The new plutocracy] were squeezing every ounce of blood through a system of corruption so gross that it was worthy of any banana republic. I know it's impossible to share why one of the oldest civilisations in the world has turned from a source of inspiration to being the punchline of cheap jokes."

I've run out of space, but Mr Andreou's main message is that the Greek people never wanted a bailout from the eurozone. And those at least 50% responsible are the banks and finance houses who showered the country with easy money, without asking themselves whether it could ever be repaid. Poor, poor Greece.

July 2011

OWN GOAL

I thought you might be interested in a few quotes. Take this one from David Beckham: "My parents have always been there for me, since I was about seven." Or this one, from Peter Shilton: "You've got to believe that you're going to win, and I believe we'll win the World Cup until the final whistle blows and we're knocked out." That's the spirit…

Let's try one from Mr Graham Watson MEP (rumoured to have been ennobled but that's just not credible): "The best way to protect British jobs is to get Britain into the euro – fast!" Nice one, Graham. Hang your head in shame, then apologise to everyone in Britain.

Or this one from singer Jason Donovan, reflecting on his career: "In retrospect there's no looking back."

Or this 1996 one from Kenneth Clarke, Justice Secretary at the time of writing, but watch this space: "I look forward to the day when the Westminster Parliament is just a council chamber in Europe." Makes you wonder why David Cameron gave him a job.

On a happier note let's return to footballers. "If you don't believe you can win, there's no point getting

out of bed at the end of the day." (Neville Southall)
Or: "I faxed a transfer request to the club at the beginning of the week, but let me state that I don't want to leave Leicester" (Stan Collymore),

Or: "I can see the carrot at the end of the tunnel." (Stuart Pearce).

If there's anybody out there still reading this, I'll finish with my favourite, from Ade Akinbiyi: "I was watching the Blackburn game on TV on Sunday when it flashed on the screen that George had scored in the first minute at Birmingham. My first reaction was to ring him up. Then I remembered he was out there playing."

August 2011

LORDS OF ALL THEY DEPOSIT

Here are some of the so-called 'Euro Big Beasts' who sit in the House of Lords, swaddled in ermine, taking huge sums of money from Brussels, whilst voting on matters concerning the EU.

Neil and Glenys Kinnock (Lord and Baroness) have earned nearly £8million from the EU and now get a combined pension of £164,693. Lord (Peter) Mandelson had a golden handshake of £311,000 when stepping down as a commissioner, and now receives an annual pension of £35,543.

Lord (Leon) Brittain has a jolly useful £83,000 a year, whilst Lord Clinton-Davis has been paid a very handy £12,150 per annum since 1989. All pensions are index-linked, of course, but you probably expected that.

In the House of Lords in early June these same

'Euro Lords', along with other pro-EU Lords such as Heseltine, Howe, and Gummer, voted down a bill designed to guarantee British voters a referendum on any further loss of sovereignty.

There's only one problem. Under a Brussels 'loyalty clause' anyone receiving an EU pension can lose it if they speak out against the EU. In other words those in receipt of such pensions have a vested interest in voting to defend the EU.

As reported by the Mail on Sunday (19/6/11) this has: "provoked an angry backlash from Conservative loyalists who say the 'usual suspect' Euro fat-cats in the Lords are biased because they receive big pensions from the EU. Unlike other outside income, they can keep the payments secret and do not have to declare them in the Lords' register of interests." You'd have thought there would be a conflict of interest here, but perhaps I'm just being naïve.

August 2011

I'M NOT ALWAYS WRONG

Sometimes I get it rong. I once saw two people standing in the park flying radio-controlled aeroplanes but when I looked up there was nothing there. Strange. Turns out they were doing Tai Chi exercises...

And it took me years to understand why Dr Who's robot dog was called K9, but there you go.

On the EU, sadly, I'm usually right. The plan was to build a country called Europe and if the citizens didn't want it, that was tough. They'd get it anyway. Common currency, flag, anthem (Ode to Joy if you're interested), common legal system, foreign policy, armed forces, police, etc. Much of this has either happened or is underway. Have you noticed that the naval fleet currently patrolling the waters off Somalia is now referred to as the EU Navy?

The whole project was sold to us as a 'Common Market' but like a cyclist going through a car-wash we got more than we bargained for. Who would have thought that the 'Common Market' would have ended up telling us to ban light-bulbs, how to dispose of our rubbish, and how to run our own immigration policy?

August 2011

EN ROUTE TO CASTLE VLAD

The Trago Column goes into thirty or so newspapers throughout the South West, with a readership of possibly 1.25 million. So I'm always grateful when readers send in clippings, cuttings, and letters highlighting the lunacies they have uncovered.

Here's one now. Jane from Totnes sent me a piece from the Forces Pension Newsletter (April edition): "I'm informed that the RAF sends Puma helicopters by road all the way from RAF Benson to Romania for maintenance. Convoys of low-loaders, with RAF markings disguised, stay overnight at USAF Framstein, near Frankfurt. A few weeks later they do the journey in reverse, because flight testing is not allowed in Romania. Meanwhile larger RAF aircraft fly to France for painting because the French do not enforce the EU COSH (control of substances hazardous to health) and thus it is cheaper than using British labour with full COSH coverage."

Or try this one from Mr Clissold in Gloucester: "Eurocrats' pension bill to cost us an extra £170m" ran the headline in the Mail, and Mr Clissold saw crimson, because his own pension is barely enough to feed the cat (and after Chris Huhne sends our energy bills sky-rocketing I suspect that Mr Clissold's cat is in deep trouble).

The Mail article described how the EU has just voted itself a massive pension hike. "The average Brussels official will now enjoy an income of more than £60,000 a year when they retire – more than double the average working wage in the UK."

As Mr Clissold put it in his letter to me: "More bad news from Brussels. Will Cameron do anything about it? Of course the silly useless fool won't."

I'll second that.

August 2011

EATING UP YOUR GREENS

There's a saying: "One tequila, two tequila, three tequila, floor."... And that's where I'm heading now, with the latest news from Brussels. They banned lightbulbs, reduced the power of flat-screen TVs, to stop ice-caps melting on Mars, and are trying to force bikers to wear Day-Glo jackets, but now the EU is shoving its nose into vacuum cleaners.

Some popular vacuum cleaners are 2,000 watts. Other bestsellers are the 1,300-watt Dyson DC33, and the 2,300-watt Miele S5211 (You probably wonder how I know this stuff. Amazes me, too). All these vacuums will be banned under the new proposals, which reduce the motor to 900 watts.

There's another saying: "If you spin an oriental person three times in a circle, do they become disorientated?" No idea, but I certainly felt dizzy when I heard that Brussels had fined Nottingham University £56,000 for not displaying the EU flag on a board outside the college building, because British taxpayers' money had helped refurbish it. UKIP MEP, Derek Clark, said: "This is a disgrace and an awful thing to do to a university. These European officials insist on having flags put up to tell people how wonderful they are. They're nothing of the sort." Thanks for that, Brussels.... But just remind me: when did I give you the power to tell me what size vacuum-cleaner to buy? And tell me again, how do I vote you out? ...

August 2011

THUS SAYETH THE LORD

It's been said that Atheism is a non-Prophet organisation, but I thought you might like to hear a few gems from the Church Bulletins, the local newsletters produced by church ladies with typewriters (Never let it be said that the Trago Column goes in for stereotyping).

"The Fasting & Prayer Conference includes meals" was one. Or: "The sermon this morning: Jesus Walks on the Water. The sermon tonight: Searching for Jesus.". Or this one: "Miss Charlene Mason sang 'I will not pass this way again' giving obvious pleasure to the audience". Or: "Irving Benson and Jessie Carter were married on October 24 in the church. So ends a friendship that began in their school days."

On the subject of ending a friendship, the UK Independence Party seeks an amicable divorce from the EU, before the household bills cripple the entire country. Total annual cost of EU membership is approx £120-billion, which includes all the expense to UK business of having to obey all those rules, directives, and regulations.

Let's return to the Almighty because we're going to need Him whilst David Cameron is in No10, shovelling money at Pakistan and the eurozone... "Low Self Esteem Support Group will meet Thursday at 7pm. Please use the back door."

Or: "Weight Watchers will meet at 7pm at the First Presbyterian Church. Please use large double door at the side entrance." Or my personal favourite: "The Associate Minister unveiled the church's new campaign slogan last Sunday: 'I upped my Pledge – Up Yours'"

September 2011

FOUR'S COMPANY

If you visit Bradford Moor Community School (an area of Bradford rarely described as 'desirable') you'll discover a strange and worrying fact. As described by the Daily Mail in August 2011 there are four hundred pupils in that school, but only four of them speak English as their mother tongue. That's right. Just four. Guardianistas might think this is fine, but then...

Bradford Moor is an extreme case, but the official figures show what is happening across huge (mainly urban) swathes of the country. A quarter of all primary school children are from an ethnic minority, an increase of almost half a million since 1997 when Tony Blair got the keys to No10.

This isn't a question of skin colour. Britain has a long and honourable tradition of giving immigrants a warm welcome, though we'll always have racists. The problem is the numbers (in 2010 net immigration was 220,000, the population of Stoke-on-Trent arriving here in just 12 months, which is insupportable) and also Multiculturalism where we teach people that their culture is as valid as our own. Sorry, but they aren't. This is Britain. Forget about tikka masala and Chinese take-aways; we don't practise female circumcision, stone people for adultery, or truss cats and dogs up in the local farmer's market, alive and ready for the pot. For good or ill, that's not our way.

UKIP's position is simple. If you want to come and settle here (and if you satisfy the other criteria such as leaving your AK47 at home) then you must learn the language and fit in. If not, don't expect the taxpayer to fund your own personal life choice. And if that is unacceptable then you can always take advantage of another great British freedom. The freedom to leave.

September 2011

INSERTING THE PLUG

Here's a quote from Roman philosopher Cicero:

"The budget should be balanced, the Treasury should be refilled, public debt should be reduced, the arrogance of officialdom should be tempered and controlled, and the assistance to foreign lands should be curtailed, lest Rome become bankrupt. People must again learn to work, instead of living on public assistance."

He wrote that in 55 BC, before somebody stuck a large sword into him whilst he was relaxing by his pool... (Cicero was too sensible and kept saying the things no-one wanted to hear, so they eliminated him)

Unfortunately, similar idiots are still in charge and still making the same mistakes. And what a shame, because two thousand years have passed, and still there they are... incapable of running a bath, even if you inserted the plug for them.

October 2011

FAREWELL GRAHAM

On behalf of all at Head Office I would like to pay a brief tribute to former MEP Graham Booth, who died recently.

Graham was a true gentleman, in the proper sense of the word, and a driving force in UKIP.... Everyone who knew him held him in great affection. A kind, just, truthful, loyal man, with a will of steel when required, who will be sadly missed. Our hearts go out to his widow, Pam, and to all Graham's sons, daughters, and ten grandchildren.

Here is one of my pieces from 2003 (which appeared in The View From Here) which gives a brief flavour of him: "It had been a busy day in Parliament, and the media were clustered on Westminster Green.

Chancellor Gordon Brown had just announced the failure of his economic tests for joining the Euro. Among those being interviewed on the Green that day was Graham Booth, MEP for the UK Independence Party.

The interview, on Radio 4's "PM" programme, began with a briskly self-assured question from the lady-interviewer: "And now I'm talking to Graham Booth from the UKIP... Mr Booth, surely you're not suggesting that it's in Britain's national interest to withdraw from the European Union, with all the benefits we get from it?"

Graham replied: "Yes, I am......... Would you mind telling me what the benefits are?" upon which the poor girl did a very good fish impression, mouth working soundlessly, even over the radio; Graham finished her off:

"Exactly. Nobody ever can."

He was a lovely man, and we'll all miss him.

October 2011

WHERE TO FILE THE BRIGHT IDEAS

As you know, (along with many others in UKIP) I trawl the EU news so that you needn't bother. Here's a few snippets possibly of interest: "Million drivers face losing licence under EU diabetes diktat" ran the headline in the Daily Mail (22/08/11).

Diabetes sufferers who have been driving for decades without problems could now be banned from the wheel thanks to new EU proposals. People who occasionally suffer 'hypos' (low blood sugar causing blackouts if not dealt with at once) may lose their licence, even if the hypo happened in bed.

Let's be honest. If someone is constantly suffering blackouts or feeling asleep in the middle of a conversation, it's sensible to stop them driving. Tough perhaps, but preferable to meeting them head-on at the next bend. But there are limits. (By the way, I'm not diabetic, and this isn't 'special pleading').

Let's try another one: Daily Mail again (28/09/11): "Brussels plan to enforce 20mph zones and replace Highway Code with European laws." MEP Dieter-Lebrecht Koch wants to introduce 30km (18.6mph) speed limits in towns throughout the EU. Along with this will be harmonised road traffic rules, road signs, and blood alcohol limits. Oh, and the MoT test will possibly be held every two years.

Thank you Dieter. If you have any more bright ideas, leave them on the table on your way out please.

December 2011

DEFENESTRATION IN ATHENS

As somebody once said: 'I may be schizophrenic but at least I have each other.' The recent news is enough to send anyone over the edge. The Greek Prime Minister, Mr Papandreou says: "I know, we'll give the Greek people a referendum!" and then suddenly isn't the Greek Prime Minister anymore. The Germans and French shove him out the window.

Three days later, Italian Prime Minister Silvio Berlusconi says: "There 'ees nothing to worry about. Everything 'ees bella!" just before his chair tips up, dropping him into a shark tank in the basement. There is brief splashing, then silence.
Both politicians were replaced by EU technocrats, unelected and unaccountable. In effect puppet governments, owing allegiance to the EU, not to their own people. As Nigel Farage MEP said: "It's like an Agatha Christie novel. You wonder who'll get bumped off next."

It's been said that Heaven is where the police are British, the chefs are French, the mechanics are German, the lovers are Italian, and everything is organised by the Swiss. On the other hand, Hell is where the police are German, the chefs are British, the mechanics are French, the lovers are Swiss, and it's all organised by the Italians.

December 2011

2012

CARPET BOMBING

An American F16 fighter was patrolling the skies above Afghanistan when the pilot noticed a flying carpet on each side of his plane, both with a machine-gunner on board. Without hesitation he shot them down, but when he got back to base he was threatened with a court martial. Apparently they were Allied Carpets...

Sorry about that, but I thought you probably needed cheering up. It's been a rough few weeks. Inflation and youth unemployment are UP. Business confidence is DOWN. And the Germans have just taken over mainland Europe. Berlin might protest this to be unfair, but let's be clear. They pushed the euro down the throats of countries that should never have joined, and when the inevitable collapse came along, as predictable as a Number 9 bus, they refused to open the bank vault.

In a sense, you can't blame them. Even the European Central Bank lacks the cash to fund this one. The euro (in its present form) is doomed. Greece, Italy, Spain, and Portugal will probably leave, and then Le Grand Project will be gravely wounded. And that's when the EU will be at its most dangerous, enough to make Allied Carpets seem like a pussycat. Or a cat on the mat.

January 2012

DUNNO

Richard Littlejohn (Daily Mail columnist) pulls no punches. I like that. We're not here long. Better to get to the point. Back in January he did an excellent piece on 'Awkward questions children ask their parents', such as: "Why is the sky blue?" I thought I'd share a few...

"Mum, why do bald men grow ponytails?" Dunno....

"Mum, why is a Tory-led government spending £-billions carving a railway line through an area of outstanding natural beauty, packed with Tory voters?" Dunno...

"Dad, why have we imported millions of foreigners to fill job vacancies when millions of people in Britain are unemployed and living on benefits?" Dunno...

"Dad, why are we letting convicted Lithuanian rapists into Britain?" Dunno, son. Ask your Mother...

"Mum, why can't we deport foreign terrorists who want to kill us?" Dunno...

"Mum, why do we let unelected foreign judges tell us what to do?" Dunno. Ask your Father...

"Dad, Why don't so-called 'travellers' want to travel?" Dunno, son. Ask your Mother...

"Mum, what do we get out of the European Convention on Human Rights?" Dunno. Ask Dad...

"Dad, what do we get out of belonging to the European Union?" Dunno, son.

"Dad, what is the point of the Leveson Inquiry?" No idea, son. Dunno. Not a clue. Ask Mum…

"Mum, how did Ed Miliband ever become Labour Leader?" Dunno. Why don't you ask David Miliband?

January 2011

OLD HAT

In 1987 the rock musician Chris Rea wrote the song Gonna Buy a Hat. You'd like it. Here's one verse: "Look at all those leaders, desperation in their eyes. Despite their smiles they cannot hide it. They know no more than you or I." My next sentence was about to be: How true. But it's so blindingly obvious I needn't bother.

In their mad or misguided dream to achieve European Unity, our politicians led us into a nightmare, where it doesn't matter how you vote (unless it's UKIP) because they've all signed up to Le Project. As a result we've been (forgive the technical term) 'screwed'. Good and proper.

Where to start? Destruction of the fishing and farming industries; VAT (a European tax); the approx £120-billion a year cost to the UK of EU membership; subjugation to the European Court; postal network flogged off (If you still have a local post office you're a lucky bunny); rampant immigration, and of course the £-billions we're still paying to bail out the eurozone, even though we don't belong to it.

And yet Prime Minister Cameron still trots out the mantra that membership of the EU is vital to our national interest. No it isn't. We should leave tomorrow.

Let's hear from Chris Rea again: "So I'm gonna buy a hat, like that Mr Gorbachev. And when it's raining all this crap, well then my hat will keep it off." Dear Chris, when you've finished with that hat, any chance of borrowing it?

February 2012

TAXING AT SAUCE

I suffer from kleptomania. When it gets bad, I take something for it. Just like Brussels. When things go wrong for the EU it just presses on, taking even more, for "ever greater union".

Unless you've been living on Mars, you'll know that the eurozone is collapsing and (among others) Greece and Italy are in financial chaos, with their governments being run by Gauleiters sent down there to kick the locals into shape.

Britain isn't in the eurozone but via the IMF we are borrowing £-billions, and pledging it to prop up the euro, shelling out money that could be spent on Great-Aunt Nellie's hip operation, or to save the local day-centre.

What you possibly don't know is the EU's latest wheeze for robbing us. It's called the Tobin Tax, a tax on all financial transactions. Whenever a bank transfers funds to another bank, it will pay a sum to Brussels. The City of London is a huge financial trading centre, employing thousands, generating vast tax revenues which then pay for nurses, teachers, lollipop ladies, and diversity awareness officers.

If the Tobin Tax is introduced, with an estimated 80% of monies raised coming from here in the UK, the financial institutions in London will "run to the sun", to the Cayman Islands, to Hong Kong, to Singapore...

You might think bankers are clankers and we'd be well rid of them. But you'd be wrong. Even the anti-capitalist campers outside St Paul's need a financial system to process their giro cheques. The Tobin Tax will inconvenience the rich, impoverish the employed, and kick the poor further into the gutter.

February 2012

GRAVY TRAIN OR SAUCE BOAT?

Henry Lawson (no relation to Nigel Lawson) once wrote: "Beer makes you feel the way you ought to feel without beer." And I know where he's coming from. I'm with him. But sometimes a beer comes in handy, and here's why....

Last September, PublicServiceEurope.com reported that EU diplomats are allowed to keep excess pay. I quote: "European Union diplomats who are accidentally paid too much are allowed to keep the money. Recovering all sums owed by Catherine Ashton's External Action Service would be a 'great disincentive' for recruitment and 'contrary to the principle of legal certainty' says the European Commission."

If you or I claim benefits or tax rebates – and are over-paid – we have to pay it back. Maybe we shouldn't (we can argue about that) but that's the system. Rubbing caustic into the wound was that the EU's trade union (Equipe d'Union Syndicale, if you're interested) is now objecting to any staff working more than 40 hours a week.

And don't forget that many of them are already entitled to one third of the year off. Paid. Nice. But if Henry Lawson is pulling the pints I'll go for a Jail Ale or Doom Bar.

February 2012

STRIDES AHEAD

I was sitting in a Greek restaurant when I got hit on the back of the head by a prawn cocktail. I looked around. The man who'd thrown it - and it LOOKED like Mel Stride (Tory MP for Central Devon) - shouted: "That's just for starters!" I think that Mr Stride possibly doesn't like me, because although he calls himself 'fiercely eurosceptic' he always votes for deeper EU integration, and I tell people about it.

If you don't believe me please visit www.peoplespledge.org and type in any postcode for Central Devon. Mr Stride's voting record on EU matters is all there, documented. And if you live in Central Devon (or anywhere else for that matter) you can sign up to the Pledge.

On the subject of Greek holidays I came across a few complaints from disgruntled tourists whining to Thomas Cook, and here we go:
"I think it should be explained in the brochure that the local store does not sell proper biscuits like custard creams or ginger nuts."

Or: "On my holiday to Goa in India I was disgusted to find that almost every restaurant served curry. I don't like spicy food at all."

Or this one: "We booked an excursion to a water park but no-one told us we had to bring swimming costumes or towels."

Or: "I was bitten by a mosquito. No-one said they could bite" (that's the spirit of the empire).

Or my personal favourite: "The brochure states 'NO HAIRDRESSERS AT THE ACCOMMODATION'. We're trainee hairdressers. Will we be OK staying here?"

Perhaps Mr Stride should answer these. On the other hand, he's got enough questions to answer already, so perhaps not.

March 2012

WE HAVE YOUR CHILDREN

UKIP has often accused the EU of brainwashing children into approving the "European Project". Some critics have scoffed at the accusation.

Well, if you have access to the internet, please try this and judge for yourself. Google: "EU brainwash our children" and you'll come to the Daily Express online. And if you click on there (sorry, but you do have to sit through a brief advert) you will see one Judith Schilling, EU Publication Manager. Ms Schilling is at a trade fair, all smiley and corporate smart, peddling her EU children's books to the delegates.

She is asked: "Why is the European Union here at this trade show?"

And she smiles again, and says: "The EU has picked up on the idea that we will never succeed to convince people of the value of European membership if we do not start early enough with the young people before their prejudices are misinformed by other sources."... In other words, "The parents might have seen through us, maybe we'll have better luck with their kids"

I'm not a parent, but if I had children at school I'd be very interested to know exactly what material was being imposed onto their young and impressionable minds, and whether Ms Schilling had persuaded my own local school to give her space on their bookshelf. If you are a parent, do you share that concern? Over to you.

March 2012

YES WE CAN

As the O said to the 8: "What a great belt you're wearing!" It's a good job the 8 wasn't travelling with author David Jones, creator of children's character Fireman Sam, when he was flying out through Gatwick a few weeks ago...

As Mr Jones passed through the security scanner at the airport, he placed his belt, shoes, wallet, and scarf into the tray. As he did so a Muslim woman in hijab passed through beside him without showing her face. Mr Jones quipped: "If I was wearing this scarf over my face, I wonder what would happen."...

After passing through the gates he was confronted by Security, accused of racism, and marched off to an interview room. His two daughters were left waiting in the departure lounge wondering where he'd gone...

Mr Jones explained: "Something like Orwell's 1984 seems to have arrived at Gatwick airport. I said that I had said nothing racist. She took my passport and boarding pass and proceeded to question me, saying that one of the Muslim staff had been offended. I again stated that I hadn't made a racist remark, purely an observation that we were in a maximum security situation being searched thoroughly whilst a woman with her face covered walked through."...

At this point Mr Jones demanded that the police be called. Along came Plod, earnest and politically correct, about as useful as an ashtray on a motorbike. (By the time you read this he's probably been fast-tracked to Chief Constable). This cop told Mr Jones he would only be allowed to continue his journey if he apologised to the Muslim guard...

Eventually, one BA Manager and two hours later, Mr Jones agreed to accept that his remark "could" have been considered offensive by a Muslim guard. And so, with his fingers crossed under the table, and through gritted teeth, Mr Jones apologised on that basis, and caught his flight. It strikes me that the only thing Orwell got wrong was the date.

March 2012

REAL TUNES

If you're partial to classical music, you'll like this one. Or maybe not. Bach, Vivaldi, Purcell. All wonderful composers. As reported by the Daily Mail (28/11/11) "Performers warn it may soon be impossible to play such music as the composers intended it to be heard because of EU rules restricting the manufacture of traditional cow-gut instruments."

Brussels is worried that musicians might catch 'mad cow disease' from the strings of musical instruments, despite the fact that they are bleached, processed, and you'd have to eat several yards of the stuff before being faced with even a remote risk of getting ill.

Quoting the Mail again: "Among those potentially affected is the British-based European Union Baroque Orchestra, who said: "It would be catastrophic if gut string production ceased. We would have to close. Gut strings are essential to our music."

It occurs to me that if the EU was really serious about building a new empire it should be run and administered by people with brains, judgement, and political nous. Instead, it drops more bricks than a hod-carrier with St Vitus' Dance and the sooner we get out of it the better for everyone in Britain (and I include all Scots in that, with the possible exception of Mr Alex Salmond).

March 2012

QUESTIONS QUESTIONS

If a mime artist is arrested, can they remain silent without prejudicing their case? And should 50% of all female impersonators be women? And is there another word for 'synonym'?

These are all good questions, but (like principles) if you don't like them, I have others.

"Why does Mel Stride MP (Con, Central Devon) call himself a eurosceptic when he keeps voting for deeper EU integration?" Or how about this one: "Why was Alphonse Semo (raped a woman then dumped her onto a rubbish tip) freed two hours before he was deported home to the Congo (after serving 8 years for rape) and then allowed to stay in Britain and given permission to marry his girlfriend?" Search me, but possibly because the girlfriend (also from the Congo) became a German citizen, which means we're lumbered with both of them until we can regain control of our own immigration policy and chuck both out.

Or how about this question: "The Met. Office has just announced that there has been no increase in global temperatures since 1997. So why are we worried about Global Warming? And if CO_2 really does increase warming and if we are now heading for a mini Ice Age (which many scientists are now predicting) will there be grants for building CO_2 factories?"

April 2012

ROBIN PETER TO PAY TOBIN

A man walked into a public library and circumspectly approached the desk. He lowered his voice: "Have you any books on Conspiracy Theories?"

The Librarian leaned forward and murmured into his ear: "They're behind you."

I'll offer a conspiracy theory of my own, but it's pretty obvious to anyone in UKIP. Late last year Prime Minister Cameron went to Brussels and said: "If you promise not to hit me [with the Tobin Tax] I'll sign your piece of paper." Angela Merkel and Nicholas Sarkozy looked back at him: "Sorry. Can't do that. We ARE going to hit you. That's the whole plan." And so Mr Cameron came home, pretending that he'd vetoed something.

Eurosceptics not in UKIP rejoiced, tails wagging and wiggling. If they'd been puppies we'd have been following them round the house, laying down sheets of newspaper. "Cameron has proved his eurosceptic credentials!" ran the message. To misquote the rock group The Who, the poor boobies had been "Fooled again".

'm glad that former RBS boss Fred Goodwin has been stripped of his knighthood (personally I'd now go after his £625K annual pension) but I'm not anti banker nor anti the City of London because it makes lots of money for Britain, keeps our pensions industry going, and pays shedloads of tax so that we can employ teachers, nurses, cops, and diversity awareness officers. But the Tobin Tax will crucify all that. And now it seems possible that David Cameron has rolled over, legs waving. In the words of Roger Daltrey, he was: "Just a boy - giving it all away".

More money leaving Britain, to prop up the doomed eurozone, even though we don't belong to it, and all being borrowed because we're broke. Incredible.

April 2012

In fairness to David Cameron (so far at least) the Tobin Tax has not been introduced. I am very happy to have been proved wrong.

MIND THE BALLS

If you're crossing the Champs-Elysées on foot at rush hour you'll need more than a badge from the Tufty Club to keep you out of trouble. But no need for Tufty (nor Willy Weasel for that matter) at Harewood Junior School, in Tuffley, Gloucestershire. In a health and safety crackdown head-teacher Andrea Mills has banned footballs. Yep, that's right. Banned them.

The children can play with sponge balls but not leather or plastic ones. Ms Mills explained: "I have purchased some sponge footballs for each year group so that the children can still play their favourite games and am happy for them to bring in something similar if they wish. There were a number of incidents when someone kicked the ball but ended up hurting someone else"

You can guess the reaction of the parents. One said: "People have been doing it for years and they have never had any fatal accidents because of leather footballs. I think it's quite stupid." Another mother said: "They might as well keep them in strait-jackets."

It strikes me that Ms Mills might qualify for the SW Region's "Silliest Teacher of the Year" award. In fact, I'm considering nominating her. Even worse, Ms Mills is failing her own pupils, because when they emerge blinking into the real world they'll be like lambs to the slaughter, without "teacher" there to protect them. They'd be far better off with Tufty the red squirrel.

April 2012

THE SLOW SOLDIER

An army marches at the speed of its slowest soldier. But when they wait for him and he catches up, everyone sets off marching again so he never gets a proper rest until camp. Prime Minister David Cameron could be described as that slow soldier. He is a committed Europhile and will never take this country out of the EU, but he is playing constant catch-up with France and Germany, who are losing patience with him.

The eurozone is destined to break apart, with everyone in denial, pretending that Greece, Spain and Italy can repay their debts (They can't of course. They're broke; despite all the freebie cash we showered over them).

I read somewhere that if we all threw our problems into a pile and saw everyone else's, we'd grab ours back. It's a good point. We're not in the euro (thanks to Gordon Brown's dislike of Tony Blair) and that gives us a fighting chance. But rather than constantly dragging along at the rear of the column, never getting a proper rest, yet still exposed to enemy gunfire, how much simpler if we just lagged back a bit, waited for the EU Army to disappear around the next bend, then dodged into the nearest hedgerow and made our own way back at our own pace.

May 2012

MARKED DOWN?

Like Oscar Wilde, I'm not young enough to think I know everything. But I thought you'd like these exam answers from a Catholic school bible-test... "The Egyptians were all drowned in the dessert. Afterwards, Moses went up to Mount Cyanide to get the Ten Commandments.". Or this one: "Lots wife was a pillar of salt during the day but a ball of fire during the night." Or: "Jesus was born because Mary had an immaculate contraption." Lucky Mary.

Or: "Christians have only one spouse. This is called monotony." Or: "The Jews were a proud people and throughout history had trouble with unsympathetic genitals". Or try this one: "One of the opossums was St Matthew who was also a taximan."

And I'll finish with my favourite: "St Paul cavorted to Christianity. He preached Holy acrimony, which is another name for marriage."

May 2012

999

In September 1988 Prime Minister Margaret Thatcher famously went to Bruges (in Belgium) and made a speech to the European Community. Basically she told them: "No, NO, NO!" meaning that she didn't want Britain to be absorbed by a European empire.

Two years later her own colleagues knifed her in a palace coup. Then John Major came along and signed the Maastricht Treaty (the Labour Party sat on its hands, allowing it through, proving they were unfit to govern either) and the rest is history.

We now have an election in France where Francois Hollande has just won an election, is now the Socialist French President, and wants to "re-negotiate" a deal on eurozone austerity measures. Bored? Stick with me. It gets interesting....

German Chancellor Angela Merkel has now just stated that the "deal" cannot be renegotiated. The French are stuck with it. "Don't like it, Francois? Tough. Sarkozy should have won".

Think about this. The French people have just had an election, voted for M'sieu Hollande, and he has a legitimate democratic mandate (He might prove to be a disaster but that's none of our business). Yet the Germans are now telling France that elections don't matter: "Sarkozy signed a deal. Forget your new government. It doesn't matter."

In effect, Fraulein Merkel is telling the French people: "NEIN, NEIN, NEIN!"

Translated into English, this means 999, and is yet another emergency.

July 2012

PINING FOR THE FJORDS

A lady I know in St Austell took her pet duck to the local vet. He examined it, looked at her, and shook his head. "I'm very sorry but your duck is dead."

The lady was very upset. "Are you sure? He might just be in a coma. Can I have a second opinion?"

The Vet sighed. "Very well." And then went next door, returning with a Labrador dog, which sniffed at the duck, then looked up with big sad eyes and shook its head. Then the Vet brought in a ginger cat and placed it on the table. The cat sniffed the duck, then meowed mournfully and jumped off the table.

"As I told you, I'm afraid your duck really has passed away." Then he went onto the computer, punched out a few keys and produced a bill of £89. My friend was astonished: "How much? £89 just to tell me that my duck is dead? How do you justify that?"

The Vet pushed his glasses further up his nose. "I'm very sorry but if you'd just taken my word for it. With the Lab Report and the Cat Scan"...

Which is all a very long-winded way of saying that if only the political establishment had listened to UKIP many years ago then it would have saved us hundreds of £-billions, and we wouldn't now be in the situation where Brussels is about to force the UK to extend social security payments to Turkish citizens. The only escape is for us to leave the EU, and nothing else will work, because they will never give up asset-stripping our country until we are deader than a St Austell duck. Deader, indeed, than a Norwegian blue.

July 2012

BEAUTIFUL GAME?

A football joke I don't understand: "How do you get the cork back into a champagne bottle?"..."I don't know, but ask a Man U fan." (I think Man U were about to win the League recently or something, but lost at the last minute)...

Personally, the only time I'm interested in football is when it's a quickie (World Cup etc). But when England gets knocked out, I reach for the remote control.

Tonight it's Friday 22nd June, and Germany and Greece have just filed out onto the pitch, with the crowd roaring and Germany the runaway favourites to win this semi-finals of the Euro Cup. But this is not just a football match. This one is different. With the collapse of the Greek economy, there's a political element. The Germans have lent Greece billions and the Greeks are broke, and both are to blame.

And suddenly there she is, the cameras dwelling on her. Petrol onto a fire. German Chancellor Angela Merkel, supporting the German team. Sitting there in the VIP box, applauding every German goal. This is bad politics. Stupid politics. And done deliberately. Even ITV's commentator John Motson wondered how it would look to Greek viewers.

Why did she do it? Why turn up? Bad advisors? Nope. She knew exactly what she was doing. She was rubbing Greek noses in it. Please remember, this wasn't the final, where one might expect a leader to attend a match. Without her presence it would have been just a game of football. She changed that. She ruined that, and did more. On behalf of Germany and the EU she was making a political statement: "We're in charge; even in football."

How did Merkel think it would play in Greece? I think she'll find out. Politics lasts for more than 90 minutes. But if you're interested the Germans won 4-2.

July 2012

HEAVY HORSES

Jane Beeson's wonderful poem 'The Grey Carthorses' captures the arrival of tractors on her mother's farm during the last war: " 'He's scared' my mother said, 'scared of the horses. He admitted to me he couldn't work them'

My father picked a tooth: 'We could get a tractor'... 'A tractor?' My mother, wedded to horses, expressed her shock. 'A tractor will never work those fields – they're much too steep.'"

But a month later there it was, standing in the yard, a brand-new Fordson, ready for action. The new age of farming had arrived, a 'modern' approach. Across Britain hedgerows were ripped out, enlarging the fields, and chemical fertilisers and insecticides became the 'conventional' way of farming.

And a few years later along came the Common Agricultural Policy, jangling its purse of gold. Who can really blame those who took up that offer? But since then agriculture has gone into steep decline, with the average age of a farmer now 62 years, and some 70% of small family farms sold off for development.

If we want a future for British agriculture then we need to actively help and encourage youngsters back into the industry, and frankly right now very little is being done.

The last few lines of 'Carthorses': "'When are the greys going? my father asked.

'Next week. To Dulverton.' My mother's voice was tragic. 'It's the end for horses' she prophesied. And so it was.'"

GOOD MONEY AFTER BAD

I was late for work the other day. Overslept. I was having this marvellous dream where I worked for a boss who couldn't tell the time. Another dream I had recently was that Britain would slash its overseas aid budget. Then I woke up. That one wasn't true either.

At the moment we are giving £billions in aid to countries across the globe, much of it wasted. India has just become the world's largest importer of arms, yet we'll be giving them 1.6billion until 2015. We also give money to China and Pakistan, yet all three are nuclear nations, with two of them running their own Space programme.

A UKIP government would take an axe to this, slash the aid budget, and ensure that any aid we do provide will go directly to those who need it, not into some dictator's Swiss bank account nor to fund his own personal war with one of his neighbours.

We will also link aid with trade and not be embarrassed by it. If a country needs 4x4s then we will provide Landrovers built here in Britain, not give them cash to buy Toyota Landcruisers built in South Korea (nothing against South Koreans. Lovely people. Some of my best friends are South Koreans, but this is business).

At a time when the Army is being reduced to little more than a joke, it seems incredible that unlike other Whitehall departments, the Department for International Development has recently had its budget increased by 37% to more than £12billion a year. You work it out. I can't.

August 2012

FEEDING THE FLAMES

I've a feeling that most readers of this Column are a sceptical bunch already. But if you're not, I'd like to touch on events in Syria. Nobody pretends President Assad's regime is a pleasant one. It's not. But the media (and the British government) clearly believe that it should be toppled, despite the risks.

May I urge caution. This is an Arab civil war between States, and (as in Libya) we have no business interfering. It's as if we've seen a fire and chucked petrol onto it. "There! That helped!"

The Israelis do not want Assad to go, because they fear the alternative, and millions of Syrians also back Assad because (along with the Russians) they are terrified either that Islamists will seize power or the whole country will collapse into all-out civil war. It is probable that some of Assad's militias are committing atrocities and he needs to rein them in. It's no excuse, of course, but the other side are also committing massacres. If they get hold of tanks then the whole country will explode.

There is something else. Significantly, the terrorist group al Qaeda recently issued a fatwa against President Assad, encouraging the Faithful to kill him. If the West topples the President we will be doing the work of the really evil people who want us dead.

There is another theory, which might even be true. Here it is: What is really going on is the creation of a new "Union" (like the EU and the African Union, etc) and this one stretches from Morocco in the west, along the North African coast, through Libya, Egypt, Israel, up as far as Syria, then across to Iraq. But with all those independent Arab leaders in the way the project was stalled, so they had to go. Gaddafi, Mubarak, Saddam, Assad. I wonder who'll be next?

September 2012

A PRESENT FROM BIGGLESWORTH

The other day my cat brought in a mouse, dropping it at my feet. I looked at him and said: "How thoughtful. Just what I wanted. A dead mouse. Thank you, Biggles". I felt a bit like that the next day when someone emailed me, asking me to sign a petition abolishing the BBC licence fee.

The BBC does lots wrong, and needs a good shake-up. And I'll volunteer for the job. But the last thing I want is for adverts to start appearing on the Service. And without the licence fee, they'd need income from somewhere. The thought of Radio Three or Four constantly interrupted by commercial breaks is not a pleasant one, and I'm sure that fans of Radio One and Two feel the same. As for the TV channels, most of them are bad enough already, without adverts.

The best way to curb the BBC is to control the purse strings. As a publicly funded broadcaster they need to remember that we pay the bills, and they must start obeying their own Charter. They could do worse than go back to the principles of Lord Reith: "Inform. Educate. Entertain," And as long as they do it in an open, unbiased, non-partisan way, that's enough for me. To put it bluntly, right now it's stuffed with lefties pushing their own agenda down our throats, and anyone who strays from the internal party line is ridiculed, condemned, or ignored.

There is plenty wrong with the BBC, and there are some brave campaigners like UKIP's John Kelly, who for years have withheld payment of the licence fee until the BBC obeys its Royal Charter in reporting matters of political importance such as the EU. But in my view if we abolish the fee and send the Beeb down the commercial route, the cure will probably be worse than the illness.

I consulted Biggles and his brother Scraggy on this. Both were in agreement.

September 2012

POUNDLAND

As the Telegraph cartoonist 'Matt' put it a few weeks ago: "I was on my way to panic-buy stamps when I ran out of petrol". This was during the recent fuel-strike and a hike in the price of postage. It just goes to show how ones efforts can be frustrated by events. Take Cait Reilly (22). She took a degree in Geology at Birmingham University in 2010, and is currently unemployed because she can't find a job. Nothing unusual there, but Ms Reilly was informed by her local Jobcentre that she had to join the government's 'back-to-work' scheme or lose all her benefits.

Ms Reilly, at the time a volunteer at her local museum, was sent to work at the high-street shop Poundland, stacking shelves and sweeping floors. This went down badly, and she is now taking the government to court, claiming that this treatment breached Article 4 of the European Convention on Human Rights, prohibiting slavery and forced labour.

I really can sympathise with a graduate who leaves university, hoping to begin a career in their chosen field, then finds themselves sweeping floors, unpaid. It must be frustrating and disappointing. But equating that with slavery is ridiculous. We all have to do things we'd rather not. As Bill Gates once said: "Your parents did not call 'flipping burgers' demeaning. They had another word for it. Opportunity.".

September 2012

NOT SUCH A BIG ISSUE?

Firuta Vasile (27) is a Big Issue seller in Bristol. She came here from Romania in 2007 (thanks to our EU membership which allowed her to take up residence, despite the fact that she didn't have a job). She WAS claiming £25,547.60 in tax credits, child benefit, and carers' allowance, but that's all about to change.

A court has now ruled that Miss Vasile is also entitled to Housing Benefit (at a minimum of £2,600 a year). No wonder she's smiling like a basket of chips in those newspaper photos. She's done very nicely out of the EU's expansion into the east. This was the one where Tony Blair predicted that 13,000 or so migrants would come here annually. In the very first year 130,000 pitched up here.

This isn't just about Miss Vasile, who has done nothing wrong and has acted within the law. This is really about two other things. A case like this becomes a "landmark", meaning that it opens the door for many more. It's also about a country having control over its borders, and exercising that control.

In times of plenty, it is silly to throw open the doors to thousands of migrants (They could be issued with temporary work-permits). But in days of austerity and cut-backs this is sheer lunacy. The problem is, whilst we're in the EU unfortunately we're stuck with it.

October 2012

TURTLES TURTLES

The philosopher Bertrand Russell was on a lecture tour of the USA, addressing an audience in Chicago. He explained that the universe began with a 'big bang' and that all matter was now rushing outwards in all directions at incredible speed.

When it came to questions afterwards, an old lady rose to her feet: "Young man. What you have told us is very interesting. But do you not realise that the Earth is supported at each corner by a gigantic turtle?"

The great man stood up and hitched his thumbs into his waistcoat pockets. He levelled his gaze: "And what, Madam, are the turtles standing on?" She replied: "You are very clever, young man. Very clever indeed. But it's turtles all the way down!"

I'm no philosopher but I know how Bertrand Russell must have felt. I feel the same way whenever David Cameron spouts his mantra that Britain must stay in the EU because "millions of jobs depend on it". We've seen the failure of the euro, and the economic consequences to those who never even joined it, and with the emergence of China, India and Brazil we need to be seeing the big picture, not handcuffing ourselves to an economic bloc whose share of world

GDP is forecast to fall to 15% in 2020, down from 36% in 1980.

Time to bale out. Right now. If not... turtles all the way down.

October 2012

QUERYING THE BILL

"But apart from that, Mrs Lincoln, how did you enjoy the play?" is one of the world's silliest questions. Others are less so. How about this one? When did Peking suddenly become 'Beijing'... and Bombay go to 'Mumbai'? I pose the question: does this mean that Exeter should revert to 'Isca'? and London to 'Londinium'? And if not, why not?

Or try this one: When did "global warming" suddenly become "climate change"? Perhaps after two successive freezing winters with hundreds of motorists stranded overnight in snowdrifts on Haldon Hill near Isca (sorry, near Exeter)?.

"Climate change" is nice and vague. Rain or shine, we can blame awful weather on human activity, completely ignoring that big yellow thing up in the sky, without which all life on the planet would be utterly extinguished within a few (rather dark) weeks.

Here's another question: "Did you know that each family in Britain is now paying approximately £86 a year on their fuel bills in a secret 'hidden' green tax?" This to subsidise a shift to wind power and other renewables. The government's Climate Change Committee (encouraged by then-minister Chris Huhne) was behind the announcement that

£150billion should be spent, cutting Britain's carbon emissions by 80% in 2050.

Professor Ian Fells of Newcastle University was scathing: "Households already pay an average of £80 a year to subsidise wind farms. There is also going to be a surcharge on household bills to fund research into carbon capture and storage for coal-fired power stations. Bills are just going to go up and up in a startling way".

Yes, you're probably right. That's enough questions for now.

September 2012

HAPPY BUT QUITE MAD

They're coming to take me away, hah, hah. Off to the old Jim-Jam hotel where the cutlery's made of rubber and there's no wine list...

This follows the recent Lib Dem conference where Nick 'Sorree' Clegg revealed that he wants to attack "tax avoidance" and anyone with assets of more than £1-million. Firstly, tax avoidance is legal. More legal than slipping your local plumber £50 cash for mending a cronky shower. And with house prices as they are, plenty of people have assets of £1-million, and some of them are the ones we need to open new businesses and employ workers...

My problem (in Mr Clegg's eyes) is that I'm a bigot. I'm a bigot because I happen to think that marriage is between man and woman. Gays have got civil partnerships and that's fine. But Messers Clegg, Cameron, and Miliband all think that Prime Ministers have the right to "re-define" words from the dictionary. I happen to think that they are wrong, therefore I'm a bigot.

I'm also a bigot, to quote "Ipcress" in the Telegraph: "because I think that the Lib Dems should know their place and stop attempting to shove socially destructive and subversive liberatti agendas onto the unwilling majority"…

I'm also a bigot because I don't believe Nick Clegg when he says: "If you don't give me your money to save the planet, you're a bad person." My reply is: "Go away. You cannot save the planet because you cannot control the climate, and you're not having my money without a fight because you plan to bankrupt the country with Green taxes and cover it with useless wind-farms and thousands of ugly pylons, none of which are needed".

And that is why I'm a bigot, and why I'm now sitting here in the "rubber room". Please ignore the fact that this is written in yellow crayon, but we're not allowed sharp objects in here.

September 2012

GOOD TIMES IN CHURCH

I was playing chess with a friend last week when he looked at me and said: "Shall we make this more exciting?" So we stopped playing…

He resorted to his Daily Express, where it was revealed that the European Union had just listed the Olympic medal table, placing itself at the very top (ahead of the USA, China, Russia, South Korea etc.) Quote from an EU spokesman: "We count and compare how many medals the EU would win if it took part in the Olympic Games as one team. The European Union is the winning team." Pass me that bucket, will you. Suddenly I feel unwell.

Eschewing the Daily Express, I returned to my collection of Church Bulletins, newsletters put out around the country by local Church groups. Here's some now: "At the evening service tonight, the sermon topic will be 'What is Hell?' Come early and listen to the choir practice."

Or: "Scouts are saving aluminium cans, bottles, and other items to be recycled. Proceeds will be used to cripple children."

Or: "Please place your donation in the envelope along with the deceased person you want remembered."

Or this one? "This evening at 7pm there will be hymn singing in the park across from the Church. Bring a blanket and come prepared to sin." Things have certainly changed in the C of E since my days...

As usual, I'll finish with my favourite: "Potluck supper Sunday at 5pm. Prayer and medication to follow." Excellent stuff. Please keep them coming, ladies...

September 2012

BEHIND BARS

A friend started at Paignton Zoo last Monday. Not a success. He was bitten by a tropical fish and attacked by a pair of chimps, so he battered them to death with a spade and threw them into the Lion's enclosure, reasoning that big cats eat anything.

Later he was collecting honey from the Brazilian Bees when they gave him a nasty stinging. Again, out came the spade, and he flattened the hive into a pulp, tossing it in with the lions.

That afternoon a new lion arrived at the zoo and my friend overheard the conversation. New Lion: "What's the food like here?" Old Lion: "It's brilliant with this new keeper. Today we had fish and chimps with mushy bees." Boom boom, Mr Derek...

Apologies for that. The Lib Dem conference is to blame. I've now retreated into levity because Mr Clegg's reality is too awful to contemplate. Wind farms. Endless pylons. Green taxes. Climate change. Taxing anyone who has put a bit of money aside. Dreadful stuff...

On a similar topic, I recently heard a conundrum on the QI programme with Stephen Fry. "Whom do you most admire?" was the question. Came the answer: "Nick Clegg. How does he manage to look at himself every morning when he's shaving, and not put a gun in his mouth?"

Sorry, Nick. But I do have a constructive suggestion. There's a vacancy coming up for an EU Commissioner. Based in Brussels. And you'd be perfect. They just LOVE wind farms out there. You'll go down a storm. At least consider it. There's nothing for you here now. Though you could always try Paignton Zoo. I've just heard one of their keepers has left.

October 2012

JUMPING THROUGH THE EYE OF THE NEEDLE

If you'd like examples of how the EU governs Britain, here's some now. Following the Arab Spring (probably an 'Autumn', but we'll leave that for now) the UK government seized £100-million of assets belonging to the regime of President Hosni Mubarak:

property, cash, paintings, cars, share certificates etc. The new Egyptian government now needs the money because tourism has dried up. But EU rules prevent us returning the assets to Cairo without making them jump through hoops that could take many years to complete.

Another example: UK prisoners will soon be given the vote in general elections, despite the Prime Minister saying this made him feel "physically sick". This comes from the European Court of Human Rights, which has now been absorbed by Brussels. Under the Lisbon Treaty all ECHR rulings are legally binding. So prisoners will get the vote. If not, they can sue our government (with Legal Aid) and receive compensation.

Final example: thanks to the EU's new "Gender Directive" men will now get lower pension payouts when they retire. Here's why. Insurance companies will be banned from taking into account a person's sex. Man or woman, Brussels says we're all the same (with the possible exception of Julian Clary). Men currently get a pension annuity rate about 8% higher than women, because men die earlier and are less expensive for the insurance companies. But that's about to change. Men's annuity rates will fall to perhaps as low as 2% whilst women's will rise by roughly the same amount. Thanks Brussels. Nice one...

You'll notice that wherever the EU sticks its nose things get worse. Yet again, the ordinary citizen has been stuffed, mounted, and displayed on the mantelpiece in a glass case, bearing the legend: "LESSER-SPOTTED SUCKER".

November 2012

ODE TO A PM

Prime Minister David Cameron was on an official visit to a hospital in Edinburgh. He was greeted by a Dr George at the main entrance, shook hands, smiled for the camera, then began a tour of the building. Shortly into the visit they entered a ward full of men sitting up in bed. David Cameron smiled at the nearest one: "Good morning. And how are you feeling?" The patient replied: "Fair fa your honest sonsie face, Great chieftain o' the puddin race." Mr Cameron smiled, glanced at George, and moved on to the next bed, where the patient stared through him, muttering: "Some hae meat an canna eat, And some wad eat that want it."

By now Mr Cameron was totally confused. He smiled nervously and moved on to a third patient, who sneered back at him: ""Wee sleekit, cowerin, timorous beasty, O the panic in thy breasty."

At this point Mr Cameron reached breaking point: "Dr George, is this a mental ward or what?"

Dr George replied (Wait for it) "No Prime Minister. This is the Serious Burns Unit"...

Boom, boom. Sorry about that. Again, I'm retreating into levity because reality is too strange. Denis MacShane MP, former Europe Minister, and the man who wrongly once accused Nigel Farage of pocketing £2million from the EU, has now been unmasked as a thief, writing cheques to himself from 'front' organizations headed by himself. He has now resigned as an MP and his career is finished.

It seems very likely that "Denis" will soon be languishing behind bars, which cheers me up no end. I will now have a Very Happy New Year, all through to Burns Night, and on that note I raise my glass to you all!

December 2012

One year later Denis Macshane (after a year of wriggling and absurd but inventive legal arguments) was indeed sent to prison for false accounting. He served six months behind bars.

2013

GIMMEE, GIMMEE, GIMMEE

I once knew a plasterer in Redruth who worked long hours, learning his trade, building up his business, buying a house, getting married. After a few years he felt able to buy his dream car, a BMW soft-top in metallic silver. Two weeks later he awoke to find that some kind soul had written the words "Nice car, mate" on the bonnet with a screwdriver.

This might seem mundane but, to me at least, it highlights a problem. Too many people are driven by envy and resentment at what others possess yet can't be bothered to work for it themselves. The world owes them a living. They 'wouldn't get out of bed' for less than £15 per hour. To me, if that's how they feel, their benefits should be scrapped.

I feel the same about beggars in Britain (not Big Issue sellers, I should add, nor buskers). But I do not understand the notion that I should hand over some of my money to a beggar without them providing some "good or service" in return, preferably something I want..

I'm in good company. The comedian Jethro recalls a girl once shimmying up to him, saying: "I'll do anything you like for fifty quid." To which he replied: "Will you go round and paint my house?" I suspect the house remained unpainted, though the plastering was probably brilliant.

January 2013

AN EVIDENCE-BASED APPROACH

In December 2011 the European Union banned bottled water companies from claiming that imbibing some water can prevent dehydration. They have now followed it up with a judgement on prunes. Yes, that's right. Prunes. The European Food Safety Authority has ruled that there is "insufficient evidence of a link between dried prunes and bowel function."

'Sir' Graham Watson MEP (not my favourite 'Sir', I'm afraid) then challenged the EU Commissioner to a prune-eating contest to settle the matter: "I have asked the Commission if it is satisfied with the criteria and methodology used for testing such claims because I know that prunes contain sorbitol and dihydrophenylisatin, which have laxative effects. But most of our constituents do not require a scientific test".

I rarely agree with Mr Watson but this time I heartily do. For such an ardent Europhile he must have been shaking his head in despair.

January 2013

WHAT'S GOING ON 'ERE THEN?

Johnathan Field was at a nightclub in Newton Abbot when he drunkenly assaulted another man, biting off part of his ear. Horrified witnesses saw Field with the segment gripped between his teeth before he dropped it and fled the scene. The entirely innocent victim, another local man, is now permanently disfigured.

Field was soon arrested, and charged with grievous bodily harm. And now Exeter Crown Court has just sentenced him to 12 months in jail. I'd call that lenient. The message to Field is that an ear is worth a year, and with good behaviour, out in six months, it's 'alf a year.

If we're cracking down on anti-social behaviour then surely biting off the bigger portion of somebody's ear deserves more than the sort of punishment you might get for not paying your TV Licence. I hate to sound like the Daily Mail but we need to get a few basics right. Here's my list...

The cops should be freed to catch criminals not get involved with social engineering projects from the government. I'm all for 'mentoring schemes' for prisoners who need help with rejoining society, but the victims must feel that they'll get support and be respected by the system, not treated as an inconvenient nuisance. As for the criminals, they must know that if convicted they will be clobbered hard. And if they re-offend, then clobbered even harder. If that means building more prisons, then great news for the UK construction industry, and it might even provide some jobs for ex-cons who have gone straight.

And if a few Guardianista readers are now groaning over their cappuccinos, please remember... a conservative is just a liberal who got mugged.

January 2013

NOT GETTING OUT ENOUGH

I was enjoying an old Chris Rea album this Christmas, a track called Love Turns to Lies, when it struck me that it could easily be dedicated to everyone who'd voted for David Cameron in the last general election, in the hope that he'd do what was needed once inside Number 10.

The song begins: "I could have stood to watch you walk away, and put it down to your uncertain ways" and goes on: "You could have pushed, I would have gently fell. I could have played the graceful one so well."... But it didn't happen like that, did it? Having finally ousted New Labour, we were left with a Prime Minister who really wasn't very much at all. Certainly not the person who had been on offer.

The song continues: "What's that you say? You were gonna leave me anyway?"... And I think that's what really happened. Cameron was always going to shift his ground, moving into the almost empty air, a straw man, blown and buffeted by the wind as he tiptoed out onto that highest wire, 'the truth to tell upon a rope too thin', leaving behind those who had supported him.

Perhaps the real problem is that Cameron, Clegg, and Miliband are essentially the same, leaving us down there in the audience below, 'munching, in our seats', knowing that he will inevitably fall, an 'ordinary man on ordinary ground'. Interesting times, especially for Chris Rea fans who possibly read too much into old songs and need to get out more.

February 2013

MORE THINGS IN HEAVEN AND EARTH, HORATIO

I heard an odd theory last week that Jesus was probably a woman, because He fed a crowd at a moment's notice when there was virtually no food; He kept trying to get a message across to a bunch of blokes who just couldn't get it, and even when He was dead still had to get up because there was work to do.

Even odder is the approach of Richard Dawkins, author of the bestselling The God Delusion, who takes a rather childish delight in pouring scorn and contempt onto Christianity. Personally I'm not a church-goer but see no sense in ridiculing personal beliefs and trashing a system that forms part of our national culture. Even the atheists are Christian, in that the God they don't believe in is the one from the Bible.

I can't put it better than physicist Peter Higgs (he of the 'Higgs Boson' particle): "What Dawkins does too often is concentrate his attack on fundamentalists. But there are many believers who are not fundamentalists. I mean, Dawkins in a way is almost a fundamentalist himself, of another kind."

February 2013

A PASSING ENTERTAINMENT

I haven't had so much fun since I rolled a pair of archbishops down One-Tree Hill, complete with vestments and staffs of office. How we laughed. Actually, none of that is true at all. It was only one bishop.

I was reading the Guardian back in November when I came across a double-page spread of how much we gave in Overseas Aid in 2011-2012, and it was eye-watering stuff...

In £-millions, we gave Somalia £102, Pakistan £216, India £268, Bangladesh £203, and the Congo £143. I won't bore you with the others. Yes I will, or at least a few of them: Rwanda got £75 (now ceased because they've been using our money to fund a war in the Congo), Mozambique got £87, and the Occupied Palestinian Territories (one of the most corrupt areas on the planet) were given £91.

We spent £8.55-billion that year, and by 2014 this will increase to £12.66-billion. At a time of austerity when we're closing Day Centres, locking up public conveniences, and sacking lollypop ladies this is madness. If we want to increase Britain's "soft power" around the world there are better, cheaper ways. We could revamp the BBC World Service and stop getting involved in foreign wars that are (a) unwinnable, (b) none of our damned business, and (c) counterproductive, as in Syria and probably Libya.

The biggest threat to the West is militant Islam, bearing in mind that the so-called Arab Spring could lead anywhere. In my view we need to concentrate on that, and on sorting out the Arab-Israeli problem – all of which will keep us busy for the next twenty years. No time to spare for rolling more archbishops down hills, I'm afraid. Much to my regret.

February 2013

SHADOWS THAT SOON PASS

I'm usually a cheerful man but do find a few odd things depressing. Walking into a church and seeing a drum-kit always does the trick, with an urge to hurl it out the door, along with the inevitable guitar and tambourines.

Another trial for me is whenever Ed Miliband opens his mouth to speak. In our household, there's always a scramble for the TV 'remote'. "Well where is it? You must be sitting on it.".

But recently my biggest bugbear has been abu Qatada, Islamic hate-preacher and former pal of bin Laden. The British government wants to pack him off to Jordan on terrorism charges, but the European Court of Human Rights – now effectively taken over by the EU – has put the kybosh on that. The recent UK Court judgment, allowing Qatada back onto the streets, quotes Article 6 of the European Convention on Human Rights, which comes straight from Strasbourg.

March 2013

A REAL EYE-OPENER

Retired bishop Desmond Tutu once said: "When the white missionaries came to Africa they had the Bible and we had the land. They said 'Let us pray'. We closed our eyes. When we opened them we had the Bible and they had the land."

Very true. A bit like 1973 in Britain when they said: "We're joining the Common Market. It'll be great for business", and when we opened our eyes they were telling us that English wine is really a 'fruit-based alcoholic beverage', and that we cannot claim that imbibing bottled water eases dehydration, nor that prunes are a laxative.

Add to that the £-billions spent on propping up the euro, the Human Rights industry from the ECHR, and the estimated £120-billion it costs Britain to belong to the EU every year, and it all gets rather silly and pointless... And that's without the possibly millions of Bulgarians and Rumanians who could be pitching up here in January 2014 because we have surrendered control of immigration to the EU.

I wonder what Bishop Tutu would have made of that...

March 2013

FEELING A LITTLE HORSE

I went to the doctor the other day and he advised me to watch what I eat, so I went home and switched on Channel 4 Racing... But I have another problem: I've been saddled with hundreds of boxes of Findus Lasagne, and after checking in the fridge, "They're Off!"

Looking more closely I see that they're fairly low in fat but surprisingly high in Shergar, which worries me because I have shares in Findus, who scored highly in a recent Gallop Poll, despite the fact that sales are expected to go down. But hopefully not furlong, after which they should stable-ise.

On a more serious note, the recent Horsemeat scandal perfectly shows the importance of buying fresh, local, British food. If a Cottage Pie is produced in stages, with meat from Bulgaria, gravy from the Republic of Ireland, spuds from Luxembourg, and tomatoes from Spain, it is almost inevitable that corners will be cut and we'll end up eating something dodgy. It's a lot simpler and healthier to buy from the local butcher and greengrocer, and probably cheaper too. Or at least it should be, because if local town centres want to survive they'll have to tell their Traffic Wardens to back off.

To put the cap on it, I've just heard that my nearest budget supermarket has introduced a new range of children's food, "My Lidl Pony". but as they're refusing to name their mane supplier this rumour must be treated as a tall tail, if not a shaggy dog story.

Sorry. Couldn't resist it.

March 2013

MEN AT WORK

I avoid clichés like the plague, though somebody once described them as a quick way of getting complicated ideas into uncomplicated heads. At the risk of giving offence, and without the use of clichés, here are a few quotes from past leaders of the European Union so that you can see what they've been up to, rather than me wibbling on about them really building a new European 'country'.

"The Constitution is the capstone of a European Federal State." (Guy Verhofstadt, Prime Minister of Belgium, 2007).

Or this, from Konrad Adenaur: "My dream is that one day we might be able to applaud a United States of Europe" (quoted by the Europe Peoples' Party, the largest grouping in the EU Parliament, in a brochure '50 Years of European Integration', March 2007).

Or this one: "It is essential for the EU to become a political power and not just a group of nation states" (Pierre Muscovici, French Minister for European Affairs, 2001).

Why I'm raking over these old quotes is because today's politicians in Britain are again pulling the wool over people's eyes. (Damn, another cliché). Messrs Cameron, Clegg, and Miliband all waffle on about 'reforming the EU' but it has 27 members, all in different situations, all with different agendas, and therefore is not 'reformable'. And if Mr Cameron etc think that they can reform that little lot, they're barking up the wrong tree. And I am unanimous on that. [That's enough clichés. We'll end there. Ed]

April 2013

THE PERILS OF POT NOODLES

I've just burnt my lip eating a pot noodle. I'm not after sympathy. Those of us who eat pot noodle deserve all we get. But it shows how a simple task can suddenly go wrong.

Here's another example. Prime Minister David Cameron recently promised an In/Out Referendum on our membership of the EU, which at first glance seemed good news but wasn't. There are so many "ifs" that the thing becomes a meaningless con trick. "If" Cameron wins the 2015 general election with a working majority, he will try to negotiate a "new deal" with the EU and then put it to the people in 2017. But he's already said he wants to stay in the EU, so if they (effectively) tell him to get stuffed, will he still hold a referendum and yet tell us to vote Yes to staying in?

Here's another "if". "If" he finds himself horse-trading in another coalition then all bets are off. And then of course there's the Labour Party, currently leading the polls because thousands of disgruntled Lib Dem voters have changed sides.

Meanwhile, back in Brussels, they were queuing up to explain to Cameron that the EU is not Woolworths and he can't Pick 'n Mix what he likes, otherwise they'd all be at it, and you can see their point. I am reminded of a song released by The Who in 1973. It was called "Won't Get Fooled Again." And we won't.

Now then, where did I put that pot noodle?

April 2013

FOR WHOM THE TOLLS BELL

Lorry drivers have hated the tachometer for years, the so-called "spy in the cab" which records how many hours they've driven, how many rest periods have been taken. Given that most road accidents are caused by driver error, and that falling asleep at the wheel of a 30-tonner is unwise, I've always felt that tachometers are a necessary evil. (I might feel differently if I was a trucker, but I'm not, so there you are)...

But within a few years things are going to get a whole lot worse. The EU is going to introduce "Road Pricing", a pan-European road toll payment system, which will make the tachometer seem like a friendly old aunt, giving a bit of gentle nagging from the back seat, and this will apply to all drivers, not just those with a Yorkie bar tucked into their breast pocket...

The technical term is European Electronic Toll Service (EETS) and it's been dreamt up by Brussels to take money from its citizens and (happy spin-off) enable it to track your vehicle at any given time, by an on-board unit....

So the next time some politician drones on about road tolls being a "good thing" just remember they're spouting the EU line, and when they deny it (they will) then you'll really know they are telling porkies, because any politician commenting on road tolls would certainly KNOW that it comes from the EU. Just say "EETS" to them and they'll go away. If only...

May 2013

THE CYPRUS JOB

The three bank robbers piled aboard the black Mercedes, scattering euro-notes across the pavement in their haste. Tyres howling, the limousine sped through the darkened streets of Nicosia, leaving the hapless Cypriot Police in its wake, frozen into shocked immobility, gaping open-mouthed, pistols in their holsters.

"The Great Cypriot Bank Job" had been performed by real professionals. But this time – little did they know it – the Robbers had gone too far.

Well, OK, it wasn't quite like that. Cyprus was broke, its banks were in meltdown, and the rest of the eurozone refused to ride to the rescue when many of the depositors were from dodgy sources in Russia. And then Brussels stepped in (actually the Germans) and told the Cypriots: "We'll lend you money but only if your own depositors also cough up.".... So that's what happened. Anyone with more than 100.000 euros in their bank account was then robbed of 40% of their savings. This is the true face of the EU, when the mask has slipped.

Jeroen Djisselbloem, chairman of the Eurogroup, blew the gaffe, describing the "rescue" as a model for the future. As a result, anyone with money and sense is now shutting their "eurozone bank account" and opening one with a bank that is not in the Eurozone. Take your pick. American, British, Swiss, State Bank of Guatemala, even Bank of Under the Mattress. Any of them is an improvement. The Cypriot Bank Job has proven that the EU steals from its citizens and lacks the brains to realise that Banking is built on Trust, and once Trust has gone then nothing is left behind.

May 2013

THE FUG OF WAR

Perhaps I've been working too hard but I have this vision of our Foreign Secretary, William Hague, sitting in the Kasbah, wearing a red fez, puffing away contentedly on a hubble-bubble pipe, dreaming up another "foreign policy masterstroke". There's trouble wafting our way again.

We invaded Iraq and left it a failed state. We toppled Gadaffi in Libya, which is now in chaos, consequently undermining Chad, Mali, and Mauritania. And now Mr Hague has announced that he wants to "give weapons to the Syrian rebels" as if it's Star Wars and it's the plucky little good guys against the might of the evil Empire.

It isn't Star Wars. The biggest Jihadi group in Syria (the rebels) has now formally announced its loyalty to al Qaeda (bin Laden's lot, you'll remember. Twin Towers? Madrid train bombings?). And our Foreign Secretary wants to give weapons to a group dominated by such people. Whatever he's smoking, it must be good stuff. I'll have some myself.

The civil war in Syria is between two sets of not particularly nice people. But at least under President Assad there is religious freedom for Christians, Muslims and the Druze. If Assad falls, then Syria will probably become an extreme militant Islamic state, along the lines of Iran, but slam-bang next door to Israel and Turkey. Surely even Mr Hague, currently transported by his hubble-bubble, doesn't want that.

May 2013

TILTING AT THE WRONG WINDMILL

There's been a hooh-hah recently about companies like Apple, Yahoo, Google, Starbucks etc not paying enough tax in Britain. Margaret Hodge MP, (Labour) Chairman of the Public Accounts Committee, came steaming out onto the tracks, puffing away like a tank-engine going up Scarfell Pike with the valves stuck wide open.

Revelling in the full glare of the media she dragged various Chief Executives before the Committee and laid into them, as being evil and immoral because they make profits in Britain but pay hardly any Corporation Tax. But Mrs Hodge, who gained a third class BSc Economics degree in 1966, is attacking the wrong people and (like most Labour MPs) doesn't understand business...

The Government makes Tax Law and businesses obey it. If businesses break the law they are committing Tax Evasion and go to jail. But if they find a way to legally reduce their tax bill then it's called Tax Avoidance, and is perfectly legal. These companies have done absolutely nothing wrong and Mrs Hodge and her Committee should butt out and do something more useful.

If the Government wants to change the Tax law, that's up to them, but they should not use Mrs Hodge to fight its battles. Yahoo, Google, etc have shareholders, and the board-members have a duty to make as much profit for them as possible. Your own pension company or bank might be one of those shareholders. It's called Capitalism, the thing that beat Communism.

Paying tax that can legally be avoided is absurd, particularly when it's going to be squandered on

Overseas Aid to our competitors, £billions to the EU, and a stupid war in Syria.

June 2013

THEY TRAVEL ON BUSES TOO

I hope you enjoy these snippets, from the Ticketing Agency at Washington DC Airport, which imply that it's not only UK politicians who shouldn't be let out alone. Our American Cousins are even worse.

Here's one now: "A Vermont Congressman complained furiously about an Orlando, Florida, package trip we'd arranged. He'd expected a sea-view from his room. I explained that Orlando is in the middle of the State and he shouted: "Don't lie to me. I looked on the map. Florida is a very THIN state!"
Or this one: "An Illinois Congresswoman called last week wanting to know how it was possible that her Detroit flight left at 8.30am and reached Chicago at 8.33am. I explained that Michigan was an hour ahead, but she just couldn't get the concept of time zones. Finally, I told her the plane went fast and she bought that".

Or another: "A senior aide for Senator John Kerry called to inquire about a trip package to Hawaii. After going through the costs she asked: 'Would it be cheaper to fly to California and then take the train to Hawaii?'

Or this one: "Senator Dianne Feinstein called and said 'I need to fly to Pepsi Cola, Florida. Do I have to get on one of those little computer planes?' I asked if she meant to fly to PENSACOLA on a COMMUTER flight, and she said: 'Yeah, whatever, smarty.'"...

Or finally this one: "New Jersey Congressman John Adler called: 'I want to fly to Rhino, New York.'

I replied: 'I've not heard of a Rhino code'.

He retorted: 'Oh don't be silly. Everyone knows where Rhino is. Look at your map'

I looked at the map and said to him: 'You don't mean Buffalo, do you?'

The reply: 'Whatever! I knew it was a big animal".

They walk among us, ladies and gentlemen, even through the streets of Westminster. Sometimes we even vote for them...

June 2013

LOOKING AFTER THOSE INSIDE

There's nothing "racist" about controlling immigration. It makes good sense. If we need migrant workers then we can give them temporary "work permits", but not citizenship with access to schools, the NHS, social services etc. Even the Home Secretary has recently admitted that 30% of new housing is because of immigration.

Britain is now in the strange situation where our own unskilled workers were allowed to lounge around on the dole, and we shipped in labour from Eastern Europeans, who were usually hard-working and full of initiative, self-selecting by the very fact that they'd had enough gumption to up sticks and come here, often for less than the minimum wage. But this led to a general downward pressure on wages ("You take that rate of pay, son, or I'll get a load of Latvians in here for half the price!"). At the same time our unskilled people were dumped onto the dole and got into the mind-set of: "The country owes me a living without me getting out from under this lovely warm duvet."

Unfortunately for them, the coalition is now ripping away that duvet, telling them to find a job. But they can't get unskilled jobs because the Eastern Europeans have it sewn up; and they can't stay on the dole because the coalition is chasing them round the bedroom with a cattle-prod.

The poverty in Romania and Bulgaria is grindingly low, and it will be the bright ones who move abroad in 2014 to escape it, exactly the sort of people who should be staying behind to rebuild their country. And if you look at the crime figures for London for the last period the crime rate among Eastern Europeans is eye-wateringly high. Sure, many of the workers are honest and decent, but I'm afraid that the organised gangs are also here, and those guys mean business. To dismiss this as racist is stupid. It's gone far beyond pointless insults.

June 2013

CRADLE OF CIVILISATION

Some of you might wonder why I keep going on about Syria. It's simple. The UK has made huge mistakes in the Middle East, costing thousands of lives, and our coalition government is about to do it again, by sending weapons to Syria. This is petrol onto a fire and is quite mad.

For two thousand years the place has been a hotbed of war, tribalism, and religion, of Christians, Jews, of various Islamic faiths like Sunni and Shia (who loathe each other) and the Islamic spin-offs such as Druze and Alawites, many of whom settled in Syria. If you recall the story of Sinan, the "Old Man of the Mountains", an Ismaili, he led the Assassins, a fanatical group of "suicide killers" operating from a remote castle high in the hills, and it was his movement that terrified Shia and Sunni leaders for centuries. Even the great Saladin was forced to receive visitors whilst seated inside a metal cage for fear of assassination.

When the Crusaders arrived in the Holy Land in 1096 they were merely another irritant in a land riven by war and religious violence (they even became allies with Sinan). The Muslim Empire had originally arisen in Arabia, sweeping westward across Egypt, northwards to Iran and Iraq, destroying vast armies sent out against them from Baghdad and Constantinople. But it soon collapsed into bickering, warring factions who are still bickering and warring today..

And our government (along with the USA) intends to supply weapons to the rebels, many of whom want to impose Sharia law across the world and believe that the only good non-Muslim is a dead non-Muslim. If you met someone like that, would you risk giving them a gun? By his actions, it seems our Foreign Secretary clearly would. This policy also ignores the complications of Israel, and of Russia, Syria's traditional ally.

This is an Arab civil war and none of our business. The Arabs have plenty of money, more religion than they can consume locally, and don't need any more weapons, from us or the Russians. We should keep well out of it...

June 2013

DUMB AND DUMBER

Of all the stupidest comments I've heard in 2013, the worst came last week. Not from David Cameron, nor from Nick Clegg. Nor, you may be surprised, from Ed Miliband. It came from me...

I was watching Midsomer Murders on TV, when I looked across to Hilary and said: "Someone's going to get bumped off in a moment." If you've never seen the programme, the parish of Midsomer has a higher death rate than Mogadishu. Agatha Christie would have had endless inspiration just by reading their village news-letter.

Tea on the Midsomer vicarage lawn (cucumber sandwiches with crusts removed, of course) is the prelude to screaming from the shrubbery or hysterical sobbing from an upstairs bedroom window. And then the bodies start falling. Burning, trampling, poisoning, electrocution, impaling, whacking on the head with a spade. It's all there, and more.

The carnage in Midsomer is so bad you'd expect the Army to quarantine the place, or bulldoze it and just start again. A glance at the postcode and no insurance company would grant cover. Yet at no time does Inspector Barnaby ever suggest opening a police station in the village. And I think I know why. I think that Peter Mandelson must have been a closet Midsomer fan, and he came to the rescue. It's the only explanation. So many Brits were getting bumped off in the parish that they desperately needed new incomers to swell the ranks, which is why New Labour encouraged all those immigrants into the country, a net increase of 2.2million between 1997 and 2010. As Lord Mandelson recently admitted: "We were not only welcoming people to come into this country, we were sending out search parties and encouraging them, in some cases, to take up work in this country." Surely this is code for Midsomer?

If the media ever gets hold of this there'll be a national scandal, to make the Leveson enquiry look like the grindingly tedious waste of time that it really was.

One possibility is that many thousands of "new arrivals" have already been fed into the Midsomer Murder Sausage Machine, and questions will need to be asked, and not just of Inspector Barnaby, oh no. There will be many other questions needing to be...

[That's enough, Ed. Normal service will resume next week when Mr Challice has adjusted to his new medication]

July 2013

WHY CAN'T WE GET IT RIGHT?

The UK's Foreign Policy in the Middle East has been a hopeless failure for many years, with all Britons paying for it, some even with their lives or their limbs... We toppled the Taliban in Afghanistan (a good thing) but then tried to "civilise" the place, when the Afghans just wanted us to go home.

We invaded Iraq and left it in chaos. We helped revolutions in Libya and Egypt and drooled over the Arab Spring, which is now soaking away into the burning desert sand.

The West simply doesn't understand the Arab Countries. Most of them might be Muslim but that's where it stops. The Sunni hate the Shia, and the

Shia hate the Sunni, and it's been mutual ever since the Prophet Mohammed died, causing a huge bust-up over who would succeed him. Virtually the only time the Arab world has been united was under the great Saladin, following the Crusader Invasion in 1096. But once the Crusaders gave up and went home the locals were at each others' throats again.

The strife in Syria is a "proxy" war. Qatar, Saudi Arabia and the Turks (the Sunni) are backing the rebels. Iran (the Shia) is backing President Assad, along with the Russians of course. Sunni against Shia, the old story.

The Gulf States are bloated with oil-wealth and can easily provide refugee camps if they want. Instead they are pouring weapons into Syria, and now William Hague our own Foreign Secretary, wants to get involved too. This will be a complete disaster for Britain. It's time we learned that military power must be used sparingly and surgically, not just to impose our values on other societies. This is Nanny-State with machine-gun slung round her neck and grenade in teeth. We are heading for big trouble down Syria way...

July 2013

KEEP IT UNDER YOUR HAT

In early February 2013 the German government quietly circulated an 'informal' paper around the halls of Brussels, suggesting that Baroness Ashton should control the European Commission's "neighbourhood policy," which covers relations with 16 countries on the EU's eastern and southern rim. The Baroness heads the EU's "External Action Service", a sort of EU Foreign Office rapidly replacing our own Foreign Service, and costing £billions every year.

The German paper suggests that Baroness Ashton should handle negotiations of EU treaties with leading nations such as China and Russia, and also take "overall authority" on EU aid to African and Caribbean countries. This paper has not yet been signed by Britain but 16 other nations have put their signatures on it, including Italy, the Netherlands and Spain.

What planet are they on? Indeed, which solar system? Spain and Italy are broke, yet seem happy to sign away their power over their own aid budget and foreign affairs, to an unaccountable organization headed by a Labour peer whose only experience of the workplace comes from once being Treasurer of CND.

As the Daily Telegraph put it: "Lady Ashton, the second-best paid female politician in the world, has in the past faced criticism for skipping most European Commission meetings because she says she is too busy elsewhere." This is polite-speak for saying that most officials in Brussels think she's a waste of space. UKIP MEP Paul Nuttall confronted her in the Parliament and told her (among other things!) to switch on her mobile phone because no-one could ever get hold of her.

August 2013

WHAT IF?

What if there were no hypothetical questions? Let's try a few. "What do you do if you see an endangered animal eating an endangered plant?" Or: "What was the best thing before sliced bread?" Or: "Why does the word 'lisp' have an 'S' in it?"

Or how about this one? "Why would a wind farm

be given money to stop producing energy?" Well I think I can help here. In April 2011 high winds were blowing across Scotland, and more energy was produced than could be used. The National Grid was at full capacity. Rather than just switching off the contribution from wind farms, (Thanks but we'll leave it until things settle down a bit. Take the night off. Have one on us afore ye go), the Scottish Government gave £300,000 to six wind farms to compensate them because their energy was not needed.

Hadyard Hill in South Ayrshire (one of Britain's most powerful wind-farms) was given £140,000 alone to stop producing energy. Lee Mooney, from the Renewable Energy Foundation, said: "Throwing the energy away and paying wind-farms to do so, is not only costly but obviously very wasteful. Government must rethink the scale and pace of wind power development before the cost of managing it becomes intolerable and the scale of the waste scandalous."

This made me mad. Madder than 'Mad-Jack' MacMad, three times consecutive winner of the hotly-contested: 'Maddest Madman of Madchester' Contest. But then I breathed deeply, and relaxed, thought of Chris Huhne, Energy Secretary, and was fine again.

July 2013

THE SNOW LEOPARD

Back in January, I paid £2.00 a month to adopt a snow leopard (under threat thanks to Chinese medicine, or something). Imagine my surprise last week when a man knocked at the front door and said: "I've brought yer leopard. Where do you want 'im? Ee's a bit frisky, mind."

On the same day I was equally surprised to read in the Guardian newspaper a perceptive article by journalist Robert Ford, making the point that UKIP's sudden surge in popularity threatens Labour more than the Conservatives, and he's dead right.

Ed Miliband has got it hugely wrong, and I predict that he will pay the price at the next election (the Europeans in 2014). The Coalition might be unpopular, but it won't be Labour scooping the pool as a reward. The meltdown of the economy, the vast number of immigrants etc. All this was the fault of recent Labour governments.

Mr Miliband can point the finger all he likes but it is traditional Labour voters who suffered most, and they are steaming with rage... They don't forgive and they don't forget.

If you gave them the choice of voting Tory or of having a sensitive part of their anatomy slammed repeatedly into a desk drawer, most of them would choose the latter. But they are very willing to vote UKIP.

There have been all sorts of stories cooked up in the media recently about UKIP making pacts or deals with Tory or Labour. Please ignore them. UKIP is committed to pulling out of the EU, and the Lib/Lab/Con is absolutely determined to stay in. In those circumstances it is impossible to arrange a deal even if anyone wanted one, which they don't, so it doesn't arise.

As for the guy delivering the snow leopard, I told him "Put it round the back with all the others, and I'll get you something to fix that bleeding." (Never say you don't get your money's worth with the Trago

Column. You don't get this kind of thing with DFS or Allied Carpets!)...

GULP

We had friends round to dinner the other night. They were holidaying in Devon and brought their little girl with them. She spent the whole meal looking at me, hardly touching her food. I tried ignoring her but finally cracked: "Why do you keep staring at me?" I asked.

The table fell silent. The little girl said: "I'm just waiting to see how you drink like a fish."
Times are certainly changing. When I was her age, things were very different, almost another world. Sauce was either brown or red. Pasta came in a tin with Heinz on it. Jason King was on TV. Oil was for lubricating your bike, not cooking. Soup was a main meal, cubed sugar was posh, and eating al fresco was known as a picnic, and Salmonella, E.Coli, and Botulism were all just "food poisoning", and very rarely happened.

Yet some things haven't changed. Flaubert once said: "Whatever happens we will remain stupid," and he was spot on. Listen to the politicians - whether it's Peter Mandelson admitting that Labour went out seeking immigrants to come to Britain as workers when we'd already got our own army of unemployed, or William Hague rummaging around in his swordware collection, mumbling "Syria. Syria. Possibly Egypt. Syria." to himself, like someone who's scoffed all the magic mushrooms and may soon require a stomach pump.

Or try this one. In the last five years the UK has given more than £100-million in grants and loans to Polish students so that they can study at British universities. Under EU law foreign students have the same rights as our own students. But unlike our own students, it now appears that most of these "foreign loans" will never be paid back. The students are skipping home and UK tax-payers will pick up the bill.

Well honestly. It's enough to make you drink like a fish...

August 2013

HEADS BELOW THE PARAPET

I recall Godfrey Bloom MEP ('Bongo-Bongo Land' and whacking journalist Michael Crick on the head with a rolled-up UKIP Manifesto) once commenting on "gender quotas". He asked if 50% of all female impersonators had to be women. Godfrey is married to a lovely Polish lady and has many female employees, so he's an expert on this subject... It strikes me that the desire to enforce gender-quotas across society is another example of the cultural Marxism that has shackled Britain for the last thirty years, and UKIP is totally opposed to it.

On the subject of raising the differences between men and women, this is not because someone hates women or thinks men are superior. It just means that there are differences that most sane people would recognise.

These days it seems one is not even allowed to voice an opinion without being screamed down as sexist, racist, bigoted... like the Salem witch-trials without the bonhomie.

Women might not be very good at backing a car, but they're a damn sight safer driving it (ask the insurance companies). Women are home-makers. Men just leave the seat up in the bathroom (and sometimes worse, but we won't go there). Women can multi-task. Men can read maps....

This is not ill-informed speculation nor ignorant generalisation.. I have discussed this at length with Hilary. Since the snow came all she's done is look through the window. If it gets any worse I'll have to let her back in again.

September 2013

FOREIGN SECRETARY FAILS TO ANTICIP

It's like challenging Tiger Woods to a round of Crazy Golf. You just never know what'll happen. Mr Cameron, Prime Minister, must feel the same way... He panicked over the Syria vote in Parliament, dragged his MPs back early from their hols (which made him about as popular as a pork-butcher in the Kasbah) and then told them: "Actually you don't need to vote on attacking Syria now because I haven't thought it through properly."

Mr Cameron's defeat in the House was totally avoidable. Like many, he is wedded to the "Something must be done" idea, without knowing what it is. And so his default position is to fire Cruise Missiles onto a powder-keg, all before the UN Inspectors had made their report.

Despite all the "Assad must be punished" stuff, it remains a possibility that the despicable chemical attack was not sanctioned by the Syrian government. It might have been Jihadi rebels, known to have used gas in the past, or possibly some ill-disciplined Syrian officer firing off a canister in defiance of orders, in which case it can hardly be described as "Syrian Government gasses civilians", and is certainly not enough to declare war.

We are meant to be at war with "terror" not the Syrian government. As Syrian officials say to Western journalists: "Look, we know you don't like our country but can't you see that by bombing us you are helping al Qaeda?"
If anyone should resign from the British government it isn't David Cameron, who at least had the guts to go to the House and put it to a vote. The man who should resign is William Hague, who even wanted to arm the rebels. He should resign now. He could take up Crazy Golf.

September 2013

YOUNG NOT AS DAFT AS THE PARENTS

Radio 1's Newsbeat programme ran a poll last June, among 18 to 24-year-olds. The results were interesting, given that this age-group is thought to be more "liberal" having been brainwashed by the PC establishment for the last two decades.

To quote the BBC: "Of the 1,000 young people questioned, 28% said Britain would be better off with fewer Muslims, while 44% said Muslims did not share the same values as the rest of the population. Some 60% thought the British public had a negative image of Muslims. An adviser on anti-Muslim hatred said the findings suggested young people needed to mix more.... The government group says constant negative media coverage on Islam is shaping people's views. A report submitted to the Leveson inquiry into press standards last year concluded there was 'a serious and systemic problem of racist, anti-Muslim reporting within sections of the British media' ".

May I suggest another reason why so many young people in Britain have a "negative attitude" to Islam? Perhaps because all around the world, from Bali to Madrid, from New York to Nairobi, London to Lahore, Muslim terrorists are planting bombs, detonating suicide vests, and machine-gunning non-Muslims, particularly those who are Christian.

Syrian Christians have fled to the "safety" of Iraq. (Things must be pretty bad if Iraq is safer than staying at home.) In Egypt hundreds of Coptic Christans have been murdered, their churches fire-bombed, their congregations car-bombed. In Nigeria the Christians are being literally butchered with axes and machetes.

On the same day as the Nairobi Shopping Mall attack (currently 60 dead, expected to rise), Taleban-linked human bombs blew up a church in Peshawar, Pakistan (81 dead, 140 wounded).

Call me unsophisticated but I must advance at least the possibility that this depressing catalogue of murder, extremism, and carnage might be why people, young and old, now view Islam with suspicion.

October 2013

ON OATH

It's nothing to do with UK politics, Syria or the EU, but I thought you might enjoy this one from "Disorder in the Courts" a record of things said by witnesses under cross-examination in court...

ATTORNEY: "What gear were you in at the moment of impact?"
WITNESS: "Gucci sweats and Reeboks"...

ATTORNEY: "Are you sexually active?"
WITNESS: "No, I just lie there."...

ATTORNEY: "How was your first marriage terminated?"
WITNESS: "By death."
ATTORNEY: "And by whose death was it terminated?"
WITNESS: "Guess."...

ATTORNEY: "Can you describe the individual?"
WITNESS: "He was about medium height and had a beard."
ATTORNEY: "Was this a male or a female?"
WITNESS: "Unless the circus was in town I'm going with male."...

ATTORNEY "Is your appearance here this morning pursuant to a deposition notice which I sent to your attorney?"
WITNESS: "No, this is how I dress when I go to work."...

Mind how you go...

November 2013

DIRTY GENERATION

The next time some eco-warrior assures you that Windpower is the future, please point them to a recent newspaper article by James Delingpole. Thousands of dirty diesel generators are being secretly prepared all over Britain to provide emergency back-up to prevent the National Grid collapsing when wind power fails.

As Mr Delingpole explains: "Under the hugely costly scheme, the National Grid is set to pay up to twice the normal wholesale market rate for the electricity they generate. One of the main beneficiaries of the stopgap plan is the Government itself, which stands to make hundreds of millions of pounds by leasing out the capacity of the generators in public-sector property including NHS hospitals, prisons, military bases, schools and council offices. This scheme is a direct consequence of the renewable energy policy adopted by the Coalition but first developed by Tony Blair in response to EU renewables directives to reduce Britain's carbon emissions by 20% by 2020."

OK, you might ask, so who will lose out? The answer, I'm afraid, lies behind the face staring back at you next time you look in the mirror. You are about to have huge hikes in your electricity bills, all in the name of 'combating climate change'. Ever been had?

Mr Delingpole again: "The scheme is expected to cost £1billion a year by 2015, adding five per cent to energy bills. As more and more wind turbines are built to replace fossil fuels, so the National Grid will become increasingly unstable because wind power is intermittent, unpredictable and unreliable"

December 2013

MORE HO HO HO'S

Here's a seasonal cracker for you. In Britain it is illegal to marry more than one person at a time. It's called 'bigamy' and carries a jail sentence. But in our lunatic world of multicultural political correctness, if someone is married abroad (as in a man marries five or six women) and then moves to Britain, bringing his family, then the (multiple) marriages are lawful and the various spouses can all claim State benefits.

Some Guardianistas might be relaxed about this. Well, I suppose they would be, but if someone moves here from abroad then they should be subject to our laws. The State should not pay a penny-piece towards such households, and should prosecute them for bigamy.

If you think that's a little harsh then may I quote Baroness Flather, the first Asian woman to receive a peerage. She was responding in July 2012 to the Universal Credit proposals which could mean an actual increase in benefits paid out to these people: "That is terrible. Why can't they see it? Why are they allowed to have more than one wife? We should prosecute one or two people for bigamy. That will sort it out."

Good old Baroness Flather. She's going onto my Christmas Card list...

December 2013

NOT AS CLEAR-CUT AS THEY CLAIMED

I thought you might be interested in this response to the recent report from the UN Intergovernmental Panel on Climate Change. Professor Bob Carter, Chief Science Advisor of the International Climate Science Coalition and former head of the School of Earth Sciences at James Cook University, Australia, said: "No-one should trust it. The IPCC has a history of malfeasance that even includes rewording recommendations of expert science advisors to fit the alarmist agenda of participating governments."

Climate data analyst John McLean of Melbourne, Australia warned, "In previous IPCC assessment reports, media were tricked into reporting that thousands of climate experts endorsed the chapter in which climate change causes were discussed. In fact, only a few dozen scientists even commented on that part of the document.

There's more: Dr Tim Ball, former climatology professor at the University of Winnipeg, observed, "Inexplicably, the IPCC have increased their confidence that anthropogenic greenhouse gases caused most of the warming of the past half-century despite the fact that all of their forecasts have failed. Sadly, this IPCC report will give governments unjustified confidence to impose CO_2 regulations so severe that the world's most important energy sources, hydrocarbon fuels, will be phased back sentencing billions of the world's most vulnerable people to the misery of energy poverty. The IPCC's reputation is now beyond retrieval."

The voice of reason, science, and sanity has not yet been drowned out, ladies and gentlemen, and I know who I'd trust, and it sure isn't the IPCC...

December 2013

2014

THE WAY THINGS ARE

Once upon a time there was a patch of government land in Wales containing scrap military equipment, nothing top secret. A night-watchman was hired, to stop the locals thieving bits of rusted Landrovers and dexion shelving...

Then the government asked: "How do we know he's been given proper instructions?" So they hired someone to write a manual and do time-studies on the Night Watchman. And then they thought some more, and worried: "But how will we know that he's actually performing his tasks correctly?" So they created a Quality Control department and employed two people: one to do the studies, the other to write the reports...

Then the government wondered: "How are these people going to get paid?" So they created a payroll officer and a time-keeper. And then the Army got into the act: "Who will be accountable for all these people? This is MoD land. The insurance implications."...

So the MoD created an administration office to oversee the project: a legal secretary, an admin officer, and a secretary. Then, as usual, the government ran out of money and demanded cutbacks. And then they sacked the Night Watchman. Does it sound horribly familiar?

January 2014

A SPRING-LOADED V-SIGN FROM VW?

You might be interested in this one if you drive a diesel car. Under new EU rules, fuel suppliers have now been ordered to blend conventional diesel with increasingly large amounts of "environmentally friendly" bio-fuels. We'll ignore just how "eco-friendly" they really are (very unfriendly, as it happens) and instead concentrate on the consequences...

Breakdown services and garages have recently reported a large increase in call-outs from motorists stranded in their diesel vehicles. The cause? A thick gelatinous deposit that clogs up the filter and fuel-line, causing the engine to sputter to a halt. A bit like what happens to people who live solely on lard sandwiches washed down by pints of pork-fat. Bad lifestyle choice. Not good for the circulation.

In November 2013 the RAC attended 600 such incidents where "bio-fuel" had clogged the engine, in some cases causing huge (and expensive) damage. That figure is double that of the previous November. Another early Christmas present from the EU, thanks to their stupid, ill-conceived, and sometimes even dangerous rules and regulations.

January 2014

WALKING EAST FROM DUNWICH

Despite the fact that the globe hasn't warmed, there are still some Green activists who keep wibbling on about "Global Warming and rising sea levels" as though we all face inundation unless we turn our backs on the modern world.

I try to refrain from personal attacks (unless it's Labour politicians, but they can take it) but I'm afraid that these Green activists seem to be in a state of hysteria. God is dead; now they're worshipping the Planet.

20,000 years ago you could walk from Norfolk to Denmark, but then it got warmer and the North Sea rushed in. Looking at history and archaeology it is quite clear that many civilisations have come and gone. Great cities similar to London, Paris, New York, populated by hundreds of thousands of people, now lie wrecked, buried, lost. Some beneath the desert sand; others submerged by the oceans.

In his superb book Underworld, Graham Hancock lists a number of underwater sites, where by scuba-diving into the depths one can see paved roads, unmistakeable flights of staircases, statues, tiled floorways, sewer systems, hot baths, dry-stone walls, and cemented blockwork, in locations spread across the world, from Malta, to Japan, to the Bahamas.

All these places were once "dry land", just like the land under your feet right now as you read this. And now they are completely submerged, to all intents and purposes lost forever beneath the waves, at least until the next ice age when they might pop up again.

Nothing stays the same. We come and we go. Things change. Climates change. But to think that any good will come from closing down all our power stations and replacing them with windmills, to my mind at least, is bad science feeding gullibility and naivete.

January 2014

LEFT-HAND DRIVE?

In December 2013 the motoring magazine Auto-Express ran an interesting story, revealing that the UK government hasn't the foggiest idea how many foreign-registered cars are driving around on British roads. Foreign plates can be used for up to six months before the driver has to register the vehicle with the DVLA, but only a tiny percentage ever do that (we don't know exactly how tiny a percentage, because the government "hasn't the foggiest").

One doesn't need a brain the size of Canada to work out why they don't. Why should they? They can evade parking fines, the congestion charge, speeding fines, the MoT, motor insurance etc etc...

Auto-Express discovered that in Cornwall, Devon, and Dorset, the total of unpaid fines for the last five years has now reached a staggering £500,000. That would pay for a couple of dozen extra lollypop-ladies, or some bobbies on the beat... or even a few extra pot-plants for the Police & Crime Commissioner's new office.

February 2014

THE COST AT THE COSTAS

I have a friend of a friend in Spain (we'll call her Kathy, retired there some years now). Here's part of an email she sent. Just a snapshot but very interesting:

"You may ask about the economic crisis here in Spain, with all those young people out of work and so much political corruption, but the restaurants and bars are still chock-a-block, the streets as full of life as usual, and although everyone talks about how many people in the family haven't got a job if one member of the household is a civil servant or a pensioner people seem to get along".

Kathy went on: "I cannot understand how the government still has given the pensioners double-pay for Christmas. There is a huge 'middling-class' range where younger people are still paid by the government , be it salary or unemployment. Brussels is lending money right, left, and centre to Spain.

How are we going to pay it back? I have no idea, but again that's me, northern European, thinking about the future when the Mediterranean people generally think about today."

February 2014

BREAKING THE ICE

Last November a bunch of "global warming" researchers hired a Russian icebreaker, the MV Akademik Shokalskiy, to ferry them down to Antarctica to demonstrate how Mankind is warming the planet and melting all the ice. They went in Summer when the ice is melting anyway (more dramatic effect for the cameras and the public, one supposes). But then they got trapped in the ice, unable to move.

Diesel generators whirred to keep systems going, adding pollution to the pristine Antarctic environment. They awaited help, but expressed neither apology, nor regret, let alone embarrassment.

French-flagged L'Astrolabe came to the rescue, also with chugging diesels, but had to turn back. The ice again, you see. Too thick.

Along came the Xue Long, a Chinese icebreaker, owned by the nation environmentalists hate the most. As a recent (unnamed) commentator observed: "Hooray - the Chinese ship has a helicopter. Then the Chinese ship itself became stuck. When conditions cleared last week the chopper had rescued 52 and placed them aboard Australia's Aurora Australis which had stayed clear of the ice.

A fifth ship, the US Coast Guard's Polar Star ice-breaker is now on its way and will give the region's clean air more carbon to think about. The Antarctic sea is beginning to look like a diesel regatta".

An inconvenient truth is that Antarctic ice has been steadily increasing since 1987, and at the other end of the planet a million more square miles of ice covered the Arctic in 2013 than in 2012 (Arctic sea-ice is up 60 percent in 2013). Thanks to these bumbling buffoons the secret is now well and truly out.

March 2014

STICKING YOUR NECK OUT

A few weeks ago, at Copenhagen Zoo, a Keeper entered the enclosure of Marius, the 18-month-old giraffe, and gave him his favourite meal of rye-grass. Shortly afterwards the Keeper placed a bolt-gun against the animal's head and pulled the trigger. Marius flopped to the ground, dead. For some reason I haven't worked out yet, the Keeper then cut up Marius in front of the public and fed him to the lions.

Marius was perfectly healthy. No disease, no deformity, no illness. So why was he killed? The answer, I'm afraid, is because of the European Union which has now passed laws to control inbreeding between captive groups of animals in zoos.

I quite understand about controlling the gene pool among a confined group of animals, but Marius had already been offered a new home by the Yorkshire Wildlife Park in Doncaster, which has a new giraffe house and previously took a male giraffe from Copenhagen.

Some 27,000 people even signed an online petition to save Marius from "death row". And if Doncaster wasn't good enough a Swedish zoo and a Netherlands wildlife park also offered to take him – but Copenhagen bosses insisted. Marius must die because of its duty to avoid in-breeding.

Robert Krijuff, boss of the Netherlands wildlife park whose last-minute offer of a place was also rejected, said: "I can't believe it. We offered to save his life. Zoos need to change the way they do business." This was all reported by the BBC on Sunday 9th Feb. In the morning BBC News explained that it was because of "EU Rules". By tea-time they'd clearly been nobbled, and all subsequent bulletins merely reported that it was because of "rules". No mention of "Europe".

This is the problem. The media makes subtle little changes, minor ones that slip past the radar, misleading their own viewers, listeners, and readers. But let's be quite clear: Marius (and thousands of other animals) are being needlessly killed, all because of EU rules, when these animals could easily be re-homed.

I should clarify that I'm a carnivore and enjoy my steak medium-rare with chips and onion rings, so I'm no animal liberation activist. I just hate to see cruelty and needless, stupid waste.

March 2014

PUSHING BILL OFF HIS LADDER

In the words of the old song: "There may be TROUBLE ahead" And here's why. Because we're all living longer and the country has run out of money, Chancellor George Osborne has decided that most working people must be seventy before getting a State pension. But I foresee huge problems.

First, it's pretty much impossible for many of us to work at physical jobs at that sort of age. Imagine a window-cleaner, a builder, hairdresser, fireman, farmer, even a cop, struggling through their day, coping with high blood pressure, arthritis, and generally feeling like they'd rather not be slogging away what's left of their energy at this age, thanks very much.. (Yes I know a few hardy souls manage it, but they're the exceptions: "Brian the Postie, Still Delivering Letters to Truro at 87). Yes, good old Brian....

Another consideration is, what about all those youngsters stuck in the queue? They might be looking up at Bill the Window-Cleaner still squeegeeing at 78, exhibiting marvellous agility for one of his advanced years, but it's a fair bet that many of them will secretly be hoping Bill falls off that ladder, making room for someone younger. In short, the old will be clogging up the system, creating resentment in the young.

And then, of course, there's the EU and its rules, the elephant in the room, so big that most people can't even see that it's there. When EU nationals from abroad can get all these State benefits, without having paid into the pot, yet the poor Brits have to slog along for another 10 years before their own government sees fit to stop taking and start giving back, that government will become about as popular as a bacon sarnie at a bar mitzvah, but Mr Osborne won't care, I assume. He'll probably have moved on to different things. But others might care to bear it in mind.

Given that our EU membership costs Britain some 11% of our GDP every year, and rising, a colossal sum, UKIP will be able to avoid much of this huge burden on taxpayers and working people, by simply pulling out of the EU, and telling foreign workers "If we need you, you can have a Work Permit, but you must have medical insurance, and if you stop working then you must leave. You will not be entitled to State Benefits..."

April 2014

WHEN THE LEVEE BREAKS

Things may be different by the time you read this, but Chris Smith is currently Chairman of the Environment Agency, the man taking the flak for allowing the Somerset Levels to be inundated with water. But the truth is more complicated. The real culprit is the European Union and I'll explain why.

Back in 2007 the EU passed the so-called "Floods Directive" 2007/60/EU. This piece of law spelt it out in plain terms. The Levels and other similar areas were to be allowed to flood.

To quote Dr Richard North: 'At the time, Charles Clover, writing in the Telegraph, was far from being impressed, complaining that, while Defra calls it "Making Space for Water", others called it "flooding". And, in those few words, the future government policy was revealed. Flood defence was to give way to "management". In EU terms, that meant more flooding'.

When people say that the government has been slow to act, they're quite wrong. Our real government, the EU, acted very quickly indeed, even inventing a new word: "Washland", an area of floodplain that was to be allowed to flood or was deliberately flooded by a watercourse for flood management purposes.

When the Environment Agency ceased dredging the rivers they were only obeying orders, and this also might explain why English Nature has encouraged Somerset farmers to maintain their land in a permanently waterlogged state to encourage lapwings and other wetland birds. All singing from the same hymn-sheet. A disaster waiting to happen.

Most striking of all is the total silence from politicians and the media about who is really to blame. Sure, in heavy rainfall the Levels will flood; that's what they do. But the EU is directly responsible for the misery and torment that has been visited on those poor, poor people in Somerset.

To read more on this please Google eureferendum.com/blogview.aspx?blogno=84683
or type in: "EU policy deliberately flooding the Somerset Levels".

April 2014

REDUCE VOLCANO EMISSIONS

The debate goes on. "Global Warming" has now been dropped (because Earth hasn't got any warmer) and "Climate Change" is new kid on the block, responsible for every gale, flood, landslide and tidal wave across the world.

Australian Geology professor Ian Plimer recently wrote a report that travelled the internet. Here's an edited part of it, concerning the volcanic eruption in Iceland: "Since its first spewing of volcanic ash [the volcano]has, in just FOUR DAYS, NEGATED EVERY SINGLE EFFORT you have made in the past five years to control CO2 emissions on our planet - all of those [green measures] have gone down the tubes in just four days".

He went on: "This evil carbon dioxide that we are trying to suppress - it's that vital chemical compound that every plant requires to live and grow and to synthesize into oxygen for us humans and all animal life. And there are around 200 active volcanoes on the planet spewing out this crud at any one time - EVERY DAY."

Prof. Plimer has been fiercely criticised by the Climate Change lobby, of course (no surprise there). UKIP's position on "climate change caused by Man" is one of extreme scepticism; partly because the predictions and models that are produced, regularly fail, are alarmist, involve vast sums of money, and are based on a pre-determined assumption, which is the extreme opposite of the true scientific, academic method.

We also dislike the religious fervour of the so-called 'alarmists' who denounce any opponent as heretics, deniers, or unbelievers. It's as if, having killed God, they are now worshipping the planet. All very odd.

May 2014

TORN CURTAIN

The EU and NATO have spent years undermining the Ukraine until the democratically elected president fled the country and his government was then toppled by a mob. At that point Catherine Ashton, head of the EU's Foreign Service, flew to Kiev announcing her delight at events...

So the West has engineered a coup in the Ukraine, encouraging a split between its population; some favouring the West; some favouring the East. The European Union (assisted by the USA) tried to push its borders right up to Russia itself, threatening Russia's own borders, and the continued existence of the Russian Sevastopol naval base which gives their fleet access to the Black Sea and the Mediterranean beyond.

Anyone who seriously expected the Russians to roll over and lie down in the face of such a threat, was very wrong, and making a miscalculation of monumental proportions. President Putin was never one to allow the EU to prod at him without reaction, and if Brussels isn't careful they might find the lights dimming all across Europe as Putin turns off the gas.

May 2014

COULD DO BETTER

I came across a few old school reports the other day, so I decided to share them with you: "Since my last report your child has reached rock bottom and started to dig." or "When your daughter's IQ reaches 50 she should sell" or "This student has delusions of adequacy. He has a full six-pack but lacks the plastic thing to hold it together".
Or: "I would not allow this child to breed. They are depriving a village somewhere of an idiot."

It's not just school reports, of course. Here's a few from the Armed Forces: "His men would follow him anywhere but only out of curiosity" or "Couldn't organise 50% leave in a two-man submarine" or "He has carried out each and every one of his duties to his complete satisfaction".

Or try this one: "He is so dense, light bends around him" or: "He would be out of his depth in a car-park puddle", or "This officer can be likened to a small puppy. He runs around excitedly, leaving little messes for others to clean up." My personal favourite of all: "Fell out of the stupid tree and hit every branch on the way down."

I realise that none of the above has anything to do with getting Britain out of the EU and running our own country again. It just makes a change from castigating William Hague, who to quote another one, "Has a photographic memory but has the lens cover glued on".

May 2014

GAGGING CLAWS

The Government often says: "Britain can't leave the EU because we won't survive on our own". The following is therefore ominous...

Iain Mansfield, 30, is a highly intelligent British diplomat - Director of Trade and Investment at the UK's embassy in the Philippines, who previously worked for the Department of Business, Innovation and Skills. In April he won the Brexit Prize for his submission: A Blueprint for Britain: Openness No Isolation. Lord (Nigel) Lawson awarded him the €100,000 prize for his winning entry, which outlines a blueprint for Britain outside of the EU.

This calls for us to join the European Free Trade Association and introduce a 'Great Repeal Bill' to review many EU regulations, reducing the burden on British business and unshackling the wider economy. He calculates that the UK economy will get a £1.3bn increase in GDP.

And then the Foreign Office stepped in, refusing him permission to even discuss the document. As reported by Get Britain Out, who are calling for the Foreign Secretary's resignation: "William Hague and Iain's bosses have now decided to intimidate and silence him. Multiple press interviews have been cancelled as a result and he has effectively been put on lockdown."

UKIP MEP William Dartmouth reacted furiously to the silencing of Mansfield: "It is ludicrous that William Hague and the Foreign Office are hounding this man and censoring his voice simply because he put forward a case for Britain to leave the EU. It seems to me that the government are getting increasingly twitchy about the possibility of Britain leaving the EU as it becomes more and more compelling to the British people."

Nothing new there then. They say we can't afford to leave the EU and when one of their own guys presents the case for the Prosecution they biff him over the head, gag him, and bundle him into the under-stairs cupboard alongside the Hoover and the cat-basket until danger has passed.

June 2014

ROMANCING THE STONE

We've just returned from a relaxing stay in Sidmouth, at the Hunters Moon. Lovely place. Georgian, elegant, civilised, no children, no music, excellent cuisine, how hotels used to be. Miss Marple couldn't make it, but you had the feeling she'd have liked to come.

Outside, suspended from the railings by a length of twine, hangs the Forecasting Stone, along with instructions:

Stone is wet = Raining.

Shadow on ground = Sunny.

White on top = Snowing.

Can't see stone = Foggy.

Stone swinging = Windy.

Stone missing = Tornado.

This could be adopted for British politics:

William Hague, lips moving = We're about to make a huge mistake in someone else's country.

David Cameron, lips moving = We're about to make a huge mistake in this country.

Lord Paddy Ashdown, lips moving = I'm just about to offer my advice despite the fact that it's always unfailingly wrong.

Ed Balls, lips moving = I promise to return your wallet when I've spent everything inside it.

Nigel Farage, lips moving = I'm the only one around here telling the truth, but many of you aren't listening. With a bit of imagination the Forecasting Stone process could be extended into many other areas, but right now it's back to the Hunters Moon for me, and more of that melt-away sponge with crème anglaise...

June 2014

A CRUISE ON THE BLACK SEA

As mentioned by Nigel Farage in the recent TV debates, we have now seen the people of Crimea voting 97% in favour of leaving Ukraine and rejoining Russia (to which it used to belong until the 1950's). This is democracy in action in response to the cack-handed foreign policy of the European Union, helped by the USA. It's not a perfect situation, no-one pretends that, but I quite understand why those in Crimea feel how they do.

To quote William Dartmouth MEP: "What Putin has done is wrong but the West has played a terrible hand. Nobody should ever ask William Hague to play poker on their behalf, that's for sure. The EU encouraged Western Ukrainians to think a future as a member state and large net recipient of funds was beckoning. The population then toppled a legitimate president."

William Dartmouth went on: "The idea that this would go unanswered by Putin was always fanciful. What the EU in particular has done is the reverse of what Theodore Roosevelt recommended as the key to effective diplomacy. It has spoken loudly while carrying a very small stick. The result was eminently predictable: annexation of Crimea and a long Russian shadow cast over the rest of the Ukraine. This was dunce's diplomacy. Putin knows that the idea of the EU facing him down in his own backyard is ridiculous. The British public will be overwhelmingly against being drawn into a trial of strength that the West is bound to lose. We'd be much better off concentrating on building up our own depleted armed forces and reducing our energy dependency on Russian gas so we can stand up for ourselves when essential British interests really are at stake."

I agree totally. But I'd also arrange a Night of the Long Knives at the Foreign Office because they clearly couldn't organise a Woodpecker's Convention in Sherwood Forest.

GIVING SANTA THE SACK

The Labour Party's campaign during the 2014 European election was "Vote for us because there's a general election in 12 month's time."...

One tactic they did use was deliberately lying to the electorate about UKIP's policies. A leaflet went out, then appeared on Facebook, claiming all sorts of rubbish, so perhaps we'd better clarify this. Contrary to Labour's claims, UKIP will not axe the charge of rape if it involves a married couple. Rape is rape, whether a husband does it or not... UKIP will not scrap Maternity Pay, nor Sick Pay. Quite the reverse... St George's Day will be added as a national paid Bank Holiday for England...
UKIP will not make people pay to see their GP, and are believers in an NHS free at the point of delivery (though if you're a migrant worker coming into the country you will need private health insurance).

When Beveridge introduced the NHS it was always intended for those who had contributed... not a gravy train for the rest of the world to avail themselves of, just because we were too soft to say "No".

And finally, UKIP does not want to abolish Christmas nor stuff small children up chimneys, no matter what the left-wing of the Labour Party might allege. So the next time they start making these claims, please just give yourself a quick Chinese burn and rejoin the rest of us in the real world.

September 2014

WORDS FROM THE PODIUM

Here is part of a speech by Irish journalist Mary Ellen Sinon at the Bruges Group. She writes "the Brussels Blog" for the Mail Online. It makes chilling reading:

"If you have a referendum in 2017 Cameron may slip out of it exactly as he slipped out of a Lisbon Treaty referendum. Still, I understand most of you believe that, if you get an in/out referendum, and the out vote wins, then - hurrah! – free at last. You've won...

Don't kid yourselves. This is where I stop speaking as someone from Brussels and start speaking as someone from Ireland. In the EU, a "yes" vote is forever. A "no" vote is only ever temporary. Trust me on this one, I'm Irish. I know. The EU has forced the Irish through this trick for idiots and more than once. So it is naïve for any of you to think that if you get a vote in a referendum to leave the EU, then that is the battle won. It is not. It is just the end of the phony war...

Some of you may recall that the prime minister admitted in an interview with the Spanish newspaper El Pais last April that he would not take Britain out of the EU just because a referendum result was a vote to get Out. The reporter asked Cameron, if in the case of a victory in the referendum for the "out" vote: "Would you be willing to leave the Union?" Cameron's reply was: "I would not"...

The interview was circulated at the European Commission. It was further confirmation to the EU elite that Cameron is one of them. He is a collaborator..." END OF QUOTE.

October 2014

BOOTS ON THE GROUND

We are now in a Middle East military coalition fighting ISIS. That mob of religious lunatics and criminal psychopaths must be obliterated, but I'm afraid we won't do it merely by dropping bombs down their chimney.

ISIS has waged a religious war against Christians, Sunnis, Shia, Wahabbis, and even Yazadis, of whom I'd never heard until ISIS chased them up onto a mountain. They've even fallen out with al Qaeda because they think bin Laden's people lack commitment (!).

The problem with the coalition is that because it doesn't recognise President Assad as leader of Syria it will be about as much use as a one-legged man in a backside-kicking contest. If we don't involve the Syrian government ISIS will melt away into the Syrian badlands, only to pop up again in a few month's time. Somebody needs to put "boots on the ground" and if it's not NATO then the official Syrian Army is the perfect candidate. The Kurds and Turks aren't going to fight in Syria (they're more likely to fight each other) and the Iraqi Army has shown itself about as combat ready as Lichenstein. The last time Lichenstein went to war (1866) it sent eighty soldiers to fight the Italians. None of them were killed, and they actually returned with eighty-one men because they met him on the road and invited him home to live with them. Two years later they abolished the Army. You see what you get with the Trago Column? Interesting facts, topical analysis, pertinent political comment. Even, occasionally, the occasional joke.

October 2014

PROMISES PROMISES

Prime Minister David Cameron is slipperier than a buttered piglet. Try to catch him and "whoop" he's off, squealing between your legs, running round the room. Advance upon him and he's feinted left, then to the right, then shot back to the left in the sort of manoeuvre that any prop-forward would be proud of.

DC is a very good politician because he has the ability to promise the earth without anyone remembering it five minutes after he's left the room.

He promised to "cut annual immigration to the tens of thousands". Last year net migration to Britain was 247,000, a city the size of Bristol, in one year!

He promised to cut the EU budget, but managed only to reduce the proposed increase from eye-watering to merely gob-smacking.

He promises a referendum on EU membership in 2017 but neglects to say that he'll never pull Britain out of the EU even if we all vote to leave, after revealing that little gem in an interview with the Spanish newspaper El Pais, last year.

Mark Reckless, former MP, left the Conservative Party and joined UKIP, not because he suddenly disliked the Tories. He left because he eventually came to realise that those running his former party have absolutely no intention of leaving the EU and simply cannot be trusted to deliver on their promises, whether on Justice, Economics, Immigration etc. Buttered piglets indeed. A whole row of 'em, in fact.

November 2014

BLOWING THE GAFF TO WHITE VAN MAN

I think I know why Ed Miliband was so cross when Emily Thornberry MP tweeted her picture of a house in the Rochester by-election with England flags hanging outside and a white-van parked on the hard standing. It wasn't because she'd "treated disrespectfully" someone from the Working Classes. No, the reason Ed Miliband was furious was because she'd blown the gaff. Let slip the true face of Labour.

Tony Blair's government engaged in a deliberate bout of social engineering to bring about a "truly multicultural" country, designed to "rub the Right's nose in diversity". It knew what it was doing but deliberately concealed it from its own Labour supporters because it knew how unpopular it would be.

Last year alone net-migration to Britain was 247,000 and neither Cameron or Miliband can do anything about it because Freedom of Movement of Peoples is a core part of being in the EU. The other 27 Member States will not compromise on this, regardless of all the hot air arising from Westminster.

November 2014

PULLING UP THE LADDER

How ironic that it was Socialist Labour politicians, most of whom attended Grammar schools, who did their best to obliterate them. "Pull up the ladder. I'm alright."

This is from Desmond Bagley's adventure story The Enemy (1977): "In Britain, the left-wing decries 'elitism'. In Russia the communists foster it. When a bright youngster is found he is whisked away to a special school where his mind is stretched. He can no longer count on having an easy time walking nonchalantly through the school subjects without effort, coming out on top while his duller brethren work like hell plodding along behind"...

Some pupils might become brilliant academics, scientists, researchers, but couldn't put up a set of shelves or change a tyre, and it is vital that we don't lose sight of the huge importance of training our own students in practical subjects. Had we done so then perhaps we wouldn't have needed all those plumbers from Poland, or those doctors and nurses raided from across the globe, just to plug our own skills gap, because we were too short-sighted or lazy to train our own people here at home.

November 2014

ON LICENCE AT THE BBC?

Plenty of people love the BBC but want to axe the licence fee. I disagree, because if the BBC loses the licence fee it will be forced to advertise which will ruin the existing programmes and dumb down all the new ones. You only need to flick around a few channels to see the "commercial" alternative. If that's the future of broadcasting, we're finished. My own solution is for the BBC to shut down many of its services and keep State broadcasting to a minimum. If people want something else they have an entire world in which to find it. The BBC should concentrate on quality and on "doing less but doing it better". Four or five TV and Radio channels each; with local news programmes for the regions, and the main website. And of course the World Service. Get rid of the rest.

The BBC should also revert to being impartial and unbiased, instead of being a home for distressed lefties unable to find gainful employment at the Guardian. In fact sometimes the Guardian's more open-minded than the Beeb, and I think I know why. Figures have just been revealed, disclosing that between 2007-2012 the EU paid the BBC nearly £20million. In 2013 alone it handed over nearly £5million.

If the EU is paying that kind of money in "grants" no wonder that a perception arises that the BBC is biased in favour of the EU and is reluctant to cover stories reflecting badly on it. More next week on the BBC.

November 2014

BRUSSELS BROADCASTING CORPORATION?

Last week I revealed that the EU mistakenly released figures detailing its grants and payments into the public domain and we saw how it had given the BBC nearly £25million since 2007, calling into question the BBC's impartiality. After all, it already gets a hefty sum from the licence fee payer.

Of course, there's no such thing as "EU money". It comes from German and British taxpayers, so UK taxpayers are paying twice for a State broadcaster that is not always seen as unbiased (and that's putting it mildly).

The multi-millions in hand-outs came to light because of the sharp-eyed researcher EU historian and blogger Dr Richard North, who says "the database is a goldmine of information...once again it brings to light the huge amount of taxpayer funding going to unaccountable NGOs, and especially (but not exclusively) climate change advocacy groups."...

Dr North went on: "Grants to the green anti-industrial lobby included multi-millions to Friends of the Earth, £3,332,220), WWF £4,252,279 and the RSPB £3,024,327. More, the European Commission has taken taxpayers' money from across the EU member states to subsidise United Nations institutions to the tune of nearly £111m, despite UN staff indulging ""in corruption, waste and abuse that carries no real penalty," according to Claudia Rosett, UN expert at the Foundation for Defense of Democracies, a Washington public policy institute. "...

So there you go. Things not exactly "transparent" at the EU these days, but then they never were.

December 2014

AND ON THAT I AM UNANIMOUS

Bad spellers of the world untie! There, that got your eye. Today's subject is Sovereignty...

If you start wibbling on about Sovereignty down the pub it's only a matter of time before someone pours a pint of Bishop's Finger over your head. But sovereignty is very important, something you don't miss until it's gone.
When we joined the Common Market back in 1973 we thought it was a trading club and signed up, but we didn't realise that it involved losing our sovereignty, the right to make our own decisions as a country.

We now have a situation where we've given huge amounts of power to the EU yet the domestic politicians still deny it. They think they still run the country, but they don't. Most of the decisions are made in Brussels, and the ones still made in Westminster are called "derogations". In other words

Brussels says: "We'll let you run this, this, and this, but we reserve the right to take over sometime in the future."

From uncontrollable immigration to the size of your hairdryer or vacuum cleaner, Brussels now calls the shots, and if you think that David Cameron is going to pull Britain out of the EU after some meaningful referendum then you're sadly mistaken. As I've said before, he is slipperier than a buttered piglet. Try to catch him and whoop off he goes between your legs running squealing round the room. It ain't going to happen on his watch.

I'd give my right arm to be ambidextrous but there's no point if I'm stuck in a strait jacket. The only way to escape the EU is to leave the EU, and the only party that wants to leave the EU is UKIP. I predict that any EU Referendum that may come along will be skewed and pre-determined, and therefore something of a farce. But let's hope I'm wrong.

December 2014

YOU OBEY OUR LAWS NOT YOUR OWN

One way that you know you've lost your country (or in the middle of losing it) is when your laws are over-ruled by someone elsewhere. Unfortunately that's what happened here in Britain, thanks to the EU. To be fair, it's not that a foreign power invaded and then imposed its rule upon us. That never happened. It was our own clueless, home-grown politicians who did that. To paraphrase Cicero: "Beware those within the walls of the city, not the enemy outside."

Brussels now holds sway over something like 75% of our laws. Some of this we've deliberately signed up to; some, we only found out afterwards but were too embarrassed to admit we hadn't read the small print.

If you are one of those hopeless Europhiles who won't believe anything until it's far too late, then please switch on your computer and enter the following (below) into your search engine. It will show you that Viviane Reding, vice-president of the European Commission, came to London recently and boasted that 70% of UK Laws are now decided in Brussels, and the British people are not informed enough to have a referendum on leaving the EU...

http://www.dailymail.co.uk/news/article-2556397/Britons-ignorant-EU-referendum-Top-official-says-debate-Europe-distorted-people-not-make-informed-decision.html

December 2014

QUOTES FROM INSIDE THE CIRCUS

Here are a few quotes on politics which I thought you might enjoy, given that we are approaching the 2015 general election and it is very important to keep a sense of perspective...

"If you don't read the newspaper you are uninformed, if you do read the newspaper you are misinformed."   (Mark Twain)

"Suppose you were an idiot. And suppose you were a member of government. But then I repeat myself." (Mark Twain)

"A government which robs Peter to pay Paul can always depend on the support of Paul". (George Bernard Shaw)

"Foreign aid might be defined as a transfer of money from poor people in rich countries to rich people in poor countries" (Douglas Casey, Classmate of Bill Clinton at Georgetown University)

"Government is the great fiction, through which everybody endeavours to live at the expense of everybody else." (Frederic Bastiat, French economist)

"Just because you do not take an interest in politics doesn't mean politics won't take an interest in you!" (Pericles 430 B.C.)

"A government big enough to give you everything you want, is strong enough to take everything you have." (Thomas Jefferson)
Food for thought, I thought...

January 2015

LONGERRRRRR WORRRRRRDS

There is a secret move underway to separate the Church of England from the State, putting it on the same level as the Roman Catholics, the Muslims, the Jews, Baptists etc. The fight-back by the C of E has a name which is also the longest word in the English language, and this is it:
"Antidisestablishmentarianism".

There is another longer word, from the film Mary Poppins (supercalifragilistic-expialidocious) but that one is invented and doesn't count. But I have just heard of a couple more that caught my interest. The longest word in German is:
"Donaudampfschiffahrtselektrizitätenhauptbetriebs werkbauunterbeamtengesellschaft"
which rather splendidly is the polish for the buttons on the jackets of the captains of the steamboats on the River Rhine (if you were ever wondering why you bother with the Trago Column, this should explain it. You just don't get this kind of information anywhere else).

And I've just found another one, dating back to the days of Mad Cow disease:
"Rindfleischetikettierungsüberwachungsaufgabenü bertragungsgesetz" which means "beef labelling regulation & delegation of supervision law". It was also 1999 German Word of the Year. So if you're compiling a pub quiz you're very welcome to pinch this one.

In English, at the other end of the spectrum, we have a shortish word which applies both to our national football team and to our Prime Minister's recent negotiations in Brussels. The word is Loser, but more on that another time.

January 2015

MORE FROM MARY SINON

This is part of a speech by Irish journalist Mary Ellen Sinon at the Bruges Group. She writes "the Brussels Blog" for the Mail Online, and spends much of her working life out there in Brussels and Strasbourg. It's revealing stuff, this…

She said: "You see, the word "country" is almost never used at the commission. About the only time you will come across the word "country" in Brussels is when you are standing by the baggage carousel at arrivals at the airport. There is always at least one suitcase with a sticker that says: "Europe is my country". Exclamation mark…

No, in Brussels one says "member state". You may imagine it means the same thing as country or state, but "member state" does not. Note that adjective. Member modifies state. Like "wooden" modifies "leg". The noun stays the same, but the essence of the thing is gone.

In particular, no one at the podium, from the commission president down, will ever speak of his own country. At the commission, any one in what used to be 28 sovereign states is only ever "a citizen of Europe". Should any eurocrat somehow find he is cornered into referring to his own country, he is trained to refer to it only as "the country I know best".

That is just one of the customs of the place I've learned in these last five years. Indeed, if I had not been obliged to wear a blue and yellow badge around my neck with the words "Journaliste Irish Daily Mail" around my neck every moment I was in an EU building – quite a handicap in Brussels, that word

"Mail", but I wouldn't have had it any other way – I might even have been taught the secret handshake.
..

Or at least I guess there must be a secret handshake. For sure there is something that allows certain journalists to be tapped from the Brussels press corps and offered a job on the gravy train itself. Yes indeed some of the people – or should I say citizens – working as reporters in Brussels today may be eurocrats tomorrow..."

END OF QUOTE...

February 2015

A CHIP OFF JOHNNY'S BLOCK

Only a snapshot, but looking in the lonely hearts column at the back of the newspapers you'll see lots of: "Non-smoker, likes dogs, country walks and trad jazz, WLTM lady for companionship", or "Blonde vivacious 50-something divorcee, likes wine, chocolate and travel, seeks soulmate"

Perhaps those two wouldn't particularly gel, but it must work sometimes or folks wouldn't advertise.

But the other day I was listening to The River & the Thread, a truly superb CD by Roseanne Cash (daughter of Johnny Cash), and came across this 19th Century lonely hearts ad, amalgamated into a song (When the Master Calls the Roll). The care, craft and poetry of this genuine ad taken from a US newspaper of the time really highlights how the pace of life has changed over the last 100 years.

Here are the words:

Girl with hair of flaming red,
Seeking perfect lover,
For to lie down on her feather bed,
Some secrets to uncover.

Must be gentle, must be strong,
With disposition sunny,
Just as faithful as the day is long,
And careful with his money"

I particularly like the "careful with his money". Some things never change....

March 2015

SOMERSAULTING THE NEWS

The BBC recently published a new survey on the attitude of British Muslims to the shootings of the journalists of Charlie Hebdo magazine which had published cartoons of the Prophet Mohammed. And they spun it their usual way: "Muslims oppose cartoon reprisals" they announced to the world.

As Telegraph journalist Dan Hodges put it: 'It's a reassuring headline. It's also wrong. Many Muslims - a majority - do indeed utterly oppose the murderous killings in Paris. But a very, very large number of Muslims don't.

Presented with the statement: "I have some sympathy for the motives behind the Charlie Hebdo attacks in Paris", 27% agreed with the statement'... The survey also found 68% of Muslims believed "acts of violence against those who published such images can never be justified". But that means that 32% take a different view, though the BBC glossed over it. Another question asked: "Do you agree that Muslim clerics who preach that violence against the West can be justified, are out of touch with mainstream opinion?" Only 49% agreed, meaning that yet again a majority of Muslims disagree with it.

Given that Muslims now form approaching 6% of the total UK population, this is extremely worrying. And it's the fault of multiculturalism peddled by the "useful idiots" of the PC brigade, which sowed the seeds for this. They are to blame, not the Muslims who merely reacted to the situation on the ground.

March 2015

ANIMAL MAGIC

If you go to the zoo and stick your finger through the bars of the cage, and then pull it back and observe that it has been bitten off, you can hardly complain. You have behaved in a silly way and now paid the price. At least you won't do it again. No? Well, British Foreign Policy is akin to this at the moment.

Whoever is running the Foreign Office seems to have sacked all the old guys who knew about foreign countries and how they do things there, and replaced them with a bunch of eager young graduates obsessed with Human Rights, carbon emissions, and shoving democracy at people who haven't the faintest idea what to do with it...

And when it goes wrong, when the finger is gnawed off at the Zoo, they react with a sort of shocked moral outrage. We messed up in Iraq, Afghanistan, Libya, Syria, and now we're doing the same in Ukraine. "Here's another finger. I'll stick it through the bars of the cage and see if THIS one gets bitten off, just like all the rest". Even Johnny Morris couldn't express that in a sympathetic Lion-Voice.

Between them NATO and the EU engineered a coup in the Ukraine, toppled a democratically elected President, and set off a pocket-sized civil war, precisely when we should have been co-operating with Putin to expunge the Islamic lunatics of ISIS from the planet. We cannot do it alone, but in a Grand Coalition across the world it should certainly be possible to cripple Militant Islam, the greatest threat facing the civilised world, and it doesn't help when we start falling out with each other over manufactured arguments like Ukraine or Syria.

March 2015

A PEEK BEHIND THE GRILLE

At UKIP Head Office we get inundated with emails, many thousands of them, from people all over Britain and further afield. I thought you might like a snapshot of how it works. First, the enquiry. Then, my reply.

"Dear UKIP, I was shocked to read in tonight's Colchester Evening's Gazette of the two Lithuanian's who stole a car days after arriving in the UK. Not only did they steal the car but also committed burglary. Why are we the tax payer paying for their stay in prison? Why are they not being deported immediately? We often read in the news of people arrested abroad and being deported - what is wrong with this country?"...

And my reply: "Dear Mrs Bloggs, Thank you for your email. The simple answer is that if we're in the EU and unable to control the borders then this story is inevitable. In fact, much worse is to come. ISIS terrorists are now in Libya and will soon be hiding among the boatloads of refugees crossing the Mediterranean to Italy, from where they will spread out across the Continent, establishing a network of terror cells. At that point people might start accepting that UKIP was right to warn about the dangers of "open borders" and that it was perfectly sensible and not "extremist". We might look back with nostalgia on the days when all we needed to worry about were Lithuanian petty crooks."...

Just a snapshot...

April 2015

ALARM BELL

There is more to UKIP than just "Immigration" but there's no doubt that it's a top concern among British people, and the other parties have totally dropped the ball on this one. They don't even want to control it...

UKIP will boost the Border Agency by at least 3,500 new officers, and drum it into them that they are our frontline protection as far as borders are concerned. Illegal immigrants coming here to work in the "black economy" is bad enough, but far, far worse is the threat posed by ISIS which people are ignoring.

These lunatics are getting even stronger in Libya. A few weeks ago they launched an attack in neighbouring Tunisia on tourists from a passing cruise ship. Be warned, they will soon be smuggling themselves aboard the boatloads of refugees from North Africa across into Italy, from where they will spread across the entire EU in a nexus of suicide terror cells. Coming soon: to a railway station, museum, or shopping mall near you... All thanks to "freedom of movement" and "open borders".

When that happens perhaps even the hopeless lefties will start to realise that there is nothing racist or extreme about wanting to control who comes you're your country. At the moment we are wide open to people who (a) want to kill us and (b) want to establish a medieval Caliphate. Call me old fashioned but I think we should be doing something practical towards stopping them.

April 2015

JIHADI JOHN... GREAT GUY. BOUGHT HIS MUVVER FLOWERS

Three East London Muslim girls get lured away to join ISIS, to try to bring down the governments of Syria and Iraq. The story hits the headlines and stays there for weeks. The three sets of parents then turn around and blame the Police for not warning them of the possibility that their own children might up-sticks and wreck their lives by joining an extremist barbaric terrorist group that has massacred thousands of fellow Muslims, both Sunni and Shia.

Meanwhile, the lobby group Cage holds a press conference in London and tells us that Jihadi John (beheader of Western hostages) was a lovely guy when they knew him, so the fact that he went bananas is all the fault of MI5 who kept hassling him and wouldn't let him go to Somalia "on Safari". If only they'd left him alone, the poor lamb.

This is the logic of the madhouse. It is not the fault of the Police nor the Intelligence services if someone chooses to join a terror group. It's no good trying to use Blame Culture and offload the guilt onto someone else. The individuals are responsible, no-one else.

As far as I'm concerned, loyalty is a two-way street, and these people have now shown how much loyalty they owe to Britain. Therefore we should not burden them with a British nationality that they have clearly rejected, and we should strip them of citizenship and rip up their passports, regardless of rulings from the European Court.

April 2015

FLOGGING A DEAD MACKEREL

I heard this recently on the TV antiques programme 'Flog It'. The expert and the seller are looking at a 19th Century Chinese porcelain vase found in a house on old Glasgow docks.

Expert: "Tell me, did your Great-Aunt have any connection with sea-faring men?"... To which came the puzzled reply: "No, she worked in a shop."

Oh well, perhaps you had to be there.

On the subject of sea-farers you might be interested to hear that the French Navy has recently been forced to pay compensation to a gang of armed Somali pirates after arresting them in the act of trying to storm a cruise ship and then holding them for 48 hours longer than stated in the rules of the European Court of Human Rights. One pirate was awarded £7,000...

If you needed reasons to withdraw from the ECHR, leave the EU, and rip up the Human Rights Act into tiny pieces then this must be one of them.
Another farce, though closer to home, is the Frank Bonefaas, a huge 118-metre Dutch super-trawler that recently scooped up 632,000 kgs of mackerel

off the SW coast, with a conservative market value of £437,000. This was way over its quota and a criminal offence, theft from local fishermen.

Unfortunately Bodmin Crown Court gave the skipper a mere slap on the wrist and fined him just £102,000, leaving a tidy profit of £335k. The maximum penalty would have been confiscation of the catch, a fine equal to the value of the fish, and the removal of the vessel's quota. A UKIP government will reclaim our fishing grounds, and the skipper of the Frank Bonefaas should bear that in mind the next time he unpacks his fishing rod.

April 2015

FOREIGN SPOUSE BARRED AT BORDER

Here at Head Office we have many email enquiries from ex pats who have married abroad but can't bring their new spouse into the country. UKIP's position on this is simple.

If a Brit marries a Russian (or any other nationality) then the Russian can apply for a British passport and become a Brit, with all the rights that go with it. Of course we have to be wary of so-called "Green Card" scams where someone tries to circumvent the system with a staged marriage, but that can probably be achieved by making the "new naturalisation" conditional for a period of time.

UKIP is in favour of immigration; it just needs to be under our own control. It is complete madness that a gifted eye-surgeon from India should be forbidden entry when everyone from the EU (including Bulgarian street-sweepers and Polish taxi drivers) has an absolute right to waltz through Border

Control waving their "ring of stars" EU passport, regardless of who they are. Frankly we have enough Bulgarian taxi drivers and do not need any more. When you lose control over who enters your country, it's called loss of sovereignty.

May 2015

LOVE THAT BBC

I've always liked the idea of the BBC, growing up with great programmes from the 1960's and 70's, from Monty Python, to Blue Peter, Animal Magic, the Generation Game, I Claudius, and Morecambe & Wise. Not so long ago those running the BBC knew what Public Service Broadcasting was all about. Good programming, keep neutral, don't alienate the core audience who pay the bills.

But I'm afraid that things have gone very wrong. The Corporation has been taken over by the Left. If one wants to know the "BBC line" just buy a copy of the Guardian and there it is.

An example: Radio 4's "The News Quiz" used to be an excellent, witty reflection of events taken from the recent news (there's a clue in the title). But now it's just a vehicle for boring Leftie comics to make snide remarks aimed at anyone who doesn't read the Guardian.

As for Newsnight with Evan Davis, it tacks so heavily Leftwards that it's now unwatchable.

The Conservative Government recently announced it was "declaring war" on bias at the BBC, and not before time. UKIP was one of the four "official main parties" during the 2015 general election. The BBC ignored that and stuck to its "three Westminster parties" line, consigning UKIP to the shadows to the best of its ability.

As far as UKIP is concerned we wish Mr Cameron the very best with his campaign to restore balance and neutrality to the BBC, but if he fails then it might be time to scrap the TV licence fee and let the chill wind of competition blast through its corridors...

July 2015

GRIPE SHEETS

As a change from politics I thought you'd be interested in reading about "gripe sheets" on aircraft. Yes, I know, but trust me. After every flight, the pilot fills out a form called a 'gripe sheet,' telling mechanics about any problems with the aircraft. The mechanic then corrects the problem, and makes notes for the pilots on the form before the next flight....

Here are a few of them: "P" means Pilot. "M" means Mechanic's response:

P: Left inside main tire almost needs replacement.

M: Almost replaced left inside main tire.

P: Test flight OK, except auto-land very rough.

M: Auto-land not installed on this aircraft.

P: Something loose in cockpit.

M: Something tightened in cockpit

P: Evidence of leak on right main landing gear.

M: Evidence removed.

P: DME volume unbelievably loud.

M: DME volume set to more believable level.

P: Number 3 engine missing.

M: Engine found on right wing after brief search

P: Noise coming from under instrument panel. Sounds like a midget pounding on something with a hammer.

M: Took hammer away from midget....

July 2015

NOT AS GOOD AS TWISTER

I have three rules in life. Never eat in a restaurant where they display pictures of the food you're about to order. Never send your food back to the kitchen (a waiter's revenge can be awesome). And never reply to nasty emails without sleeping on them overnight.

David Cameron might want to add another. Never invite the President of the EU Commission for the weekend and tell him your secrets, because on Monday he'll blab them across the world.

President Jean-Claude Juncker visited Mr Cameron for dinner at Chequers recently. Once they'd finished the meal they didn't end the evening the way most of us would (play a few games of Twister, shoot some heroin, or have a go on the train-set in the attic). No, they sat down and discussed the EU Referendum. Y-A-W-N.

David Cameron revealed what UKIP has always known. The idea of the Referendum is not to give us the choice of whether we leave or stay in the EU. The real plan is to "lock" us into it forever. Sure, there'll be a referendum. But so skewed that the result will be pre-determined to keep us locked in.

We know this because once he got back to Brussels, Mr Juncker broke radio silence and gave an interview to the Press revealing the secret: "Cameron wants to dock his country permanently to Europe.".

I can just picture David Cameron reading his newspaper and then clearing a space on his desk so that he could bang his head repeatedly until his ears sang.

July 2015

MADE IN HEAVEN

If you need convincing that British Muslims who go to fight for ISIS should be stripped of citizenship then consider this. Amira Abase was one of three schoolgirls who left via Heathrow last year, heading for the welcoming arms of ISIS. She has now married Abdullah Elmir, (known as Ginger Jihadi for his long red hair) after the 18yr-old fled Sydney for Syria last year.

This is obviously a marriage made in heaven. "Ginger" hit the news last year after appearing in sick propaganda videos for ISIS, and more recently for praising the killing of thirty British tourists on that Tunisian beach in June: "May Allah bless the man who slaughtered those filthy kuffar [infidels] and May Allah grant him the highest level in Jannah [Paradise]".

You might think this makes him an unsuitable

husband for his jihadi bride, but you'd be wrong. This charming pair are well suited. Amira Abase recently sent a message that she was "laughing out loud" after being told the 30 tourists had been gunned down. LOL, as she put it.

As far as I'm concerned she must be stripped of British citizenship and her UK passport publicly ripped up. She has made her bed. Now she lies on it.

August 2015

WHAT IS THIS THING "VIDEO-RECORDER"???

For those people like me who never use Facebook and cannot comprehend why it even exists, I should explain that I am now trying to extend my own circle of friends outside Facebook whilst applying the same principles. Therefore, every day, I walk down the street telling passers-by what I have eaten, how I feel at the moment, what I did yesterday, what I will do tomorrow, when I am going on holiday and where I will be leaving the backdoor key.

I also listen to their conversations, give them a thumbs up, and tell them I like them. And it works just like Facebook. I already have four people following me. Two police officers, a private investigator, and a psychiatrist.

I resorted to this because I understand that the Government is now introducing its own version of YouTube, Twitter, and Facebook. It's called YouTwitFace and sounds brilliant.

This is not original of course. But I got it from someone and they got it from somewhere else, and they got it... which all reminds me of an old song by Tom Lehrer. But we'll leave it there.

August 2015

PLAN OF ACTION

In the wake of the travesty now unfolding in Calais, with a "swarm" of migrants (it's more of an invading army) determined to get into Britain, I could not believe the defeatist words of David Cameron: "The Calais problems will be here all Summer".

I have never heard anything more pathetic from any Prime Minister. This makes John Major's "When my back's against the wall, I turn around and fight" seem positively Churchillian. Here is UKIP's immediate plan for how to solve the short-term situation. See what you think...

1) The UK should deploy British troops to treble border staff in Calais with authority to detect illegal migrants entering the UK and to protect British holiday makers and truckers.

2) Demand that the French authorities deploy their own troops to Calais to support the under resourced French authorities and security force.

3) UK ports such as Littlehampton and other smaller ports in the UK should prepare to filter traffic to La Havre, Dieppe and Ostend.

4) We should plan to take any illegal migrants found in the UK back into France, just as the French authorities are doing on the French/Italian border.

5) If the French fail to protect the border, our truckers and holiday makers, we should close Calais. This should focus French minds and would be reopened when the situation is eased and safety concerns are addressed...

August 2015

IT GETS WORSE

The Italians and Greeks are secretly threatening to issue EU passports to new migrants arriving on their shores. If so, then the migrants won't need to smuggle themselves onto lorries at Calais. They can just buy a ticket to Dover and stroll aboard the ferry quite legally (as an EU citizen they will have total freedom of movement throughout the Union)...

This also means that ISIS killers will be among the many, many thousands entering the EU. They have already promised to set up a network of terror cells across the EU, and those guys don't make idle threats. They mean every word they say. To be waving them through Passport Control at Dover is the height of madness, the equivalent of loading the gun and giving it to them...

There is no possibility that Merkel or anyone else will relax that fundamental principle just to let David Cameron fudge his referendum. The reason why there is a look of horror in his eyes, is because he knows there is nothing he can do about immigration. If they have an EU passport then our borders are wide open.

September 2015

STICKING TO YOUR GUNS

I recall the words of Charlie Coburn, a now forgotten music-hall entertainer. At the time he was a massive star in Britain, famous for "Two Lovely Black Eyes" and "The Man Who Broke the Bank at Monte Carlo". He was once asked the secret of his success and explained it thus: "I sang them my song and they didn't like it. So I sang it again and they still didn't like it. So I sang it again and one of them said that he might get to like it if I changed the words and altered the music. So I sang it again, without changing a thing. And then they all liked it.".

There's a lesson here. UKIP has been warning for years about Militant Islam and most recently about ISIS. Finally it seems to have permeated through, with two jihadi Britons recently being targeted in Iraq by RAF drone strikes.

Predictably there was the usual hand-wringing from Lefties, who seem to forget that these two terrorists were not members of the W.I. on a fact-finding tour of the Levant seeking out exotic new jam recipes. They were members of ISIS: vandalising butchers who hack off people's heads, burn prisoners alive in cages, and destroy ancient, beautiful monuments dating from the dawn of recorded history.

Jihadi John is apparently also on the hit list. As far as I am concerned the sooner the RAF drops a Hellfire missile down his chimney the better for everyone. I raise a glass to the pilot. And if Guardian readers and Channel 4 News don't like it then quite frankly they can always do the other thing. We've tried it their way and it didn't work.

September 2015

THE SENIOR SERVICE

Thanks to a UKIP 'mole' in the Admiralty I can now reveal plans for the new generation of Royal Navy warships. The Type 666 destroyer costs £850-million and meets the challenges of the 21st Century... In line with Health & Safety rules, it can stay at sea for days at a time; the crow's nest is accessed by a Stannah stair-lift; the guns fire highly accurate 'paintball charges' to reduce injury, and stress councillors will be on 24-hour call.

Sailors will work a maximum of 37-hours a week, in line with EU employment rules, and the crew will be 50/50 men and women in accordance with the latest Home Office directives on race, gender and sexuality. Tobacco will be banned but cannabis is to be permitted in the mess. As for "rum, sodomy and the lash", rum will be outlawed but the latter two will now be available on request. Saluting an officer will be outlawed as "too elitist".

As HMS Cautious edges down the slipway at the Polish shipyard of Remontava next year she will be blessed by a petrol bomb across the bows from Captain Hook - late of Finsbury Park Mosque but now appearing courtesy of the CIA. To the strains of "In the Navy" this (literally incredible) new fighting machine will head out on her first sea trials, advertising to the world our Prime Minister's ongoing commitment to the needs of the armed forces.

A spokesman from Jane's Fighting Ships was said to be sobbing quietly somewhere.

September 2015

EYES PEELED FOR THE DOVE

In the Year of Our Lord 2015, Noah was living above a former boatyard in Polperro, Cornwall (along with his sons Ham, Shem, and the other one nobody can ever remember) when the Lord came unto him.

"Noah, good servant of mine. Once again the world has become wicked and overpopulated. Build another Ark and save two of every creature. Then gather around a few good humans and prepare for the deluge to be visited upon the Earth in six months time. Here are the blueprints for the Ark."

Six months later God returned to Polperro, but there was no sign of an Ark, just Noah sitting dejected in his boatyard: "NOAH! Where's the Ark? I'm about to start the rain!"

"Forgive me, Lord, but I needed a building permit, and these premises were no longer licensed for boat construction. That took weeks. Then the Boat Inspector insisted I install a sprinkler system (EU Directive 97/EC/1492); then the neighbours complained I'd violated local by-laws by exceeding permitted height limitations, (that took three weeks to sort out); then I had to source the gopher wood from sustainably-managed forests... Don't even mention the nightmare of getting the animals - the trouble I've had with the RSPCA. Then the Environment Agency turned up. They want an environmental impact study on your proposed flood."

"As for the crew," Noah continued, "I had the Racial Equality lot here last week, demanding we follow correct interviewing procedures, with the composition of the crew reflecting diversity among all religious, cultural, and ethnic groups. It's doing my head in!"

Suddenly the clouds rolled away, the sun came out and a glorious rainbow stretched across the sky. Noah looked up in wonder: "Lord, does this mean You're not going to destroy the world?"

"No, I'm not", said God. "The Government beat me to it."

September 2015

HOMELAND DEFENCE?

Here at UKIP Head Office many callers have asked: "Why don't Syrian young men stay to defend their own country rather than pour into Europe as refugees?"

It's a good question. Partly it's because some of them rose up against President Assad in a civil war, encouraged by the West, funded by Qatar and Saudi Arabia (who hate Assad). When their civil war went wrong and instead they ended up with ISIS jeeps parked outside, they panicked and left the country Many others were Assad's own supporters, blaming him for being unable to protect them from the rebel jihadis, so they fled their homes.

Perhaps if they had been more prepared to fight for their country and defend it (for all its faults... I'm not pretending Assad's regime was perfect) then perhaps ancient beautiful Syria would not have been reduced to rubble and ashes.

The whole business has been a monumental mess from Day One and doesn't look like getting much better. We are facing either a protracted stalemate or a victory for ISIS. And that is not what anyone in Washington, London, or Tel Aviv wants to see.

Of course there is no way that Obama or Cameron will ever ally themselves to Assad now. They have impaled themselves on the spike of "Assad must go" but that is not the situation on the ground. Some 40% of Syrians support Assad, which is pretty good for an Arab country, where once a vacuum appears they start at each other's throats.

So it is yet another great achievement by the State Department and British Foreign Office, who seem to have cornered the market in getting things wrong, wrong, wrong. Not just "wrong". Anyone can get things wrong. It's the ability to keep it up, to nurture it, to maintain it, over such a sustained period that is so impressive.

October 2015

CHASING THE WRONG FOX

Climate Change is natural and has been happening ever since the Earth was formed. Our molten ball of rock and chemicals slowly cooled, formed a crust, and then, a few billion years later along came life, including eventually ourselves.

The reason UKIP keeps chuntering on about "climate change" is because the Green lobby is chasing the wrong fox. Had they concentrated on pollution or cleaning up the planet, or tackling the time-bomb of stored nuclear waste, many people would be in complete agreement. But they hitched their star onto "climate change" and, perhaps by accident, made an unholy alliance with politicians, who are always seeking new ways of taxing and controlling the populace.

There is no direct provable causal link between CO_2 being responsible for changes in temperature. After World War II there was a huge surge in CO_2 but global temperatures fell for the next forty years.

Throughout history the planet has often been warmer than now, with CO_2 levels sometimes ten-times higher. It is quite possible that it is changes in temperature that affect the amount of CO_2, and not the other way around. An inconvenient truth perhaps?

Think of it like this: A man catches a cold, then gets a headache and a runny nose. But it's like blaming the cold on the runny nose....

Cutting back on CO2 might be a completely false trail to follow, fighting the symptom rather than the cause, which makes about as much sense as a game of Mornington Crescent, and probably far, far less.

October 2015

THE TOMAHAWK INDEX

Here is your brief guide to how the Stock Market works. One autumn the Apache Indians on their reservation asked the new chief, "Will it be a cold winter?" The Chief pondered for a while, then said: "Yes. Very cold. The Tribe must collect much firewood."

A few days later the Chief had an idea and called the National Weather Service: "Is the coming winter going to be cold?"

The meteorologist at the weather station replied: "Extremely cold." So the Chief went back to the Tribe and told them to collect even more wood.

A week later the Chief called the Weather Service again and asked if it was still going to be cold. "You betcha", said the official. "It's gonna be a freezeout!" So the Chief collected the Tribe together and ordered them to gather every scrap of wood they could find, as a vital matter of survival.

Two weeks later the Chief called the weather station again: "Are you absolutely certain it's going to be a freezeout?"

"No question, "said the official, "The Apaches on the reservation are gathering wood like crazy, and that's a sure sign of a forthcoming bad winter."

And that, ladies and gentlemen, is how the Stock Market works.

November 2015

ABOLISH THE ARMY. SACK THE QUEEN

Jeremy Corbyn has just been elected as Labour leader. This seemed about as likely as being overtaken on the A38 by Lord Lucan riding Shergar, but now it has happened Labour must deal with it.

Tony Blair tried to warn against it. Bad move. 'Tone' really doesn't understand that after the Iraq War his bank account is glowing red, just like the Middle East. He is morally overdrawn. Every time he warned: "Don't vote Corbyn" another 500 people signed up to vote Corbyn. Corbyn's victory is partly thanks to Blair and all the other cloned, speak-your-weight politicians that voters had become sick of.

I call it the Farage Effect. You might dislike Nigel Farage but there is no doubt that he can walk into a pub, or onto the factory floor (but preferably into the pub) and chat away with anyone. He also knows how to eat a bacon sandwich and knows the difference between guacamole and mushy peas. Mr Corbyn might be a quieter character but he has a similar ability, and people recognise it. At least he doesn't put on an act.

The Labour MPs (not the rank and file members) will plot away behind Corbyn and try to oust him.. But it won't be easy. The size of his mandate (60% of the vote) means that he won't be toppled in a palace coup just yet.

Personally I give him until May 2017 and with two local elections behind him, then the MPs will see redundancy looming in 2020 and will topple him then.

But predictions can be wrong, and I might yet come to regret that. To quote Brian Sewell again: "We Shall See!"

November 2015

SOME PERFUME FROM ARABY

And the trek westward continues. A human flood of biblical proportions, surging into Europe from the Middle East. Families with children, yes of course, but mostly young men of fighting age, with who knows what aim. How many of them are in ISIS?

And the do-gooders shout "Open the borders and let them in" when we haven't a clue what we are letting in. The Germans have just said "We'll take 800,000 Syrians. We'll give them a cuddle". As a result the Iraqi, Afghan, and Kurdish migrants are throwing away their passports and shouting: "I'm Syrian" just like "I'm Brian" in Monty Python.

But there is some good news. Finally, after having caused much of this foment behind the scenes, Saudi Arabia has finally offered some serious help to the West. They have offered to build 200 mosques in Germany. One for every 100 refugees who arrived in Germany at the weekend. You can read it for yourself if you Google   http://www.independent.co.uk/news/world/europe/saudi-arabia-offers-germany-200-mosques--one-for-every-100-refugees-who-arrived-last-weekend-10495082.html

I think this is a really kind gesture and one of great significance. One that we should not forget.

BELFAST IS A KINDERGARTEN

Millions of people have been caught in the crossfire between President Assad, ISIS, and the Free Syrian Army, (of which parts of the latter recently pledged their allegiance to al Qaeda, themselves sworn enemies of ISIS). If we thought that politics in Northern Ireland were complicated, the situation in Syria makes Belfast seem like a toddler's birthday party.

The drowning of that poor little boy on a Turkish tourist beach was tragic, but there is an important lesson here. In September 1940, with Britain under bombardment, a ship called 'City of Benares' was taking 90 British children to Canada for sanctuary. It was torpedoed and sunk, with the loss of 77 of the children. I do not believe that any of the bodies came ashore, the vessel was too far from land. But the point of remembering this dreadful story today is that it prompted the British Government to end the sponsorship of attempts to evacuate children across the Atlantic, though some privately arranged journeys were still made.

In short, our forefathers were faced with this dilemma. The proper lesson to learn from the tragic loss of the Kurdi family is perhaps that escaping in unseaworthy boats is not the wisest course to take.... Personally I feel that our money would be better spent in Turkey, Lebanon and Jordan, helping them bear the burden of the refugee crisis. And given the responsibility of oil-rich Qatar and Saudi Arabia in fomenting revolution in Syria, they should be paying equal sums to help ease the disaster that they have brought about. Why should the West pick up the tab for their disastrous foreign policy mistakes?

November 2015 (with thanks to Anne Glyn-Jones)

POO-POOING THE POO-POOERS

Here's an email we received recently at UKIP Head Office and I thought you might be interested:

"I support UKIP but sometimes people say: Aren't they extremist? But once I explain that Labour leader Harold Wilson ran the 1964 election on the promise to close the "open door" policy on immigration, then I receive a different expression'

I usually go on to tell them that Harold Wilson won the election, and duly closed the "open door" policy. I also tell them he gave everyone free prescriptions, stopped us going into the Vietnam war, brought in the "open university", was the first PM to outlaw racial discrimination, and together with the French, put Concorde in the sky, made it legal for homosexuals to have relationships at the age of 21.'

Wilson also said: "If you can die for your country at 18, then you should be able to vote at 18," and brought the voting age down to that age.... I then ask them: "Do you think Harold Wilson was a racist?" I usually leave with a look of bewilderment on their faces.

It's all out there on the Internet - I wish you would make use of it! It's such a vote catcher and it puts the lie to any accusation of extremism".

November 2015

ISIS IN PARIS

Emotions are still very raw following the recent terrible events in Paris, but it is clear that the need to reclaim the integrity of our borders has never been greater. In the aftermath of such mass-shootings there is something distasteful about saying "We told you so", because it risks the accusation of trying to make political capital out of a tragedy. But the fact remains that millions of Islamic economic migrants have been allowed to stream into Europe and setting aside all the other concerns we simply have no idea how many are members of ISIS with a long-term plan to set up a nexus of terror cells, across multiple countries, to launch similar attacks.

UKIP has been warning of this for years and have been dismissed as cranks or extremists. A few months ago in the EU Parliament, Mr Farage stood up and publicly warned the rest of the EU of what would happen. I clearly recall their dismissive reaction, waving him away, gesticulating him to shut up and sit down. Well, they won't be waving away such concerns in future. It's just a shame that innocent Parisians had to die before this threat became taken seriously.

November 2015
139 Parisians had just been gunned down by ISIS terrorists in three waves of attacks across the City. President Francois Hollande finally woke up, saying: "This is war. We are at war with ISIS".

GETTING YOUR CRUMPETS STUCK IN THE TOASTER

A constituent recently wrote to her MP concerned about migrants in Germany moving on to the UK. Jo Cox MP, Labour, replied: "It is important to clarify that no refugees offered sanctuary in Germany will be issued with a passport. There are many criteria to meet to naturalise as a citizen of an EU country, the German system is not very different to ours in that respect. No European country will knowingly offer refuge or support to a terrorist. Germany will certainly not be issuing passports to terrorists. Therefore the refugees, genuine or otherwise, will not have a European passport which means they will not have any automatic rights to enter the UK. I am not sure what has led you to believe that this situation will arise but it is most definitely not the case.

Jo Cox MP, Batley & Spen..."

The simple fact is that Chancellor Merkel has invited 800,000 Syrians to settle in Germany to begin a new life. (We'll ignore the fact that a fake Syrian passport now sells for £1,000 and many of those turning up in Berlin will not be Syrian). The notion that the German Government will not issue them with German nationality is so absurd that it demonstrates a total lack of insight into what is happening. The Germans have already issued passports to previous waves of immigrants and will do so again.

Germany's population is actually falling and they need more citizens. If 800,000 are going to arrive, to replenish that demographic requirement, then it is simply beyond credibility that they will not be granted citizenship. They will then become Citizens of the European Union, with an absolute right to Freedom of Movement throughout the entire EU, and can come to Britain quite legally. Jo Cox might have difficulty in processing that information but it remains a fact. Perhaps she was distracted when writing the email... someone knocking at the door, or maybe her crumpets got stuck in the toaster?

Of course Germany will not "knowingly" issue passports to terrorists. But Germany will certainly find that she has issued passports to ISIS terrorists (and others) simply because not all of them have the word "terrorist" stamped onto their forehead. Terrorists are clever like that. They look like everyone else, except when they are at work. As they were in Paris last week.

What I find most disturbing is the blissful complacency of Jo Cox, a Member of Parliament, (an MP for God's sake) to whom none of this seems to have occurred.

November 2015

THE MAGIC ROUNDABOUT

At the chilled-food aisle in Waitrose the other day I managed to make a man laugh. He had said to me: "Oh, sorry. Am I in the way?"

So I replied, "No, that's fine. I'm happy choosing pizza from a distance."

He looked back at me over his shoulder, "I'm not sure what I'm doing"
To which I responded, "Who among us ever really is?"

At this point he laughed and moved away, probably thinking: 'They're letting 'em out early these days.'

I'd been distracted because I had been thinking... which is always dangerous.

Two things had occurred to me in quick succession, and they were nothing to do with shopping for chilled food. Firstly, that the free movement of people is great if you want a plumber but not so good if you are a plumber.

And secondly, in the Middle East we seem to be in a virtuous circle.

Here's what I mean. The West builds weapons (good for jobs). We sell them to Saudi Arabia (good for exports and balance of payments). The Saudis give them to ISIS. The West drops Hellfire missiles onto ISIS. ISIS go back to the Saudis, saying: "Can we have some more weapons please. The last lot got blown up." Then the Saudis get on the phone to the West and order more weapons, and then the whole merry-go-round sets off again.

It's odd, the things that occur to you in the chilled food section in Waitrose.

December 2015

CHEWING ON SPANNERS

The other day someone described Granola as: "Like Alpen with all the nice bits taken out". I know what he means. I was going to provide you with a link to YouTube footage of Angela Merkel being continuously booed for 15 minutes by the townsfolk in a German marketplace, whilst on the platform trying to make a speech. The crowd were drowning her out with boos. In the end she just gave up and trooped off, along with her minders...

Yet I've just gone onto there and the footage is "no longer available". What a coincidence. Like Alpen, this is democracy with all the nice bits taken out..

If you're looking for an explanation from UKIP why people like Merkel are so set on destroying Western culture then I'm afraid you'll be disappointed. We do not know. Guilt for Germany's actions in the 1940s? An anti-Christian mindset drilled into her whilst being a committed member of the Youth Wing of the East German Communist Party? Very possibly...

Remember that while East Germans were fleeing over the Wall into the West, it was Mrs Merkel's Communist father who actually moved his family, lock, stock, and barrel to the East, because the allure of the Atheistic People's Democratic Germany was just so great that the West resembled Alpen to a vegan. Too rich to swallow. No wonder his daughter looks about as miserable as a garage mechanic chewing on a spanner...

December 2015

AND FINALLY...

I hope you enjoyed this book as much as I enjoyed writing it. If you haven't read its predecessor The View From Here, then let's hope you enjoy that one too.

I decided to finish by giving a quick example of how the media manipulates things to suit their own "in-house" policy. I reproduce (page 307) a 2003 Trago piece (from The View From Here) that SKY NEWS, then the BBC etc, turned into a 12-hr media frenzy during the 2014 European Election, accusing me and UKIP of hating foreigners. "Challice thinks Greeks are vile" ran the headline. Oh really? Judge for yourself. Perhaps I should have sued. Life's too short.

David Challice
Dartmoor (not the prison)
2016

HOLIDAY SNAPS

It's only a snapshot, but I'd like to offer a reason why the European Union can never work. This comes from Brian Sewell's excellent book "South From Ephesus", an autobiographical journey through the ancient sites of Turkey. In fairness to Mr Sewell I have no idea of his opinion on the European Union:

"The road to the Turkish border is littered with dead dogs. The dead dog sums up the difference between the Greek and the Turk. The Greek driver seeing a dog in the road a hundred yards ahead will accelerate and do his damnedest to run it down for sport; a Turk will maintain his speed and course, and if the dog happens to be in the way, will run over it – the one is vile, the other fatalistic, though I do not care for the indifference.

"I once scooped a kitten from the path of an Istanbul taxi with the speed and dexterity that I thought had left me when I stopped playing rugby – as the taxi shrieked to a halt the driver's scowl changed to laughter, but in Greece both I and the kitten would have been flattened."

There's bound to be some generalisation here (not all Englishmen have bowler hats; not all Frenchmen are gifted on the accordion) but contrast this with the response of most British motorists to, say, a family of ducks waddling down the road: there'd soon be a two-mile tailback, with nobody prepared to accelerate past.

It's only a snapshot, and perhaps a family of ducks means very little to you, but this is about how all of us - regardless of political viewpoint - would hopefully react in that situation. It is not a criticism of Greeks or Turks, merely recognition of the historical and cultural differences between us.

If all three countries have such hugely different views about animals on the road, what chance with a common defence or immigration policy?

October 2003

(reproduced from The View From Here, Vista Books 2008)

ALSO AVAILABLE BY DAVID CHALLICE

THE VIEW FROM HERE

The collected Trago Columns from 2001 to 2008.
Forerunner of Elephant in the Room. A collection of
bite-sized articles covering the EU, its politicians,
and current affairs of the day. A fascinating
excursion into the recent past when Blair and Brown
were in 10 Downing Street.

Read one of these pieces and you'll want to read
another... and just one more. By the time you
have finished The View From Here your whole view
of 'Europe' and its politicians will have changed
forever... Not necessarily for the better.

Available from Vista Publishing.

ALSO AVAILABLE BY DAVID CHALLICE

HEYDRICH... A WALK IN THE BLACK FOREST

Available from Vista Publishing

In Amazon Kindle only.

The story of Reinhard Heydrich's rise to power to become the most feared man in the Third Reich and heir-apparent to Adolf Hitler himself, from obscurity to Wannsee, and architect of the Grand European Project, later the European Union, to many he is virtually unknown.

The other biographies have been academic works... straight-forward factual accounts of his career. "A Walk in the Black Forest" takes a very different approach. I wanted to know more than just what he did: I wanted to know why he did it, how he got away with it, and what happened to the people who stood in his way. I wanted to walk around Heydrich, to view him from other angles.

"A Walk in the Black Forest" concentrates on the human element, on the characters involved, many of them Nazis, who were there at the time and actually knew him. Few of them ever really understood what motivated him, but at least they left us their memoirs, or were interviewed by journalists, biographers and the military after the war. Using this wide-ranging material, I have tried to write an accessible, approachable book aimed at a wide audience, male and female, many of whom might normally cross the street to avoid "serious" history; all without compromising on research and factual accuracy. I must also thank Len Deighton for his invaluable assistance and advice

"Impressive" **Robert Hale**

"Fast moving and mainstream. Measured and illuminating" **Len Deighton**

"Well researched" **Cassell**

"Fascinating" **Transworld**